With best wishes
Joyce Bailey Anderson

IMAGES
of America

PRINCETON AN
WACHUSETT MOUN

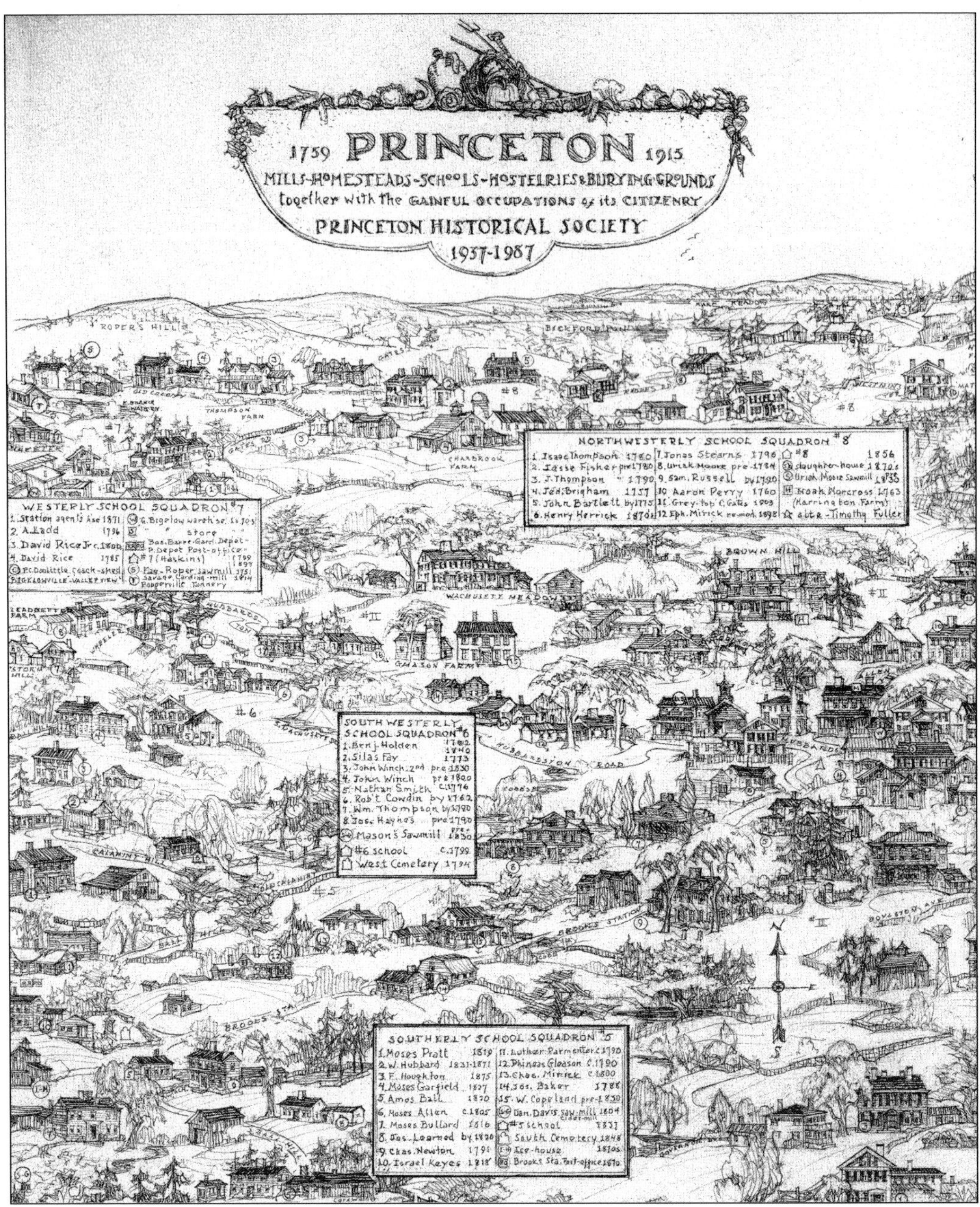

This map, created in 1987 to commemorate the 50th anniversary of the Princeton Historical Society, shows the mills, homesteads, schools, hostelries, and burying grounds as depicted in a pencil drawing by Rosalind Sturges Allen. Her love of drawing trees, houses, and maps of Princeton is evident in this tribute to the historical society. Mrs. Allen's father and brother were architects, and the love of drawing and architecture was instilled in her at an early age. Her talent has been passed down to her children. (Courtesy of the Princeton Historical Society.)

IMAGES
of America

PRINCETON AND WACHUSETT MOUNTAIN

Joyce Bailey Anderson

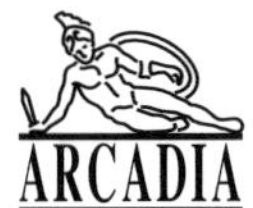
ARCADIA

ISBN 0-7385-1196-X

First printed in 2003.

Published by Arcadia Publishing,
an imprint of Tempus Publishing Inc.
2A Cumberland Street
Charleston, SC 29401

Printed in Great Britain.

Library of Congress Catalog Card Number: 2003101687

For all general information, contact Arcadia Publishing:
Telephone 843-853-2070
Fax 843-853-0044
E-mail sales@arcadiapublishing.com

For customer service and orders:
Toll-free 1-888-313-2665

Visit us on the Internet at www.arcadiapublishing.com.

To my husband, Douglas Anderson,
for his unfailing support.

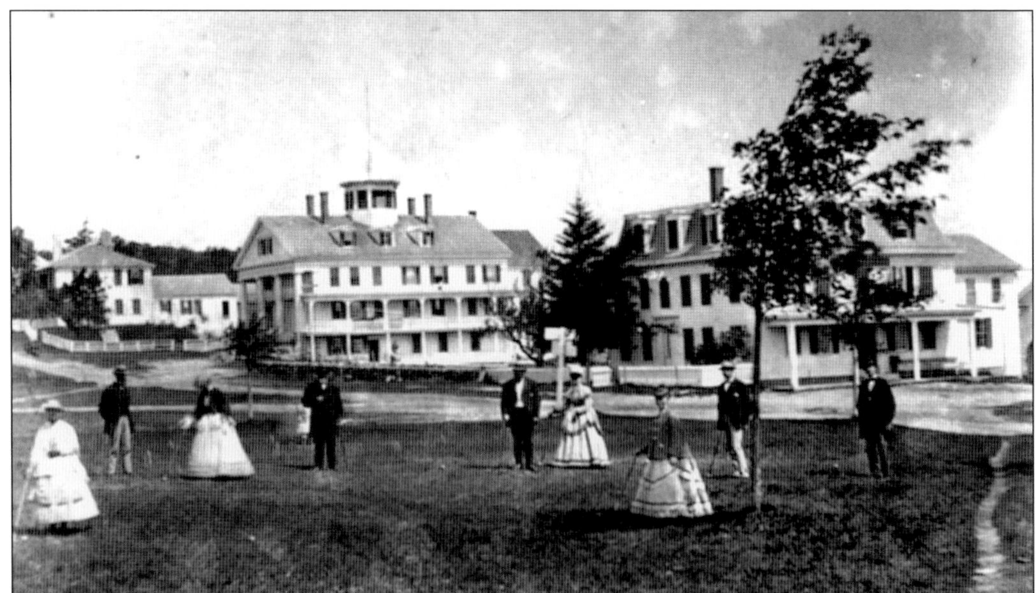

As early as the 1860s, croquet was a popular pastime in which men and women participated in tournaments to wile away the summer days. The game was popular on private courts, at Wachusett House, and on the southern end of the common. Women wore hoop skirts, and straw hats and jackets were proper attire for men. (Courtesy of Judith Chandler Chute.)

Contents

Acknowledgments		6
Introduction		7
1.	The Silent Majesty of the Mountain	9
2.	A Hilltop Town	27
3.	Factories, Farms, and Friends	47
4.	Summer Sanctuaries	59
5.	As We Grew	81
6.	Day to Day	91

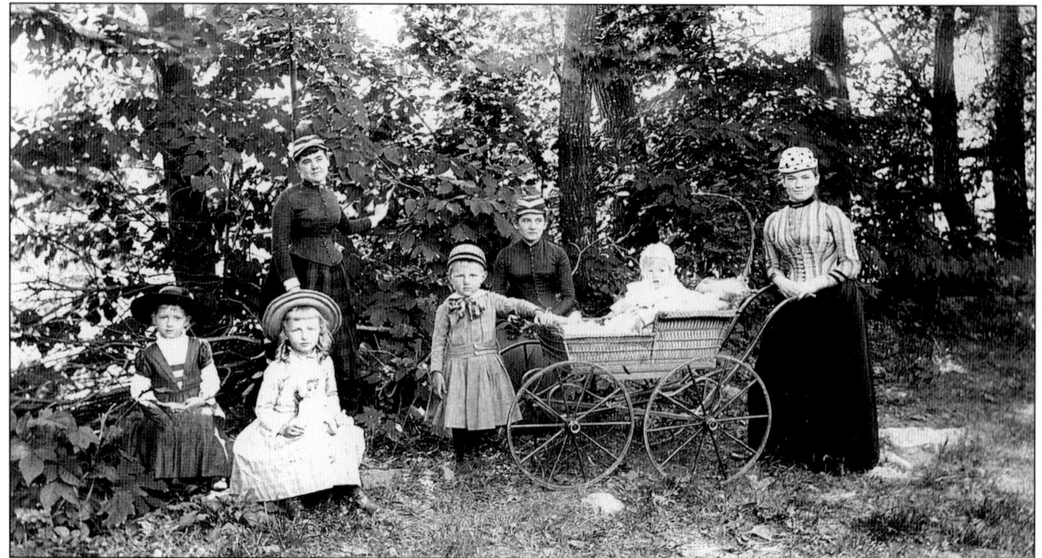
Annie Hines, hired as a nursemaid by Algernon Beaman (owner of Wachusett House), stops to pose in the summer of 1889, with baby Ralph Beaman in the carriage. Alden Beaman, older brother of Ralph, has his arm resting on the carriage, and Luella Beaman is holding a doll. The other people are unidentified and were probably associated with Wachusett House either as guests or staff. (Courtesy of Nancy Beaman Flanders.)

ACKNOWLEDGMENTS

To forget the past is to be like a brook without a source, a tree without roots.

Princeton and Wachusett Mountain became a community project when Phyllis Booth wrote an article for the *Holden Landmark* to request photographs for the book I was writing. I thank everyone who generously loaned photographs from their personal collections and the people who provided information to help me identify people and places. The Princeton Historical Society's collection of photographs and the support from the board of directors was invaluable to me. I wish to express my appreciation to the following people who helped and encouraged me throughout the writing process: Bud Brooks, Susan Ceccacci, Bruce Dean, Nancy Flanders, Susan Roney O'Brien, and Ronnie Waters.

INTRODUCTION

Above Wachusett, the mountain of the Sachems, red-tailed hawks ride the thermals as they have since before Joshua Wilder struck out from Lancaster in 1742 and built the first "house of refreshment" on Houghton Road in what is now Princeton, Massachusetts. What drew him to this unsettled area? Was it a chance to start a new life, the opportunity for adventure, virgin land, and rich forests? Who watched from the shadows of white pines that reached over 250 feet into the sky? The eyes of Nipmucks, natives of this region, followed Wilder's steps and watched as he hewed beams and raised walls.

By 1751, Robert Keyes journeyed from Shrewsbury and settled on a tract of 200 acres with his wife and five children. One April day in 1755, Martha Keyes sent her daughters Martha and Anna to Wachusett Pond for sand. Four-year-old Lucy was told to stay in the house, but when Martha and Anna returned, Lucy had disappeared. Settlers came from 20 miles away to help search, but she was never found. Her mother's cry of "Lucy, Lucy" still carries through the wind.

Twenty-five families who inhabited the newly settled territory by the late 1750s petitioned the court to establish Prince Town, named for Rev. Thomas Prince, pastor of Old South Church in Boston for 40 years. Prince was the largest landowner and one of the founders of the town. Farmers tilled, planted, and harvested, and the small farming community fell in with the rhythms of the seasons, early risings, and well-earned sleep.

Rhythms changed with industrialization and the advent of train travel. During the mid-19th century, chair manufacturers moved to East Princeton, harnessing Keyes Brook's waterpower to run machines. The village built sidewalks and installed streetlights, and for many years, a Mr. Anderson lit the lamps at 4:00 each evening, extinguished them in the morning, and brought them home to clean. On the mountain and in the center of Princeton, hotels sprang up. By 1870, there were seven large hotels in Princeton and many guesthouses to serve the summer visitors from Boston, New York, and Philadelphia who journeyed to Princeton for its beautiful scenery and healthy air, not to mention the bountiful blueberries.

Princeton is a town of strong individuals. Although the population of the town has grown and changed, the beautiful hills and clear light draws artists, writers, and independent thinkers. Many people live in Princeton because it offers a relaxed rural atmosphere and a small-town feeling. The Massachusetts Audubon Society and the state own more than 3,000 acres of Princeton land that will always be protected.

Wachusett Mountain remains. Hawks glide over the 2,006-foot peak on their migratory routes each year, and visitors standing on the summit can see, just as the Nipmucks could, 120 miles in all directions: north, south, east, and west. This book leads in yet another direction: the past.

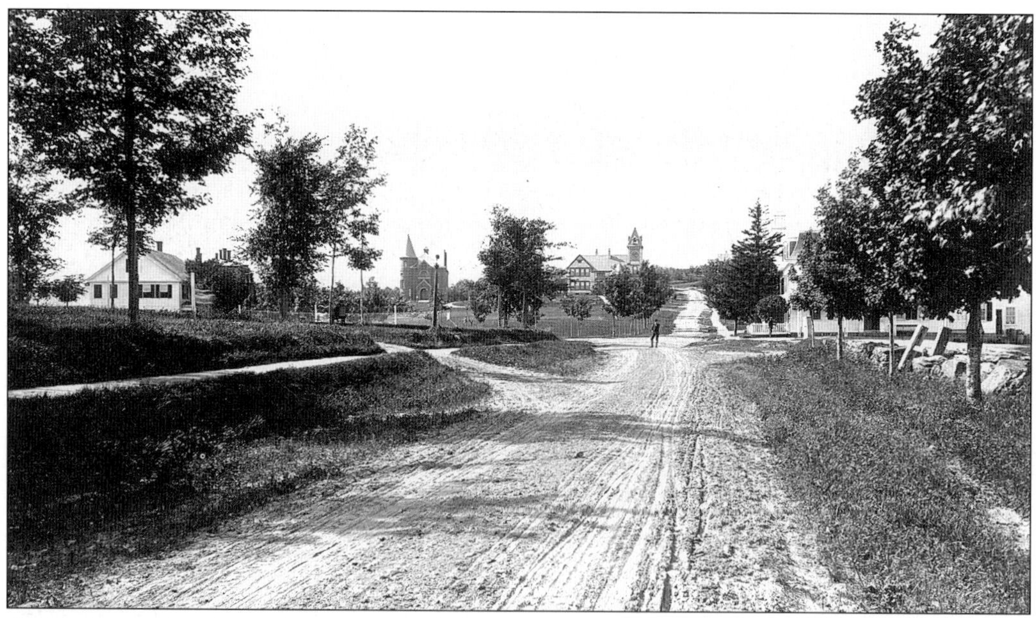

A man is standing in the intersection of Worcester and Gregory Hill Roads in the early 1900s. Behind him are the Goodnow Memorial Building (right) and Bagg Hall (left), both donated by Edward Goodnow. A deed written in 1884 for these two buildings stipulates in part, "The land heretofore used for the church shall always remain open for air, light and view and shall always be a public park or common and no other building shall be erected upon it." (Courtesy of the Princeton Historical Society.)

One
The Silent Majesty of the Mountain

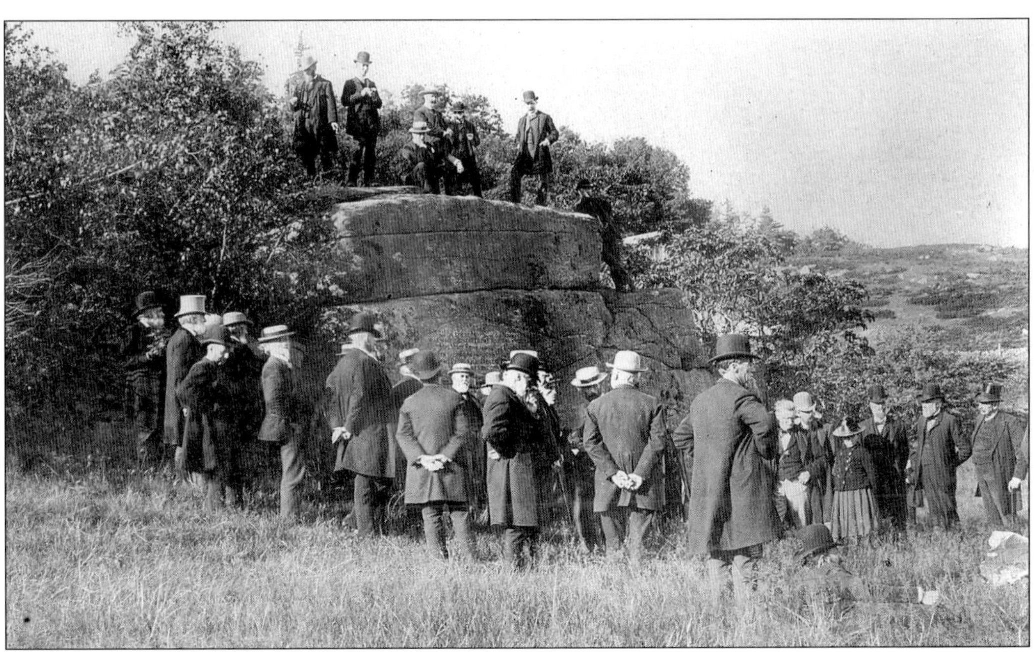

This view of a meeting of the Redemption Rock Association in 1879 shows a group of people commemorating the release of Mary Rowlandson at Redemption Rock in Princeton. The inscription on the rock reads, "Upon this rock, May 2nd 1676, was made the agreement for the ransom of Mrs. Mary Rowlandson of Lancaster, between the Indians and John Hoar of Concord. King Philip was with the Indians, but refused his consent." Rowlandson had been held captive for 12 weeks. (Courtesy of the Princeton Historical Society.)

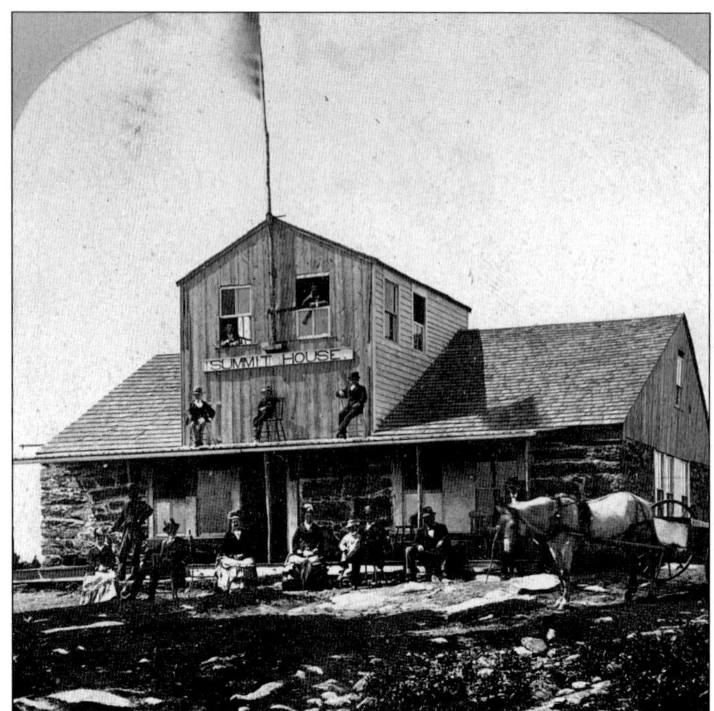

In 1825, Mrs. John Rice became the first to reach the summit. By 1866, William G. Morse had set up a small stand where he sold candy and cigars transported by a pony cart. Morse used the early Coast Survey Road, a wide, steep path made in 1833 by land surveyors to reach the stone building at the top. Business proved to be lucrative and Morse built a small stone house (pictured here) in 1870. (Courtesy of the Princeton Historical Society.)

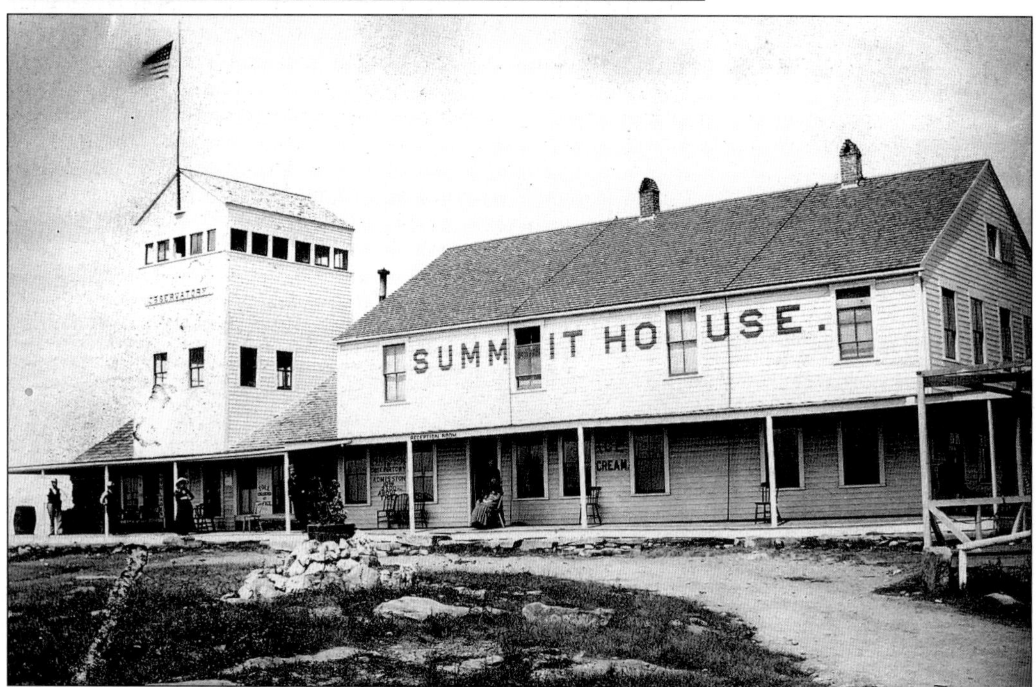

In 1874, the Wachusett Company was incorporated for the purpose of building a hotel on the summit. Eventually, the plans to build a hotel were nothing more than an addition to the existing building, but a horse barn and bowling alley were built. The Coast Survey Road was designated a toll road, and visitors were charged 25¢ to reach the summit. (Courtesy of the Princeton Historical Society.)

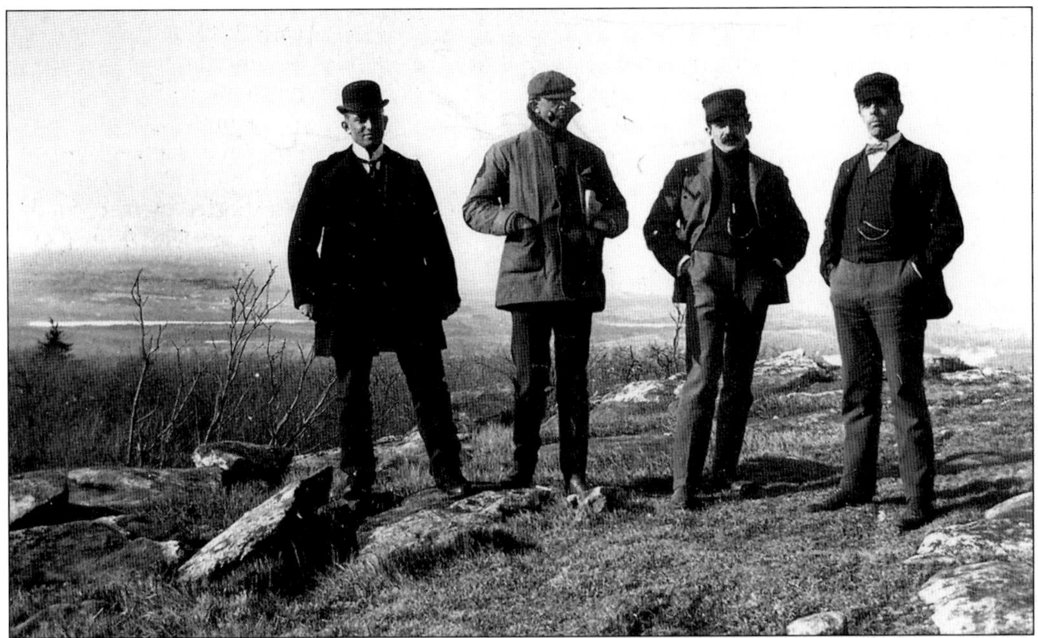

Simeon Borden was the first surveyor to climb the mountain. Following an earlier path on the eastern slope of the mountain, he began his work in 1833, and the survey results were published in 1844. This was in response to the Commonwealth's requirement that each town provide an accurate map of its territory from actual surveys. Among those pictured on the mountain in the early 1900s are Guy Chase and Everett Needham. (Courtesy of the Princeton Historical Society.)

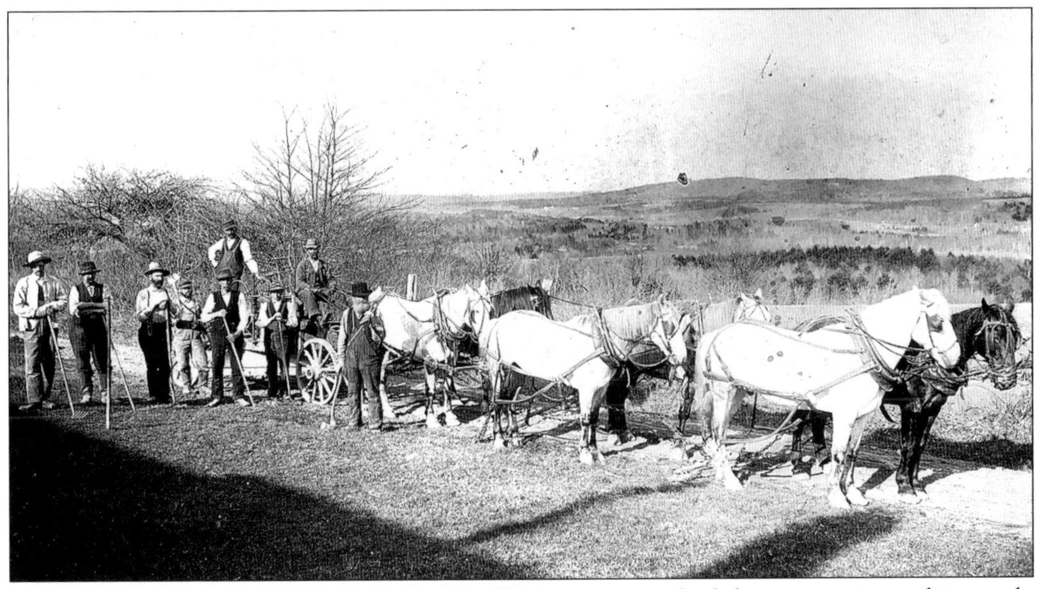

In 1883, the *Gardner News* reported, "The Westminster end of the mountain road is nearly complete. The Princeton end is much more difficult and will not be completed until next summer." This early-1900s photograph shows a team of men working on the road. Dirt and stones were raked into piles for removal by tipcart. Big rocks were rolled to the side, and rakes were used to grade the new road. (Courtesy of the Westminster Historical Society.)

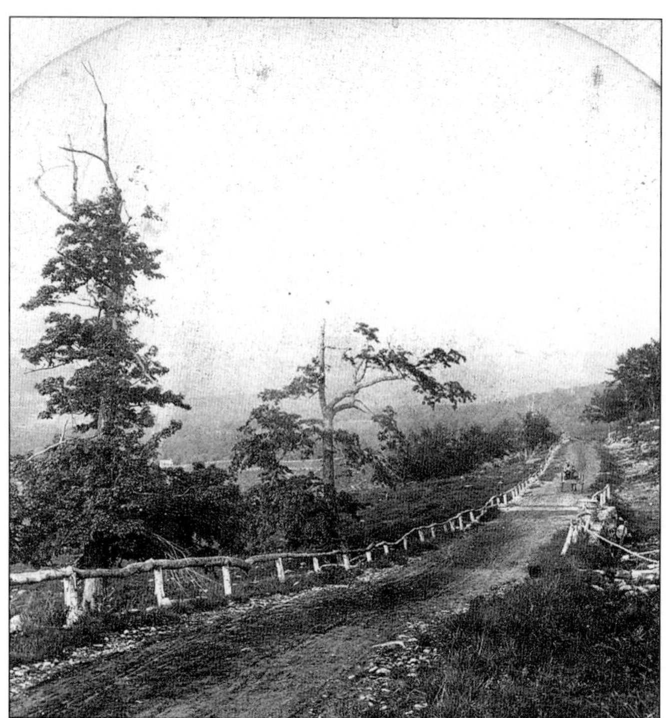

Samuel G. Bullard's book *Guide to Wachusett Mountain*, published in 1884, described access to the summit in the late 1800s by means of two routes. Both routes began at the Mountain House Hotel; one was a footpath known as the Coast Survey Road, and the other was a new carriage road running northerly from the hotel. The new road, pictured in this stereopticon view, was described as equal to one of the best roads in the country, with astonishing views. (Courtesy of the Princeton Historical Society.)

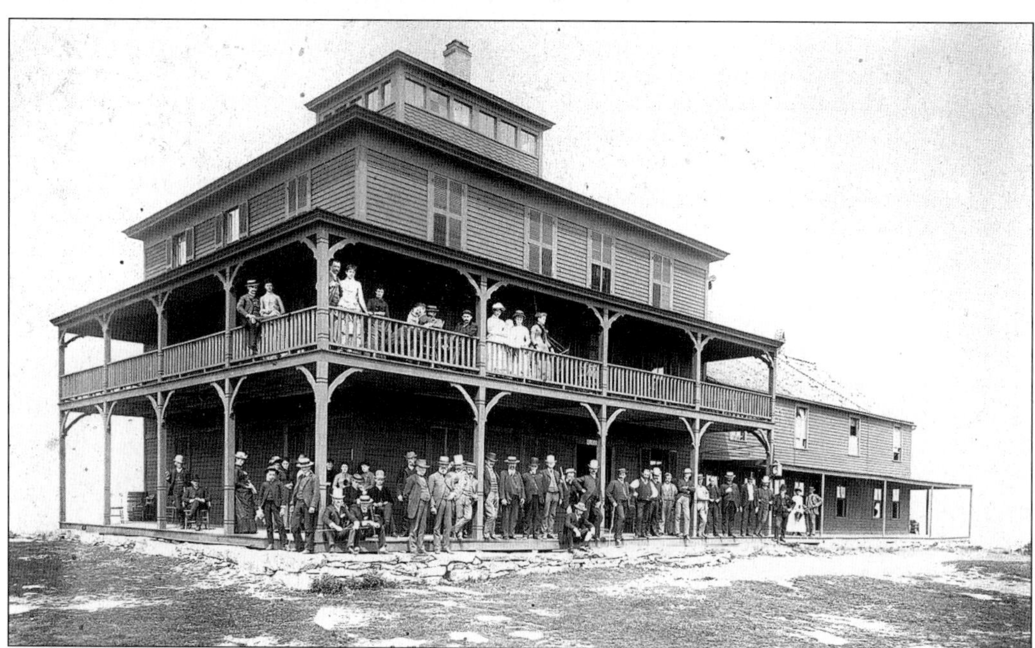

The mountain was sold to P.A. Beaman and Sons in 1882. Two years later, the second Summit House, called "Tip Top," was built. It had 30 rooms, and each room was supplied with gas and an electric bell that connected with the main desk. The season ran from May 20 to October 15. Stagecoaches picked up the patrons at Princeton Depot and at Union Depot in Fitchburg and brought them to the summit. During this time, tourism increased to 30,000 visitors a year. (Courtesy of the Westminster Historical Society.)

This brochure, printed in 1887, gave a summary of what the Summit House and Wachusett Mountain had to offer the tourist. The Summit House was described as being delightfully situated on Wachusett Mountain with numerous attractions. The brochure also described a new telescope in the observatory offering a view of ships in the harbor to the east and included a timetable with stagecoach connections at Union Depot in Fitchburg. Beginning on June 1, the stage left the station in Fitchburg at 7:30 a.m. and the Summit House at 5:00 p.m. every day. (Courtesy of the Princeton Historical Society.)

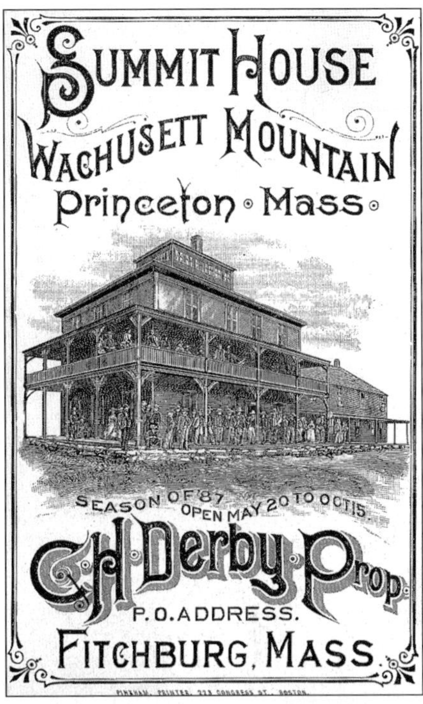

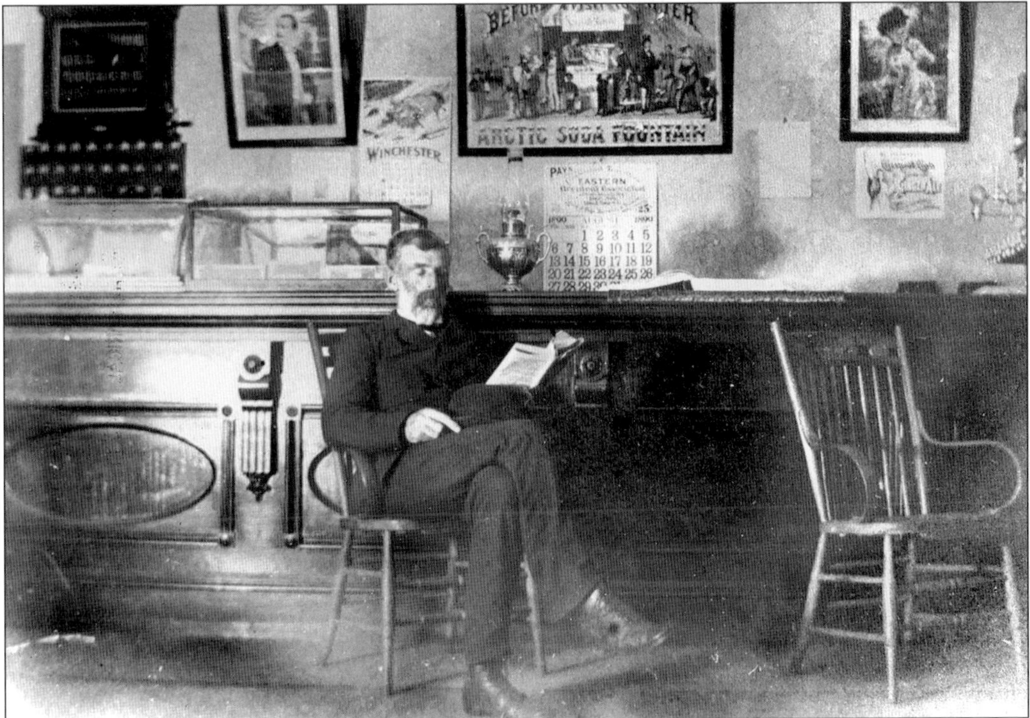

Algernon Thompson Beaman, son of Phineas Beaman, was one of the partners in the firm of P.A. Beaman, owners of the Summit House in 1884. In this view, Algernon sits in the foyer beside one of the counters at the second Summit House. The year on the calendar is 1899. (Courtesy of Nancy Beaman Flanders.)

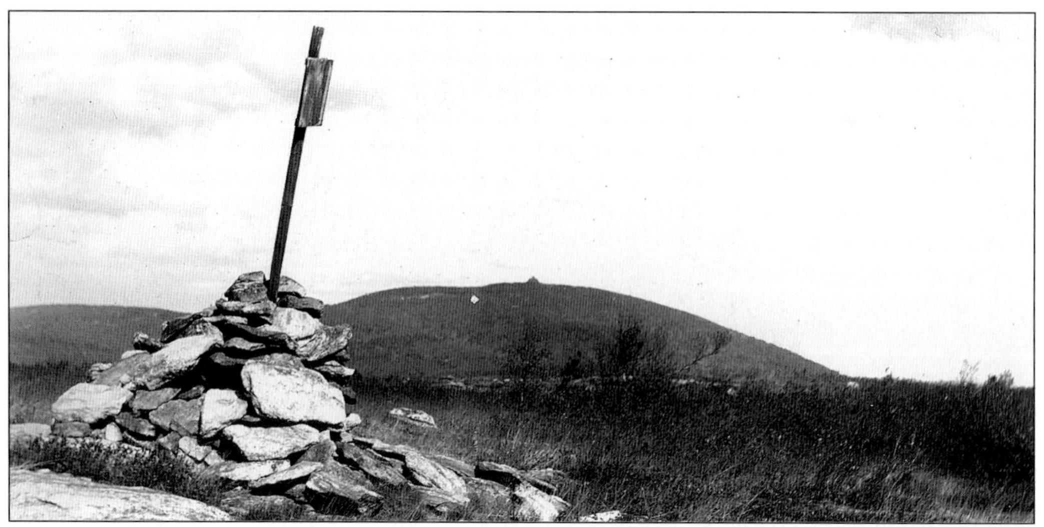

Wachusett Mountain is seen here from the summit of Little Wachusett. Susan Minns of Boston bought Little Wachusett and gave it to the Commonwealth of Massachusetts in 1926 for a wildlife sanctuary. Lois Fay, who lived near the sanctuary, was appointed guardian. She allowed visitors onto the property for the price of 50¢ a person. The Minns Wildlife Sanctuary includes Little Wachusett, with an elevation of 1,559 feet, and is now managed by the Massachusetts Division of Fisheries and Wildlife. (Courtesy of the Princeton Historical Society.)

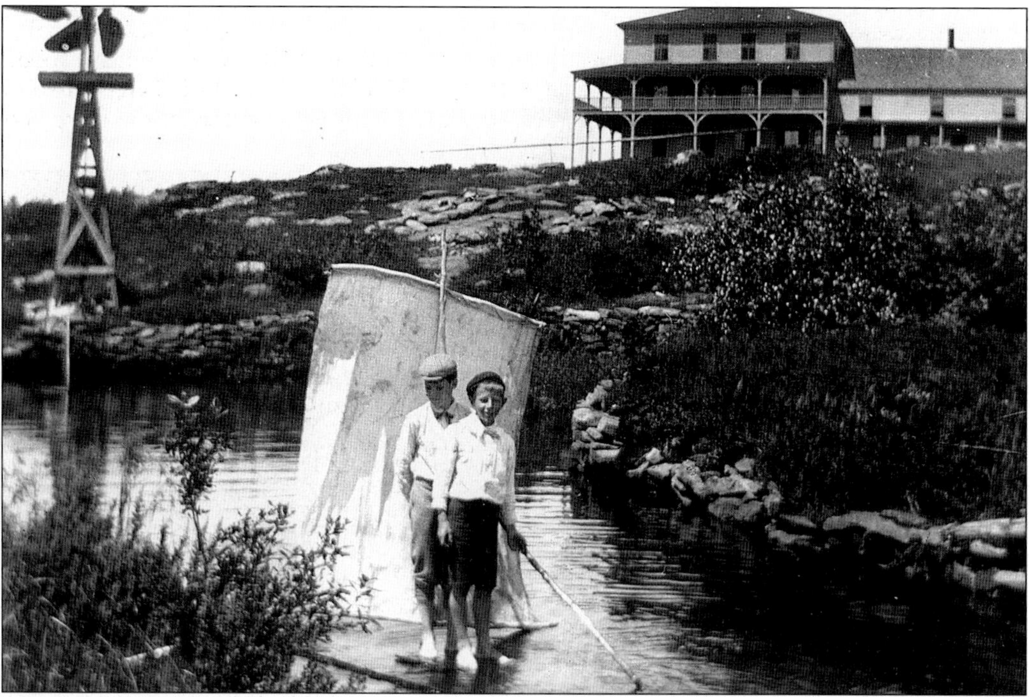

Pictured in the early 1900s, Ralph Beaman (right) and his friend Joe West are floating on a raft near the second Summit House. Summit Pond supplied water for washing at the hotel and barn. Water was pumped to a holding tank on the second floor of the hotel by a windmill. The pond also supplied ice that was stored in an icehouse on the shore. Drinking water was supplied from a spring a mile down the road. (Courtesy of the Princeton Historical Society.)

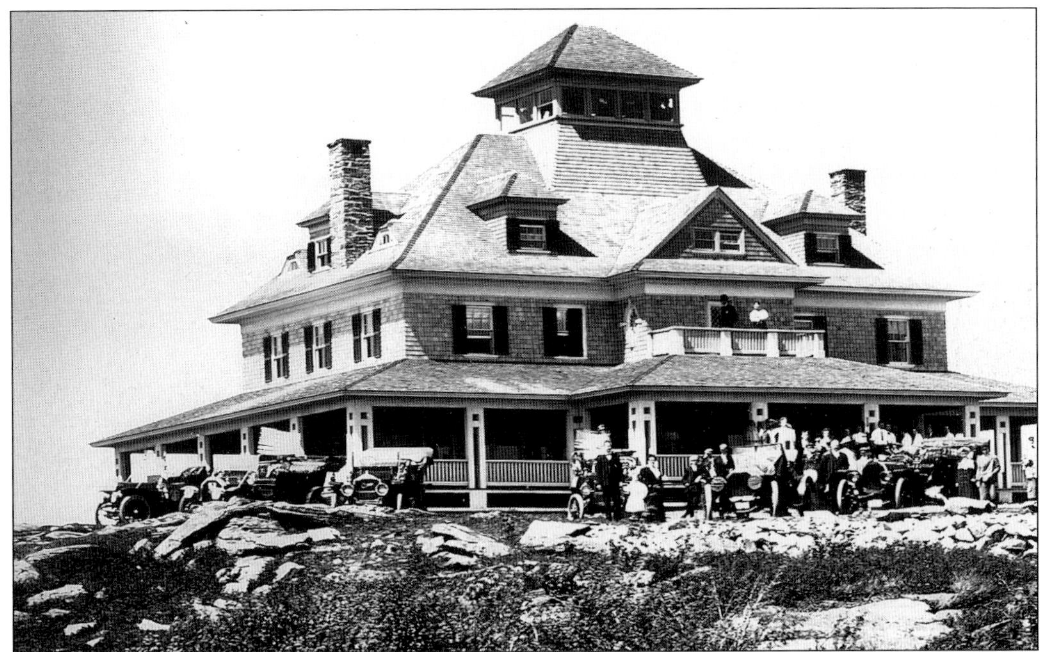

John C.F. Mirick built the third Summit House in 1907. Run by the Commonwealth of Massachusetts, the hotel opened for guests in June 1908. It had 14 bedrooms and modern bathrooms with hot and cold running water. An auto garage and stables were located nearby. In response to the increased visitation, an annex was built in 1910, with a billiard room, laundry, and several additional sleeping rooms. By the mid-1930s, overnight lodging ceased to exist. The building burned to the ground on December 18, 1970. (Courtesy of the Princeton Historical Society.)

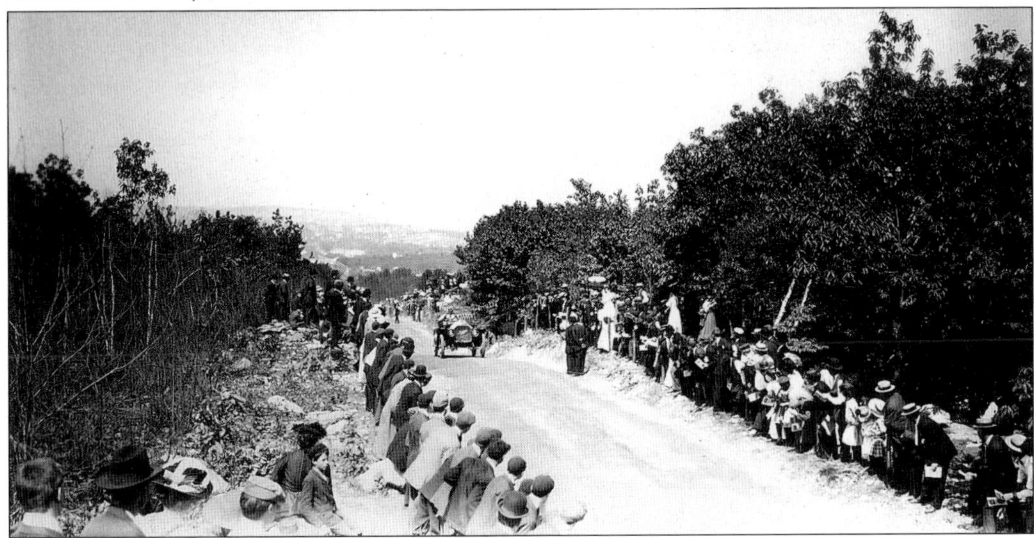

This photograph, taken in 1908, shows automobiles competing in a race to reach the summit of Wachusett Mountain. Spectators are standing along the road as they cheer the drivers to victory. A portion of an advertisement read, "The Mountain Road is open to autos from 12 noon until 2pm, and from 5pm until 7pm. The road is in good condition and auto owners all over New England are anxious to try this climb." (Courtesy of the Princeton Historical Society.)

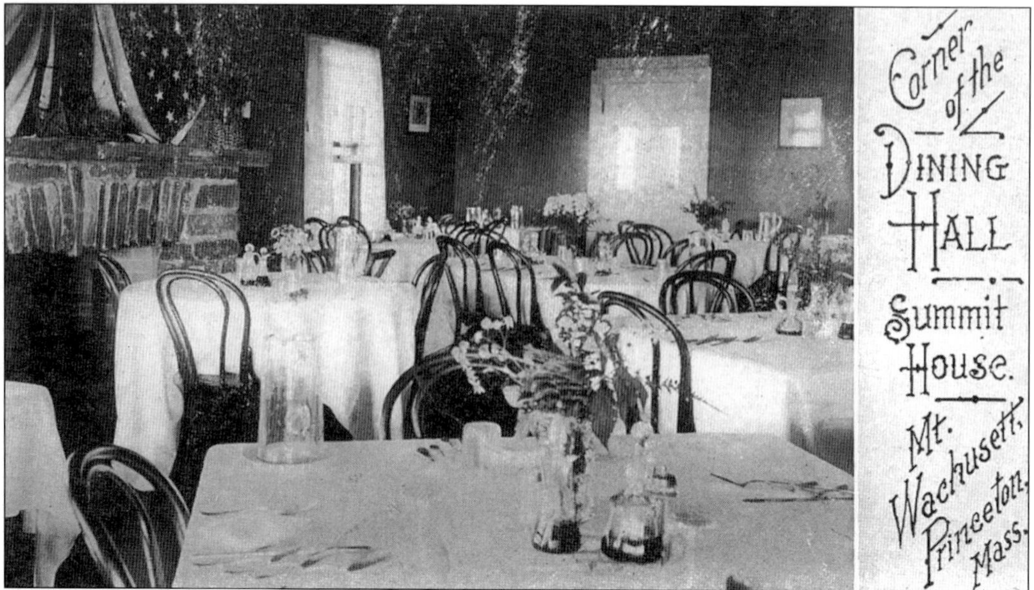

Pictured in the postcard below is the large foyer of the third Summit House. In the foyer, visitors saw counters and shelves displaying souvenirs and postcards of the area. On either side of the entrance were public rooms with fieldstone fireplaces. The postcard above shows the spacious and attractive dining room, which offered good service and excellent cuisine. On the other side of the foyer was the living room (below), where guests could sit and enjoy a cheery fire on cool evenings. (Courtesy of the Princeton Historical Society.)

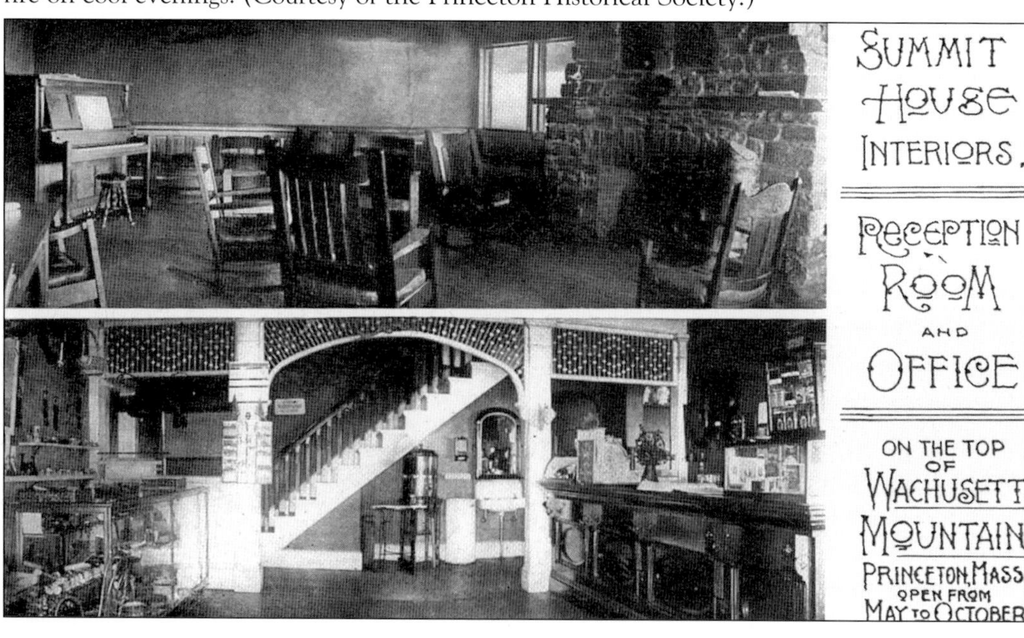

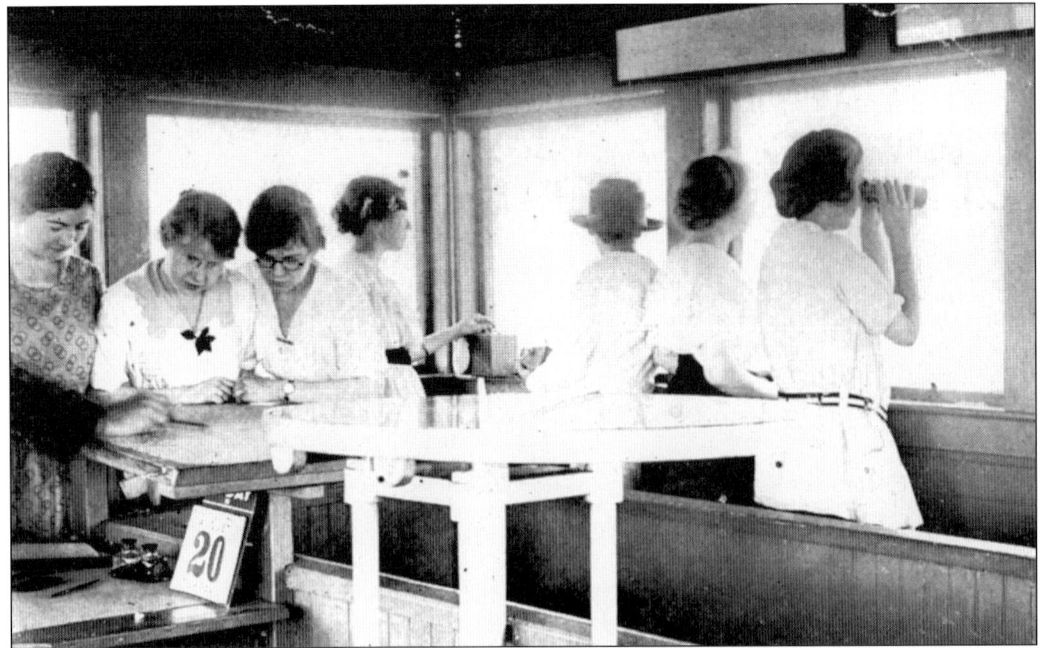

These women are in the third Summit House observatory. The date on the calendar is Tuesday, August 20, and it may have been in the 1930s or 1940s. A forest fire control station was located in the observatory of the hotel. Usually, from early April until the end of October, someone was on duty to spot fires. Just before the hotel burned in 1970, the equipment was transferred to the steel fire tower on the mountain. (Courtesy of Nancy Beaman Flanders.)

Everett Needham, superintendent of Wachusett Mountain Reservation, is shown in the early 1900s beside his Model T at the site of the Lucy Keyes home. Robert Keyes purchased 200 acres on the easterly side of the mountain and built his home in 1751. There were only three or four families living in the area at the time. Pine Hill and Wachusett Mountain Reservation Visitors Center are located where his home was originally built. (Courtesy of the Princeton Historical Society.)

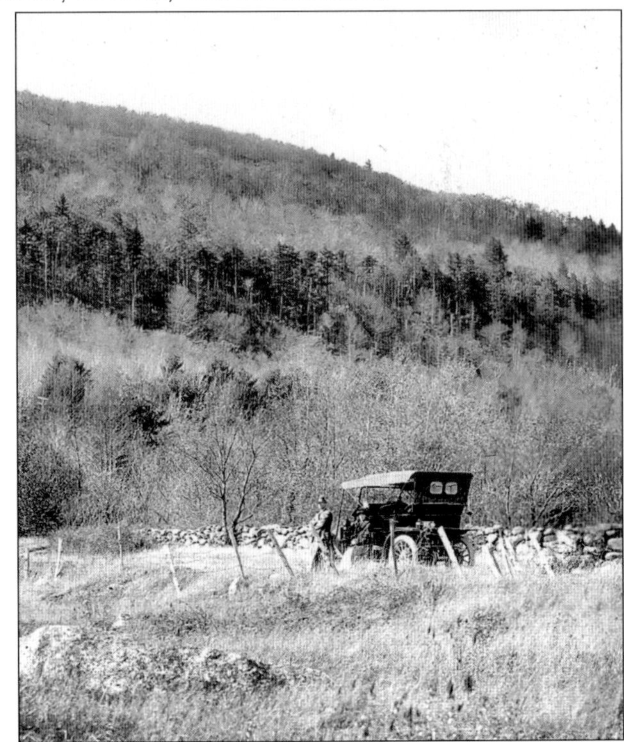

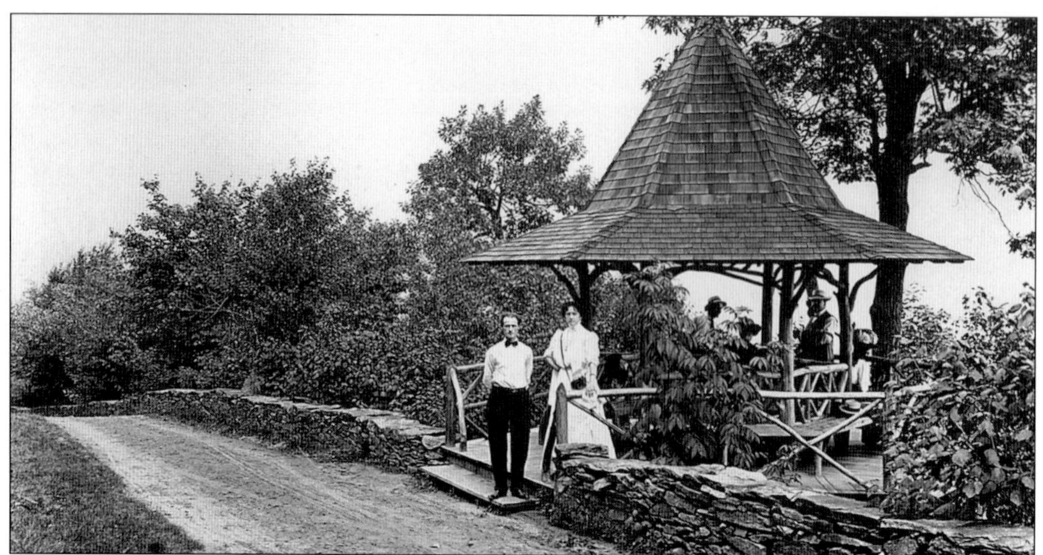

Most of these wooden rustic structures were destroyed when the hurricane of 1938 swept through the reservation. The beauty of these handmade rustic shelters was a thing of the past, too fragile to withstand high winds and bad weather. The *Gardner News* reported in June 1939 that work was to begin with clearing and replacing the rustic houses. Plans were to build a stone house, to erect stone gates at all entrances, and to develop parking areas. (Courtesy of the Princeton Historical Society.)

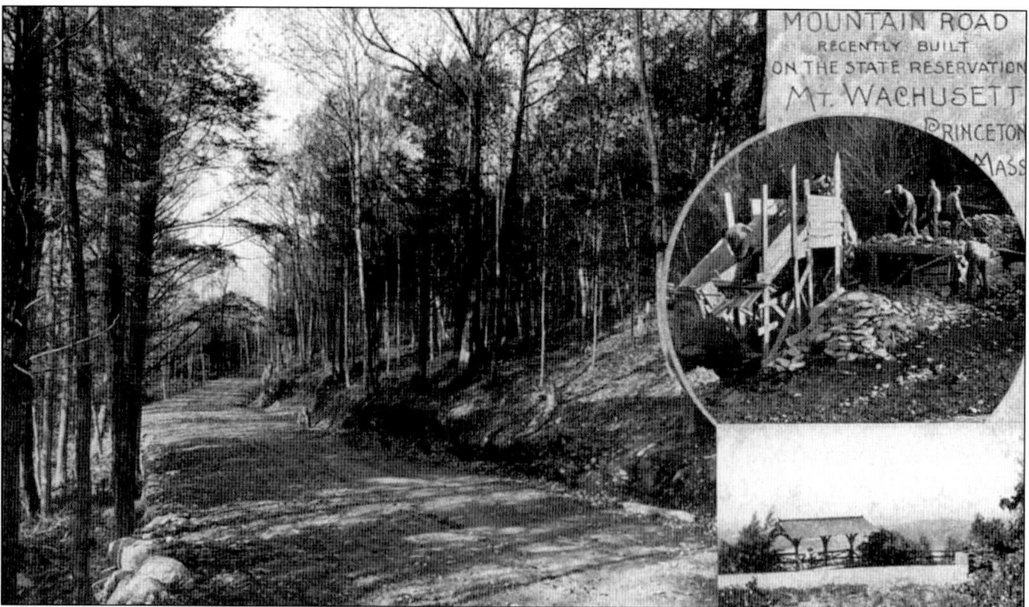

In the early 1900s, a prison camp was built near Bolton Brook on the north slope of the mountain. Ten acres of land were cleared for farming where 1,000 bushels of potatoes were grown for the Worcester House of Correction. The prisoners planted more than 28,000 pines and spruce, and logged and cleared the land. In January 1913, superintendent Everett Needham reported that 3,000 feet of new roads were built and a stone crusher had been purchased. In the inset, prisoners are operating the newly purchased stone crusher. (Courtesy of the Princeton Historical Society.)

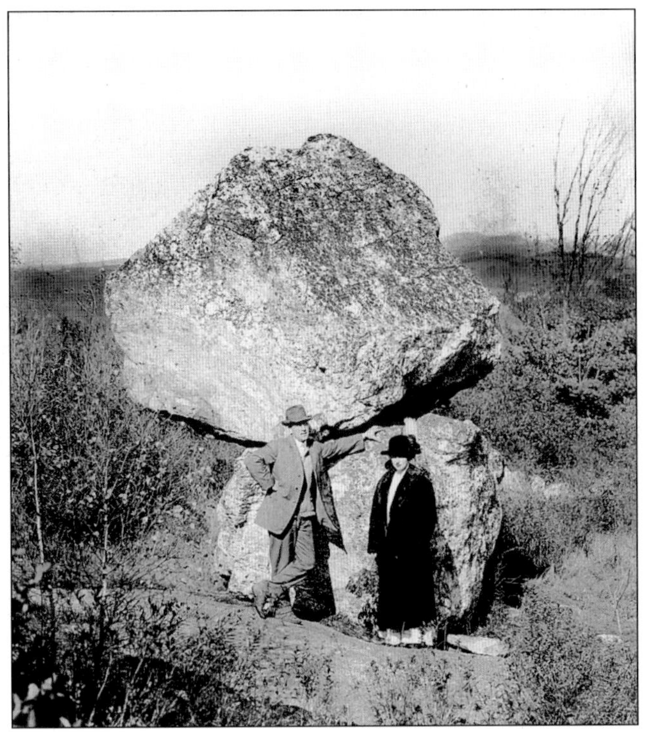

This photograph from the early 1900s shows a man and woman standing in front of Balance Rock. The rock, sometimes called Double Boulder, is a glacial erratic on the north side of the mountain near the Old Indian Trail. These huge boulders, left by the ice age thousands of years ago, are about 6 feet in diameter and together weigh about 30 tons. Balance Rock Ski Trail, named for the rock formation, was the first trail built for skiing on the mountain, in 1933. (Courtesy of the Princeton Historical Society.)

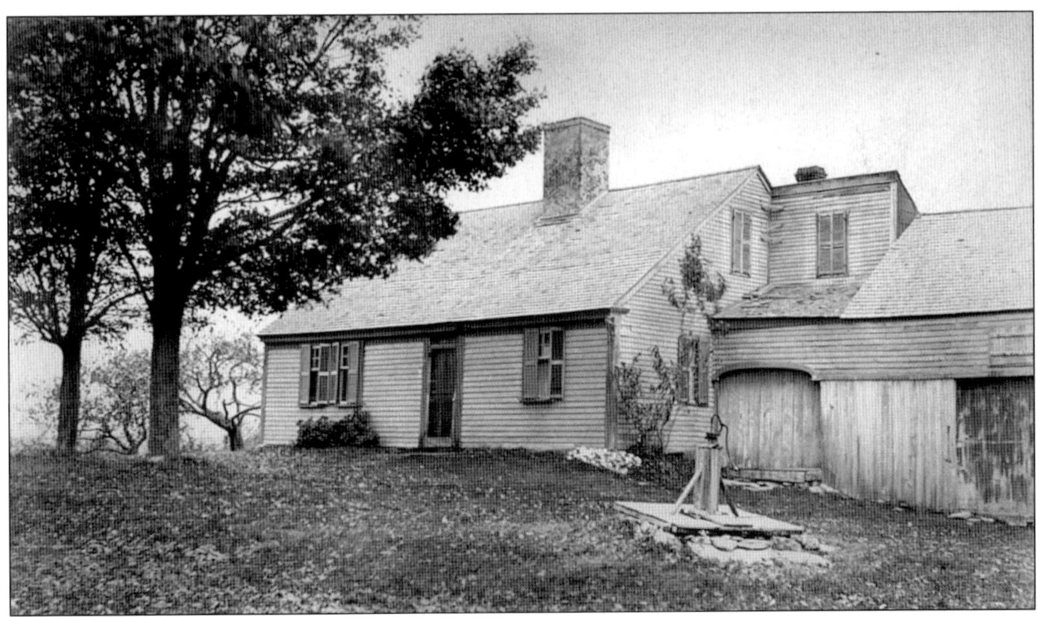

John Greenleaf Whittier visited Wachusett Mountain in the 1860s. While visiting, he stayed here at the Roper home, on the north slope of Wachusett. In "Monadnock from Wachusett in 1862," Whittier wrote, "Of far receding hills; and yet more far, Monadnock lifting from his night of pines. . . ." (Courtesy of the Princeton Historical Society.)

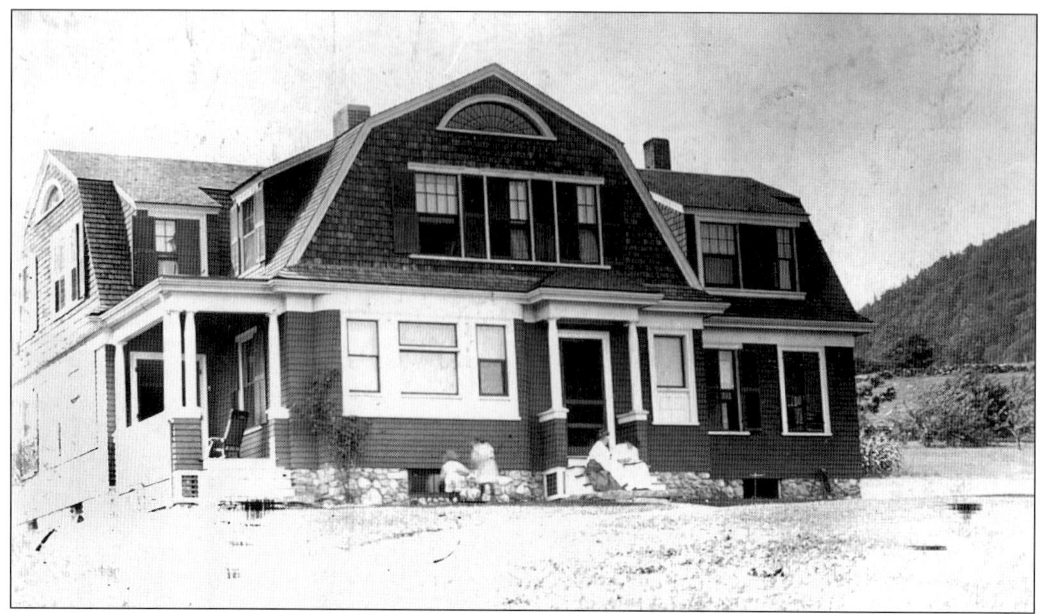

This house on Mountain Road was built in 1903 for Guy Chase, the first superintendent of the reservation. The creation of the Massachusetts State Reservation system began in 1898 in response to a concern for the preservation of lands and forests throughout the state. Purchased in 1900, Wachusett Mountain Reservation was the second park created; Mount Greylock, in the western part of the state, was the first. (Courtesy of the Princeton Historical Society.)

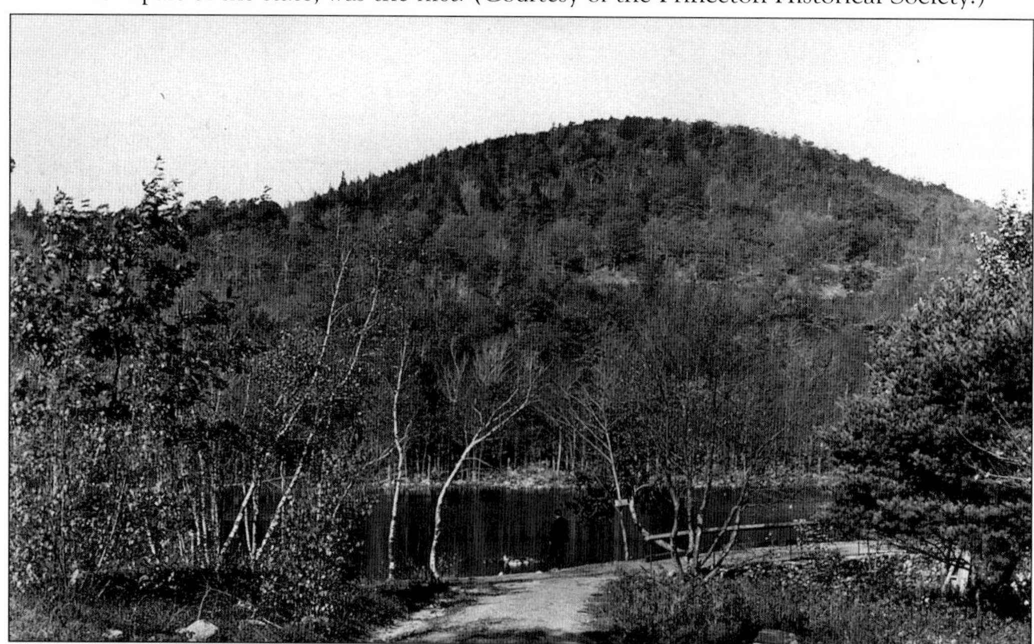

This early-1900s photograph of Echo Lake shows a beautiful two-acre spring and brook-fed pond with crystal water. Some 300 acres, including the lake, were enclosed c. 1915 for the elk and deer that were part of a park on the mountain. In 1903, Charles Hubbard's ice business supplied 20 customers with ice from Echo Lake. The job of cutting ice, sometimes as thick as 12 inches, lasted about a week each winter. (Courtesy of the Princeton Historical Society.)

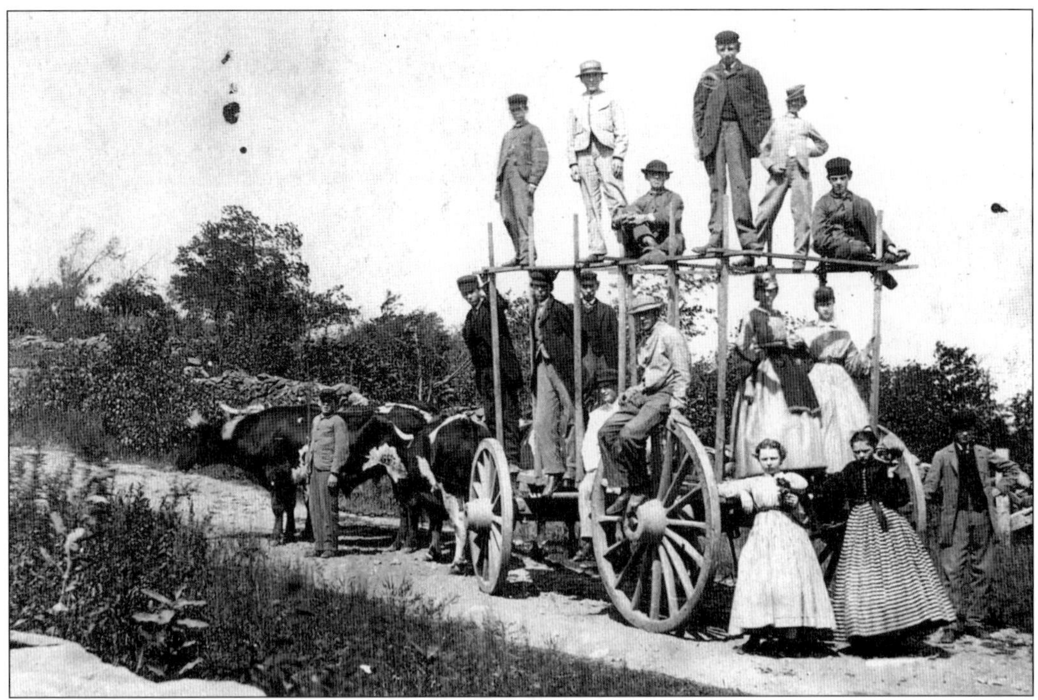

An oxcart traveling up the mountain in 1869, when this photograph was taken, was one of the early modes of transportation to reach the summit. The only road to the summit in 1869 was two and a half miles of steep and rocky terrain. (Courtesy of Nancy Beaman Flanders.)

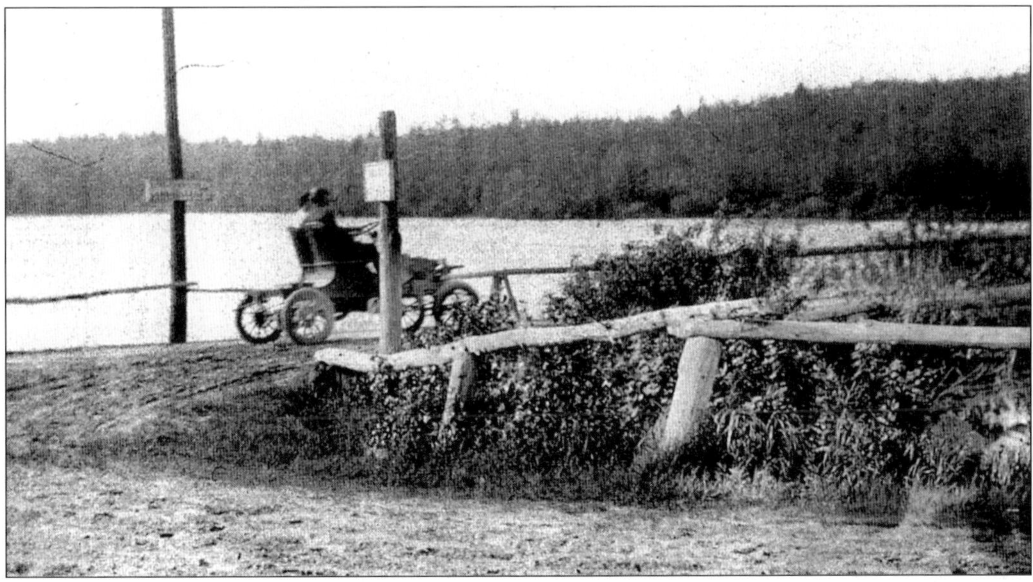

Automobile manufacturer Karl Grout of Orange drove his steam car to the top of the mountain in 1902 with John Faxon of Fitchburg. The automobile, which was 6 1/2 horsepower and weighed 1,400 pounds, made the trip in 25 minutes. Grout and Faxon were met by the police and were arrested when they returned, but the case was dismissed. This automobile, shown near Wachusett Lake, is similar to the one the men drove to the summit in 1902. (Courtesy of the Westminster Historical Society.)

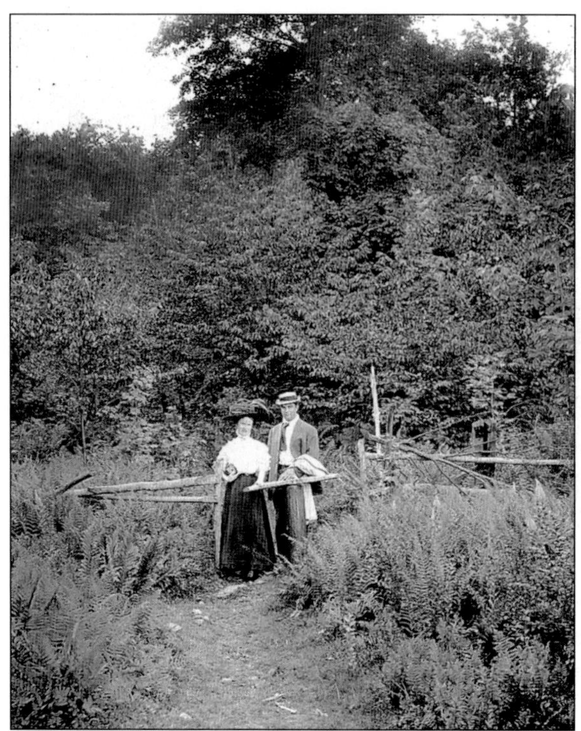

Two people are passing through the turnstile at the entrance to the Mountain House Trail in the early 1900s. Before the Mountain Road was built in the 1880s, this was the only road to the summit. Once at the summit, one can see for 120 miles on a clear day. The mountain is 2,006 feet above sea level and 1,119 feet above Wachusett Lake. It is the highest point east of the Berkshires. (Courtesy of the Princeton Historical Society.)

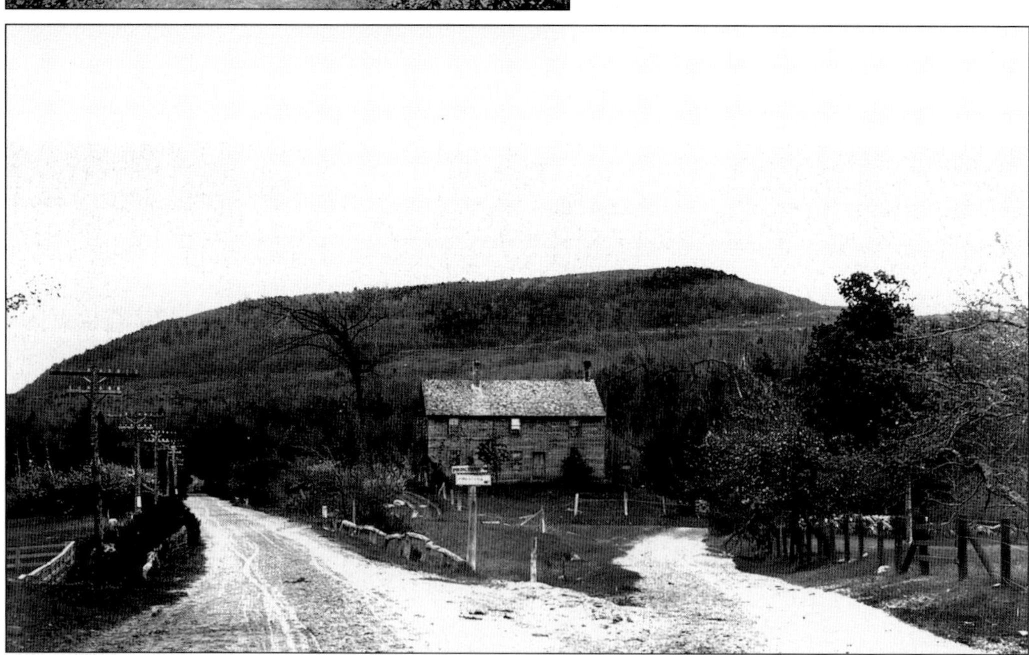

Simeon Bolton, whose family were early settlers to the town of Westminster in 1773, was the founder of Wachusett Park. He lived in this house at the intersection of Bolton and Mile Hill Roads in Westminster. Near his home he built Wachusett Park at the foot of the mountain and first opened it to the public *c.* 1873. Under Simeon Bolton's direction, land was cleared and other buildings were constructed. Wachusett Park and Griswold Park, on the north side of the lake, comprised about 35 acres. (Courtesy of the Westminster Historical Society.)

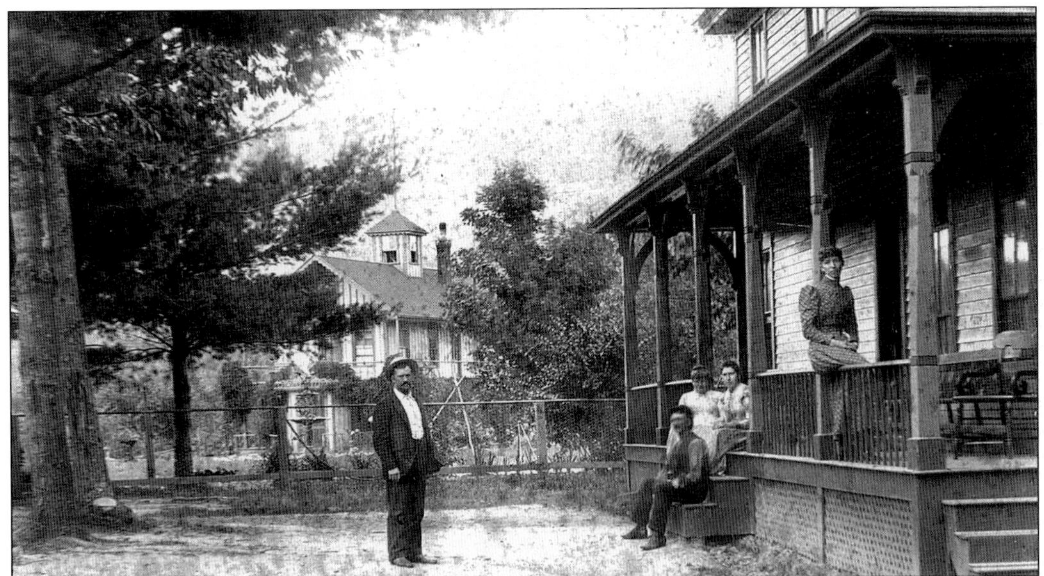

The *Gardner News* reported in May 1880 that the North View House (formerly the home of Mrs. L.G. Brown), in Wachusett Park, was nearly complete and was reported to be ready in June. It was two and a half stories high, with an office, parlor, and large dining room that seated 50 guests on the ground floor, and a second floor with seven bedrooms. Alley Harrington of Princeton managed the North View House in 1902. (Courtesy of the Westminster Historical Society.)

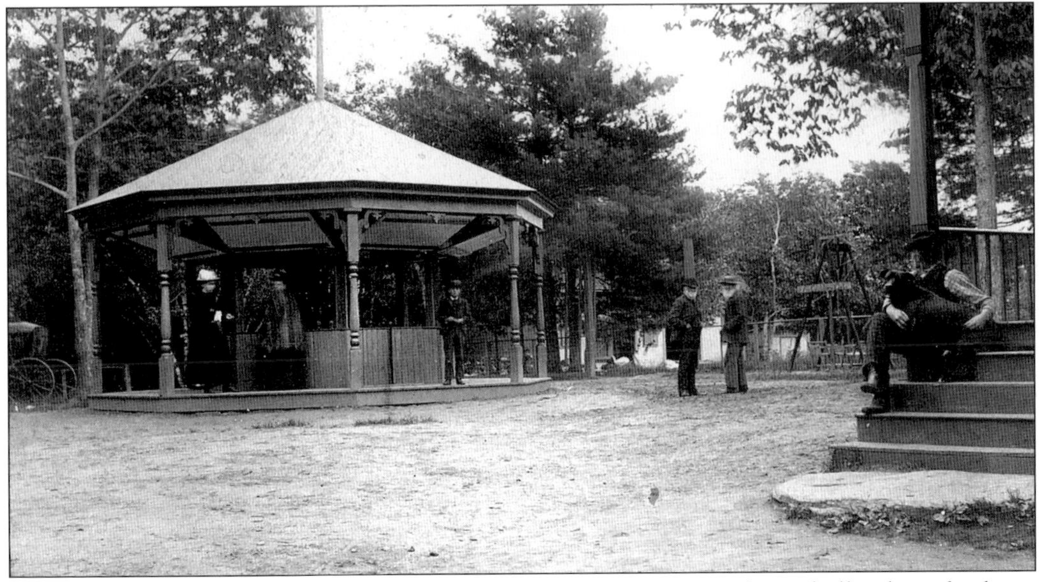

Wachusett Park had a pavilion where area bands would play, two dance halls where food was served, a skating rink, a 60-foot bowling alley, a stable, and a private fishpond. At one of the pavilions, Mary and Simeon Bolton served hornpout dinners, sometimes to as many as 200 people. (Courtesy of the Westminster Historical Society.)

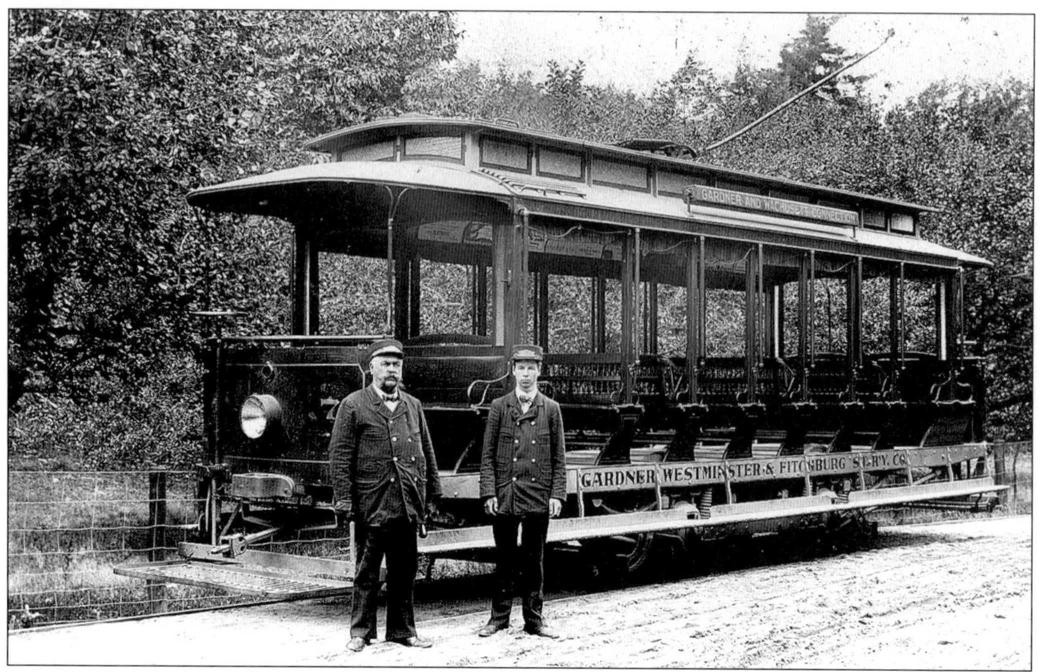

The advent of the trolley in 1899 brought many people to Wachusett Park on Sundays and holidays. The Osgood Bradley Company of Worcester made new trolley cars that ran each half-hour during the day in summer, and the last car left the park at 9:55 p.m. The trolley to Wachusett Park stopped running in 1920, and with its discontinuation, the park closed. (Courtesy of the Westminster Historical Society.)

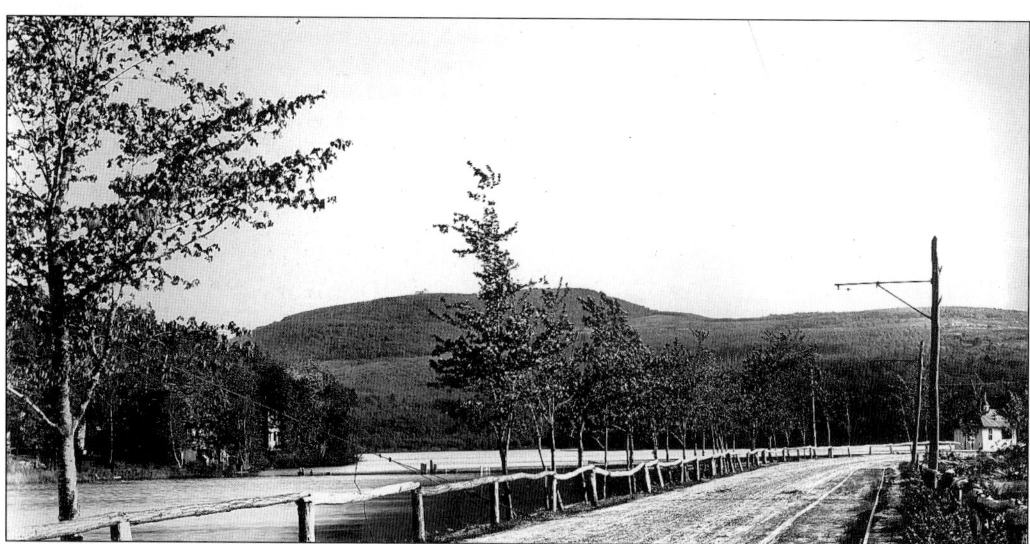

In 1902, the Gardner, Westminster, and Fitchburg Street Railway Company purchased Wachusett Park and made renovations. The railway company built a spur off the main line and provided transportation to Wachusett Park and adjoining Griswold Park. People were able to make railway connections and reach the park, where the tracks wound around the lake and stopped near the picnic grove. A plan to build a tramway to the summit was abolished in 1903. (Courtesy of the Westminster Historical Society.)

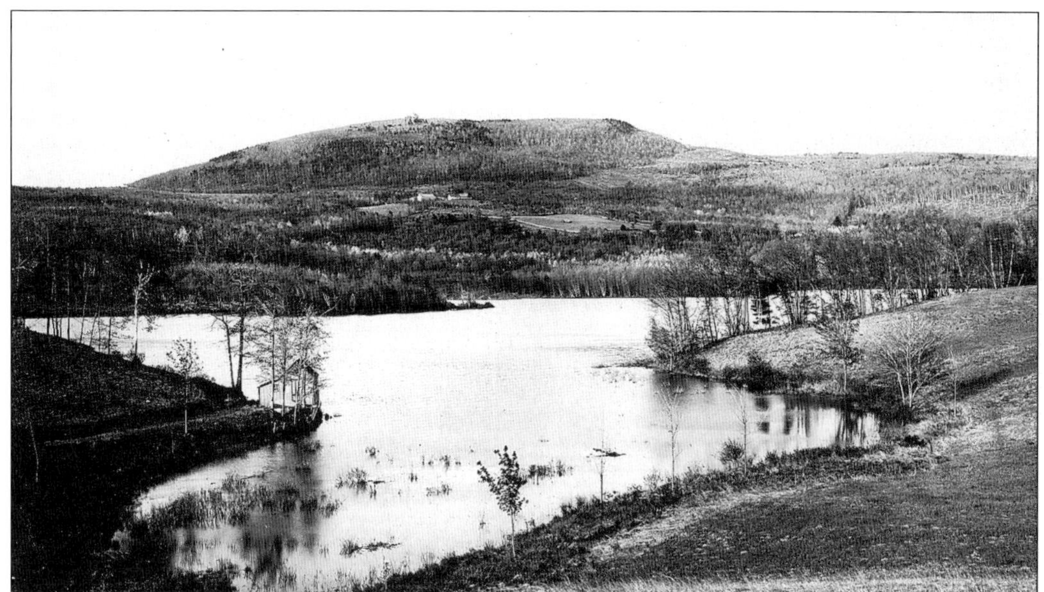

Wachusett Lake, near the base of the mountain in Westminster, is about a mile long and half-mile wide. It is spring fed and contains several varieties of freshwater fish, bass, pickerel, and hornpout. Summer homes in the late 1880s were built beside the shores of the lake. The home of L.J. Brown (later the North View House) had exotic shrubs, trees, and rare flowers, and visitors could stop to enjoy the peaceful walks and the gardens. (Courtesy of the Princeton Historical Society.)

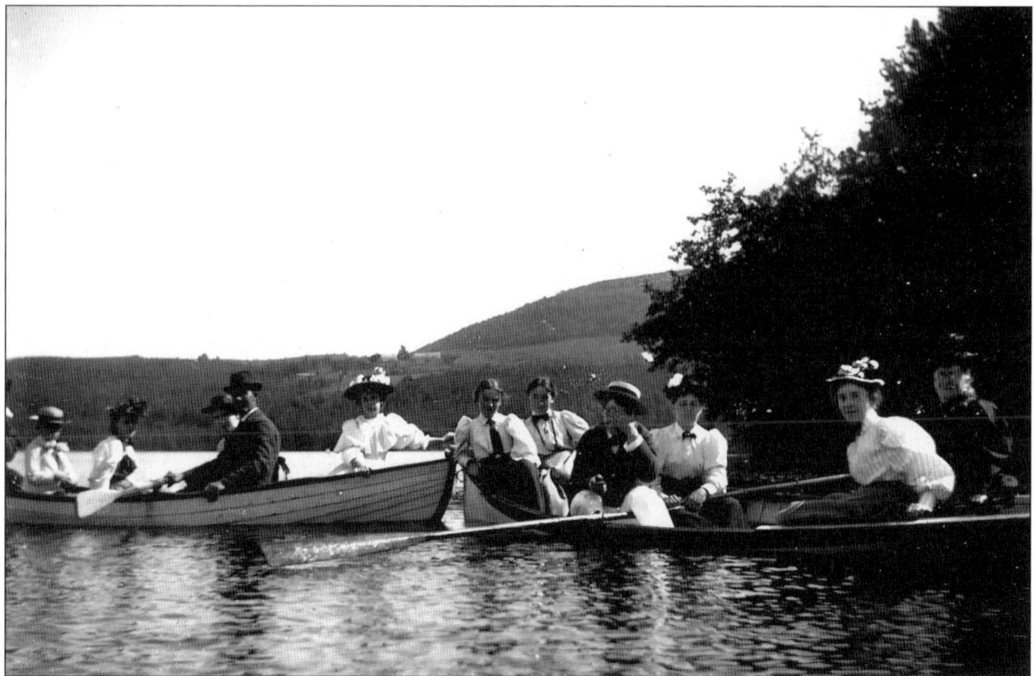

Young people are boating on Wachusett Lake in the early 1900s. Wachusett Park rented boats that allowed visitors to spend the day on the water enjoying the scenery or some of the excellent fishing. (Courtesy of the Princeton Historical Society.)

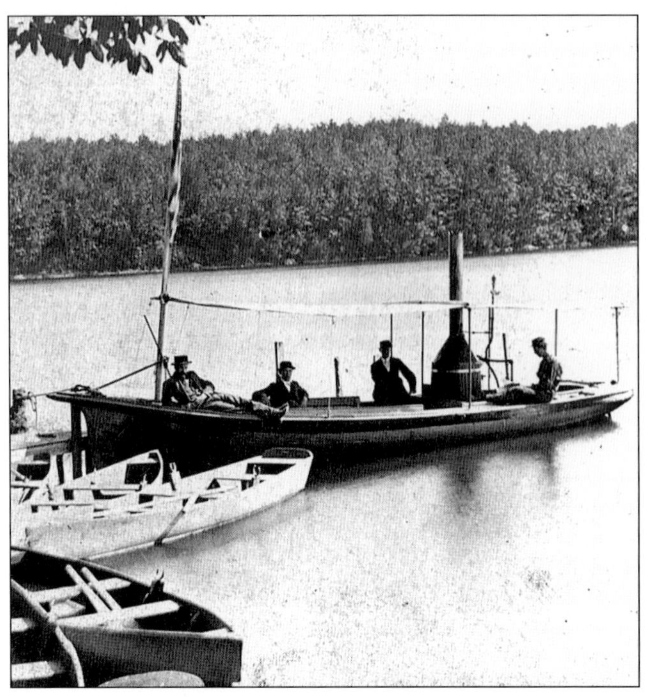

This late-1800s photograph shows one of the popular steamboats on Wachusett Lake. Mr. and Mrs. Thomas Griswold, proprietors of Griswold Park (on the other side of the lake), added steamboat rides as an attraction. An 1879 edition of the *Gardner News* said that the steamer *Wachusett* was running all day for the Fourth of July picnic, which 700 people attended. In 1880, it was reported by the *Gardner News* that the *Continental* was delivered for the Old Folks Picnic. (Courtesy of the Westminster Historical Society.)

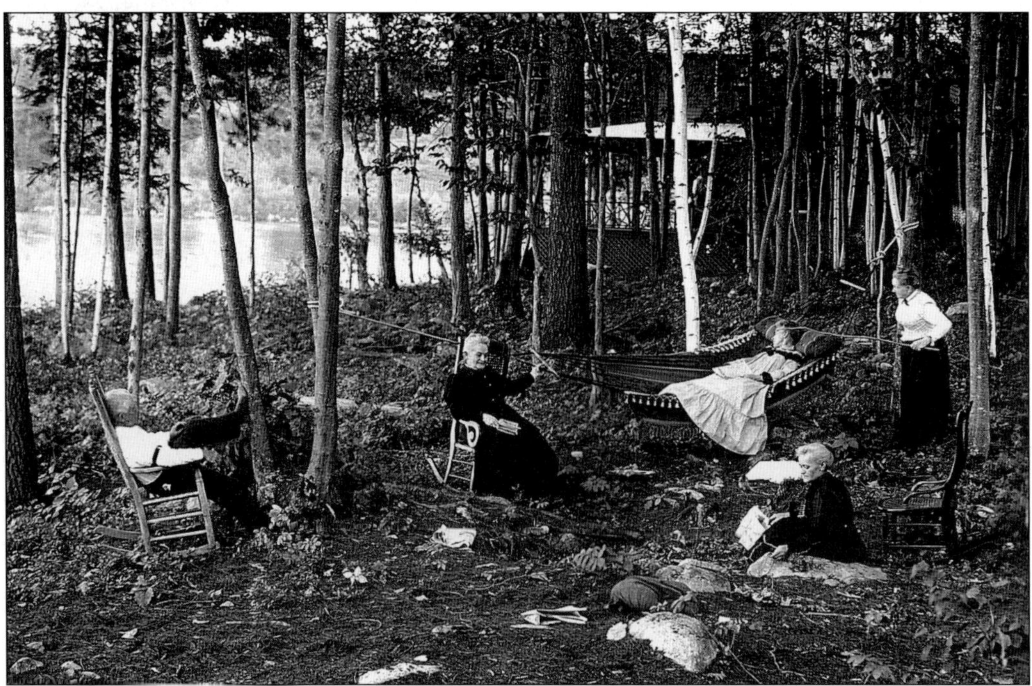

The most popular event of the season at the park was the Old Folks Picnic. Each year, several hundred people of all ages, including previous residents of surrounding towns, traveled long distances to attend. The day's activities included praying, singing old-time songs, making speeches, and telling historical stories. Pictured in the early 1900s, these people are enjoying a day at the park. (Courtesy of the Westminster Historical Society.)

Two

A Hilltop Town

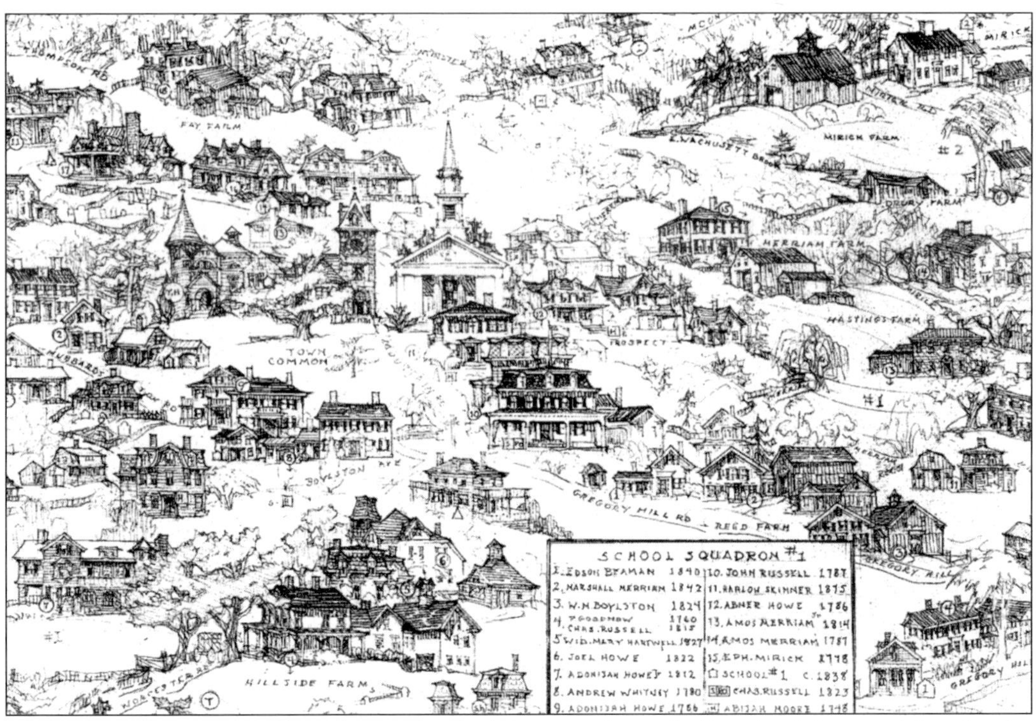

Princeton Center is seen here in a portion of the map drawn by Rosalind Sturges Allen for the Princeton Historical Society's anniversary in 1987. Princeton's beautiful landscape and interesting architecture were special to Mrs. Allen. She was a Princeton resident for 61 years and was an active member of the Princeton Historical Commission and the Princeton Historical Society. (Courtesy of the Princeton Historical Society.)

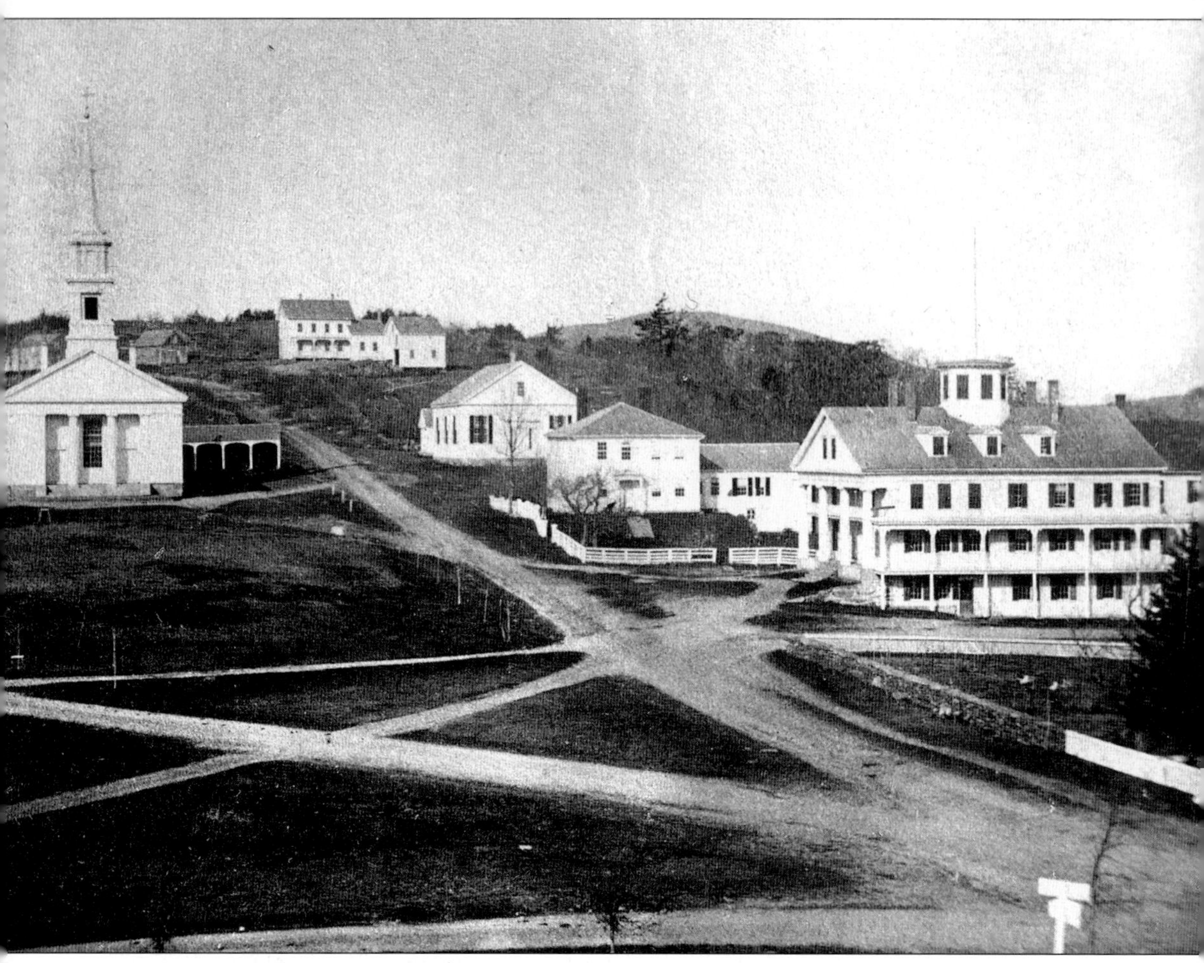

Princeton Common is pictured in a view looking north *c.* 1870. Ward Nicholas Boylston inherited Gov. Moses Gill's land holdings of 2,000 acres and, in 1819, gave the Rev. Samuel Clarke land on the common to build a house. In May 1838, the house was moved across Mountain Road, and the Union Congregational Church (along with 26 horse sheds) was built in the fashionable Greek Revival style and stood on the common until 1884. The church parsonage is farthest north on the hill. South of the parsonage can be seen a one-story building known as Boylston Hall, built in 1842 and partially funded by Ward Nicholas Boylston as a gift to the town. The hall was used for town meetings until it burned in September 1883. In the 1870s, a private school was held in Boylston Hall and was taught by a male college student. Farther south is the Rev. Samuel Clarke house, in its present location, and at the lower right is Prospect House. Originally, this Greek Revival building, built in 1840, was a Baptist church. It was sold in 1860 to Wilkes Roper and converted into Prospect House. (Courtesy of the Princeton Historical Society.)

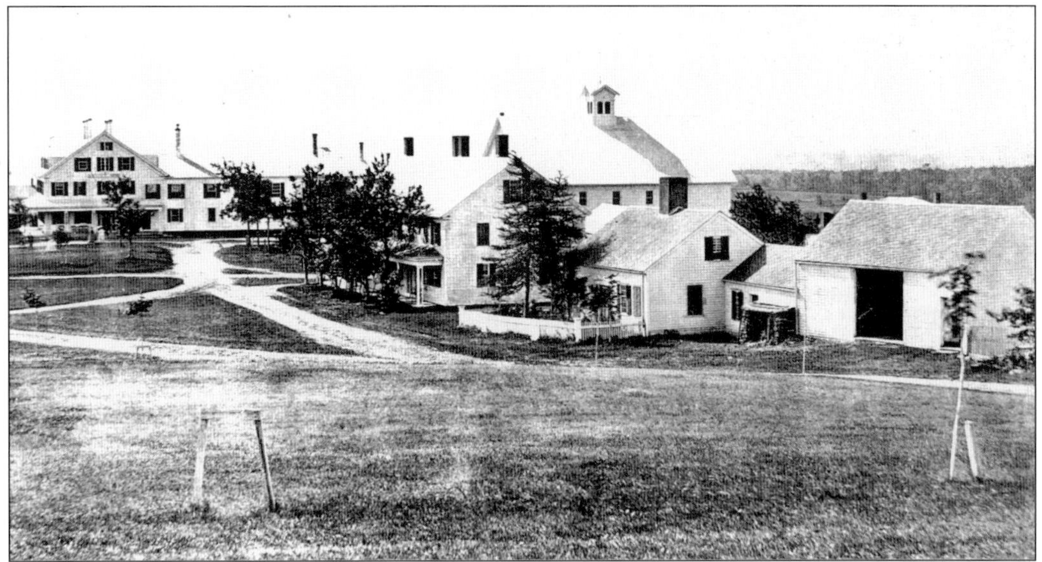

This early photograph of Princeton Common shows Wachusett House in the distance before it was remodeled in 1869. The Cape-style house (formerly the English Classical School) on the right belonged to Thomas Gill and was replaced in 1882 by a Second Empire house that belonged to Rufus Davis. The two-story house with the porch (center) is currently located at 1 Hubbardston Road. (Courtesy of Nancy Beaman Flanders.)

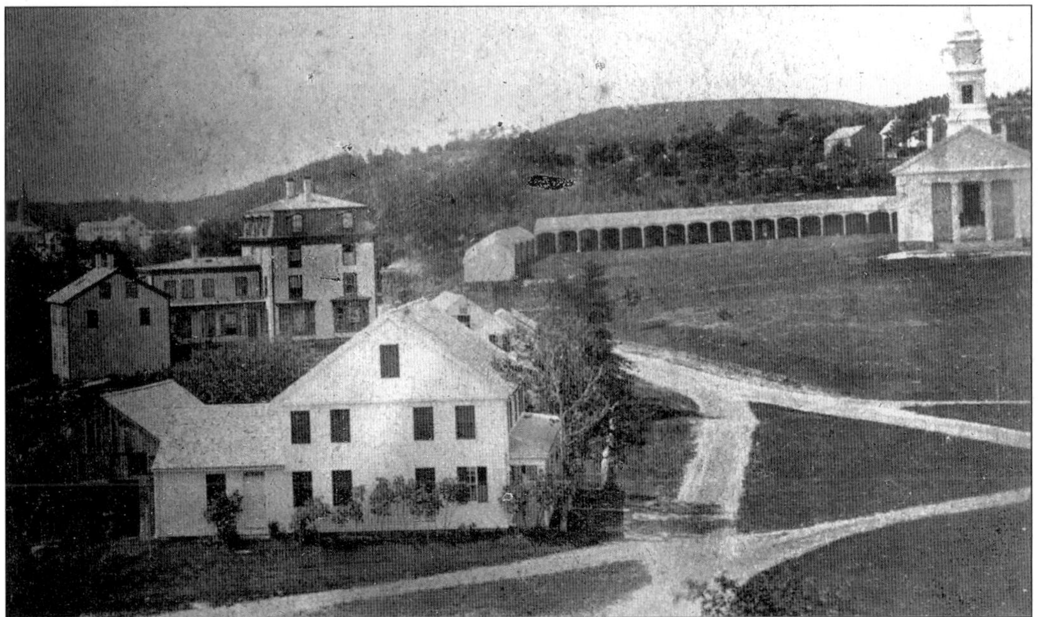

Built in 1842, the home of Daniel Davis is in the foreground. The central telephone office was installed here after the Wachusett House fire in 1910. Davis was one of the first to use daguerreotype in this country, and he invented the electromagnetic machine for electroplating in the 1840s. The house behind Davis's house belonged to Ezra Heywood, publisher of the *Word*, a liberal newspaper. Heywood was an advocate for women's rights and wrote the resolutions for the first Peace Society in Philadelphia. The Methodist church is in the distance at the far left. (Courtesy of the Princeton Historical Society.)

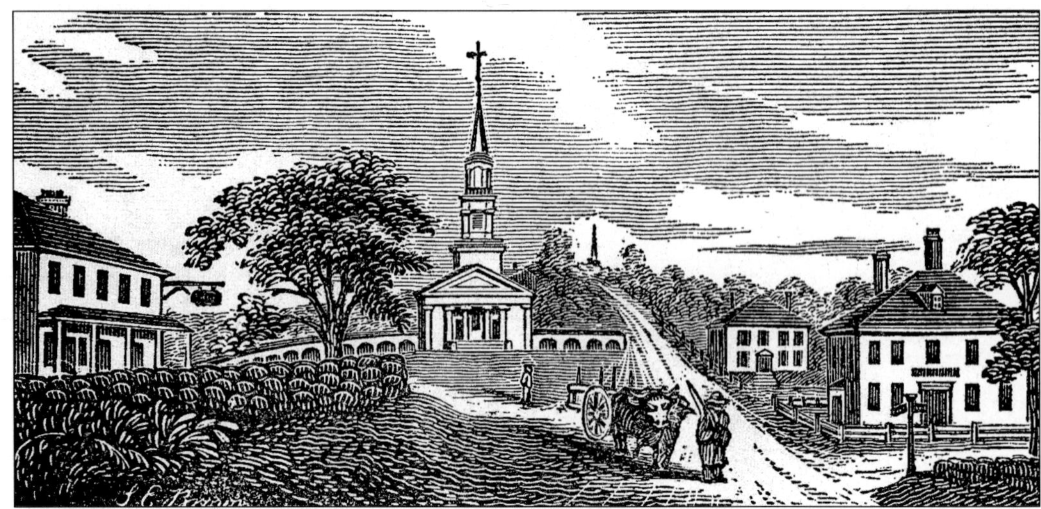

Taken from John Warner Barber's *Historical Collections*, this woodcut shows Princeton Common *c.* 1838–1839. The meetinghouse and horse sheds are at the head of the common. At the lower left is Richardson's store and tavern, possibly built here in anticipation of more business with the new stage line that opened in 1820. Blake and Allen's store is at the lower right. Farther up the hill is Rev. Samuel Clarke's house, and in the distance is the spire of the second meetinghouse. (Courtesy of the Princeton Historical Society.)

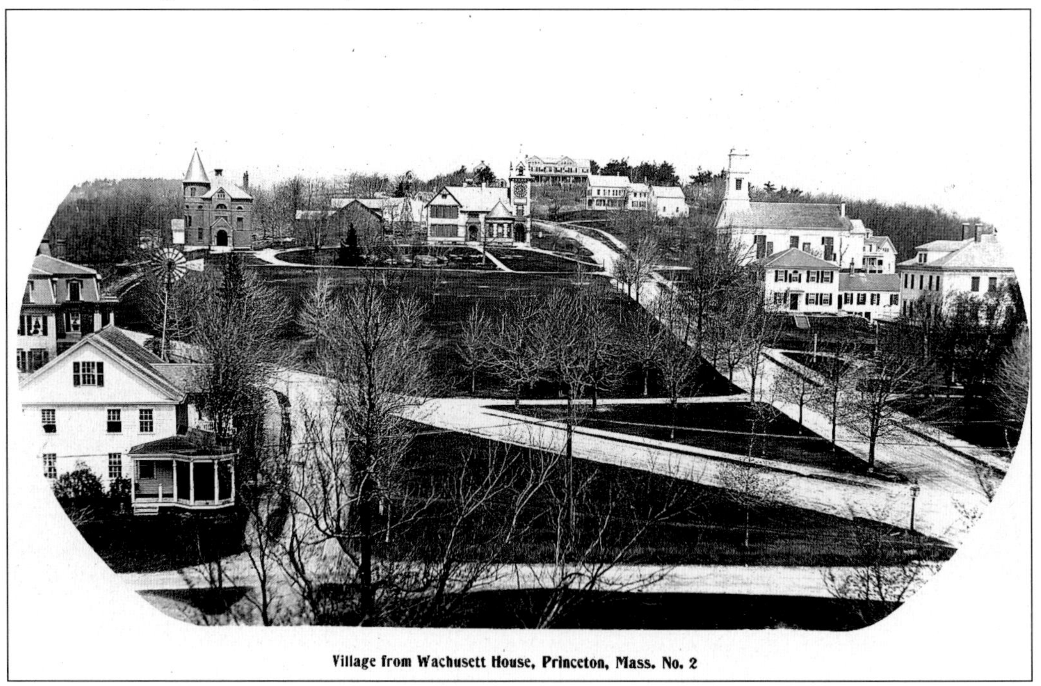

Village from Wachusett House, Princeton, Mass. No. 2

Princeton Common is pictured in a photograph taken from a window at Wachusett House in the early 1900s. Located farthest north on the hill is the Charles Washburn House, built in 1900 for the Worcester industrialist. Washburn was a personal friend of Theodore Roosevelt and wrote a biography of him. The house was converted into the Meeting House Restaurant in 1950 and was later sold and named the Princeton Inn. Today, it has been restored as a private home. (Courtesy of Bud Brooks.)

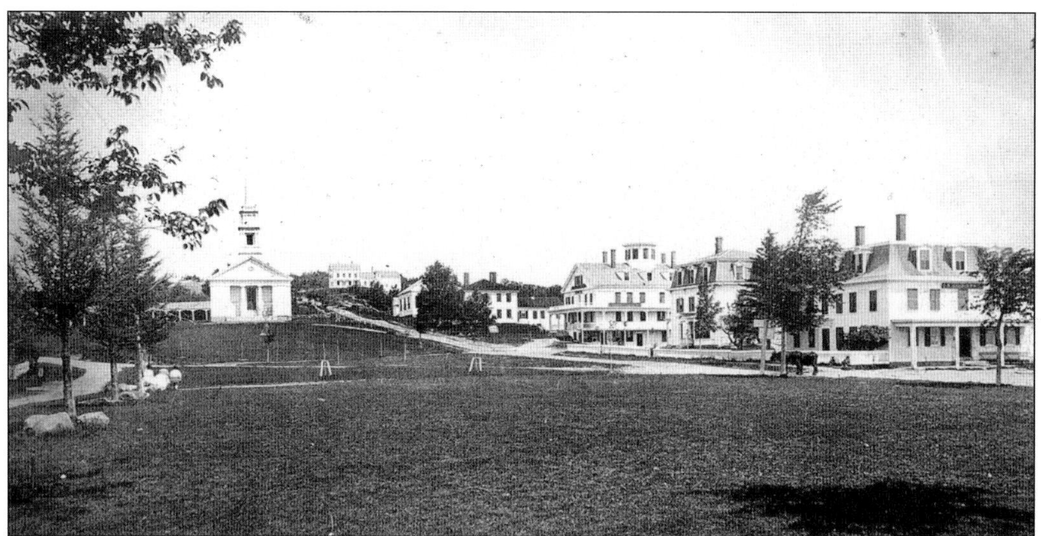

It was not until the 1870s that houses were built around the common in the popular Second Empire style with mansard roofs. The new mansard roof on the D.H. Gregory store (lower right) replaced the hip roof that dated from the late 1700s. The Gregory house, next door, was built in 1874. Across the common, two other houses were built in the 1880s. Newly planted trees surrounded the common. By the 1870s, Princeton was a fashionable summer resort town. (Courtesy of the Princeton Historical Society.)

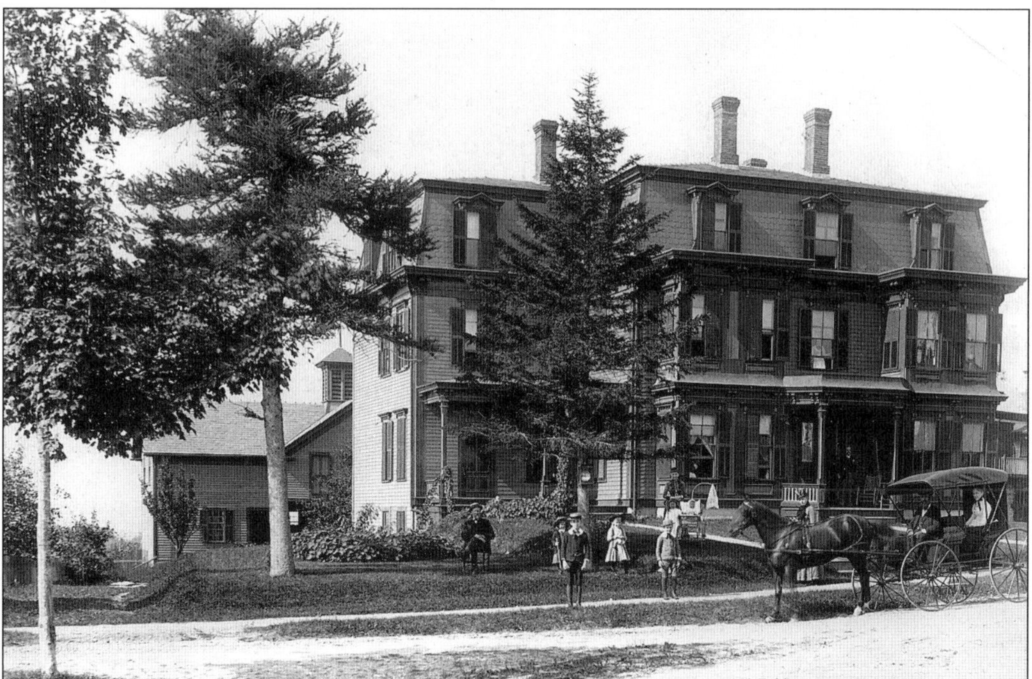

The Second Empire Rufus Davis house was built in 1882 and stood on the west side of the common in the location of the house at 5 Hubbardston Road. This house and the Heywood house to the right of it burned to the ground in 1908. The present house was built in 1909 on the foundation of the original Davis house. Rufus Davis is sitting on the lawn. (Courtesy of the Princeton Historical Society.)

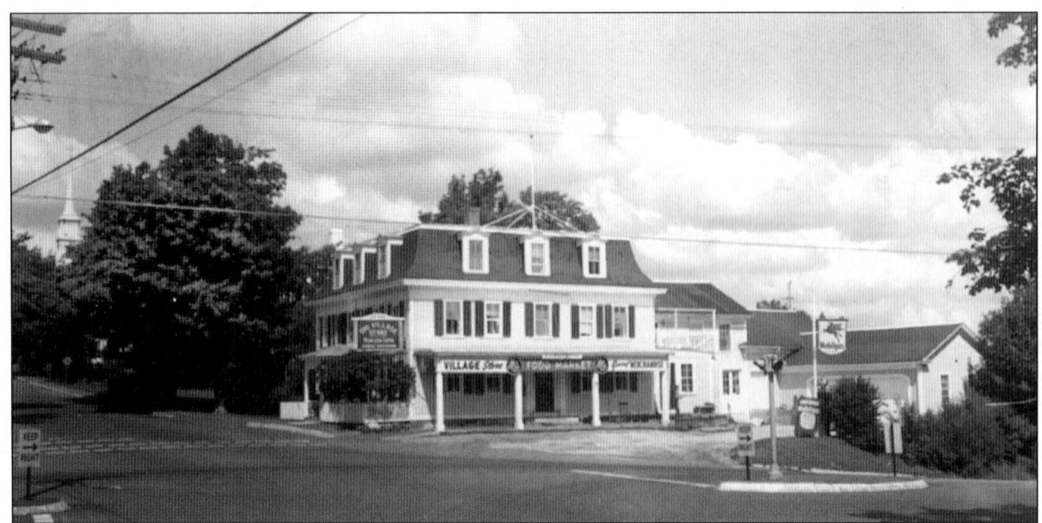

The Village Store, at the intersection of Mountain and Gregory Hill Roads, began as early as the 1770s. By 1785, a blacksmith shop was beside it on Mountain Road. David Hoyt Gregory purchased it in 1840, and it remained in the family for over 100 years. Josiah Gregory became the owner in 1865, and Raymond Gregory, third generation, was proprietor from 1915 to 1942. Pictured here in the mid-1900s, the store closed in the 1990s. (Courtesy of the Princeton Historical Society.)

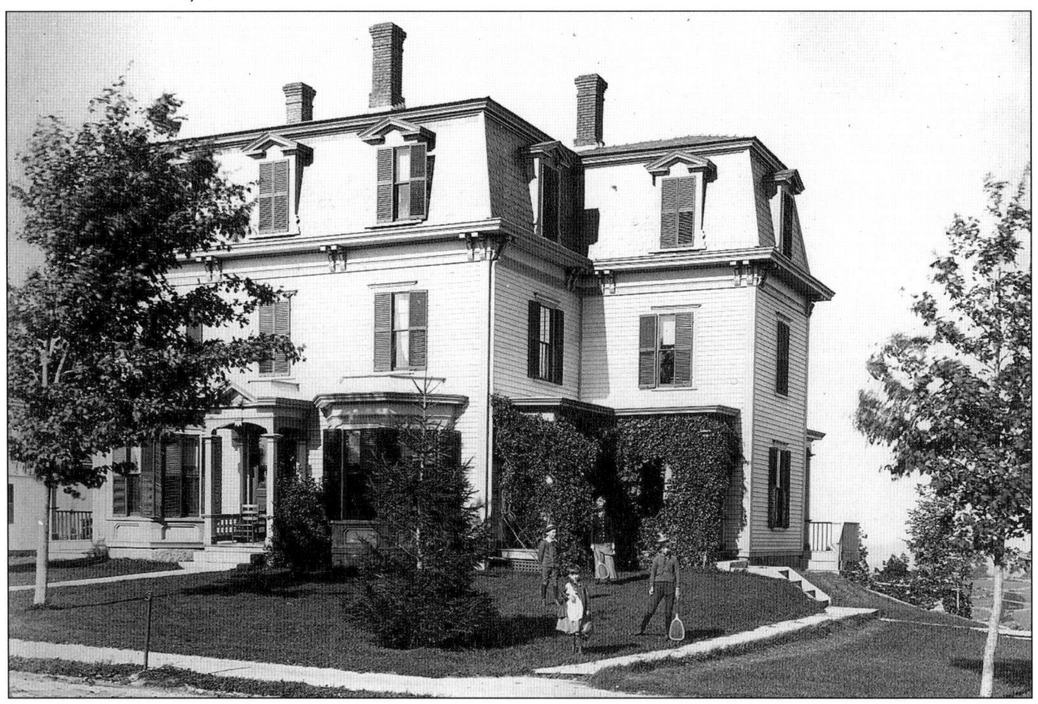

This Second Empire house, beside the store on Mountain Road, was built in 1874 for Josiah D. Gregory. Josiah and his father, David, were co-owners of the D.H. Gregory and Company general store. Outside the house are the Gregory children. Pictured are Richard H. Gregory (far left), Mary Gregory (in the back), Raymond Gregory (right), and Louise Gregory (in the front). (Courtesy of the Princeton Historical Society.)

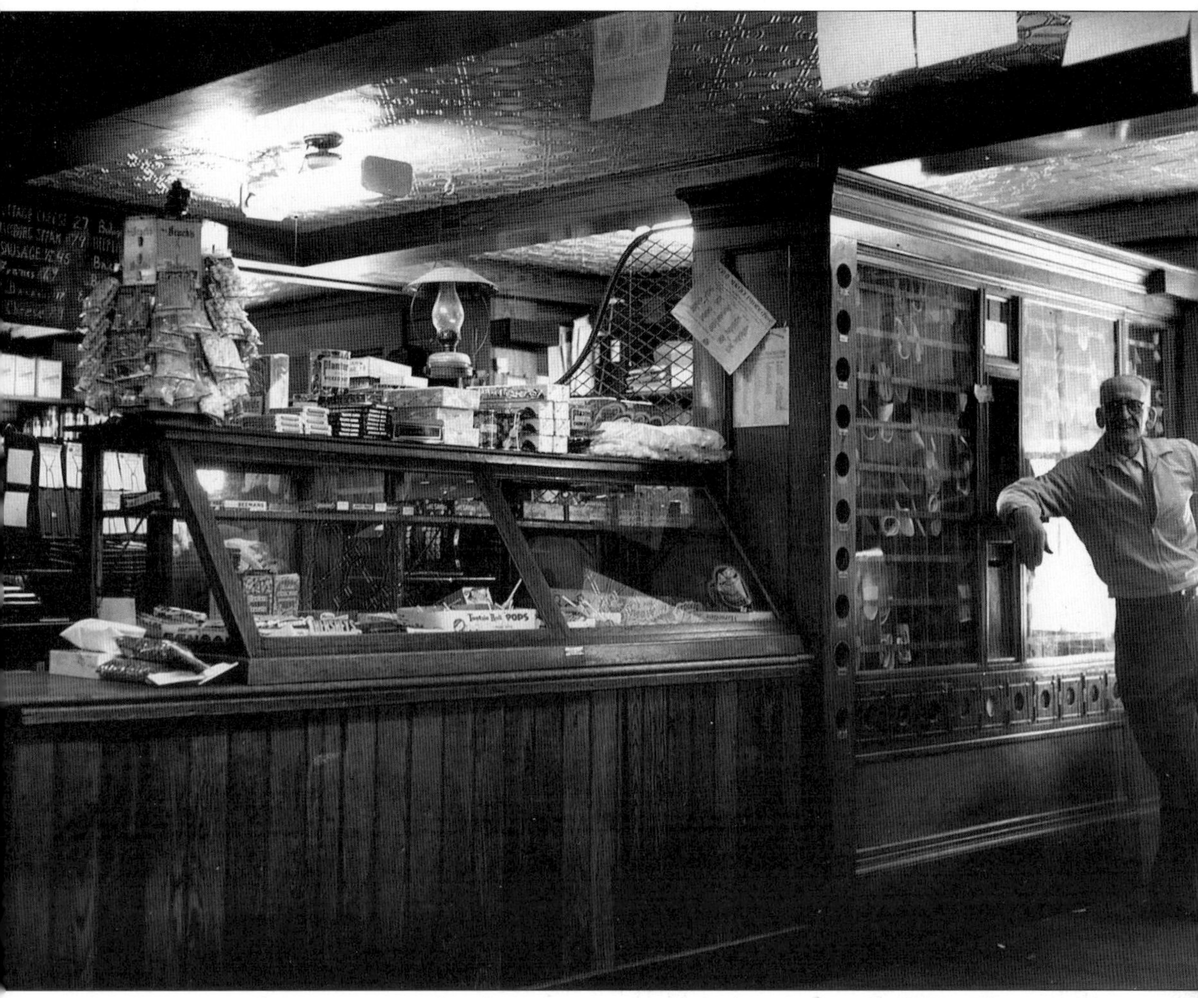

D.H. Gregory and Company was bustling in its early days, the 1840s and 1850s. The town's population was 1,400, and the store inventory amounted to $1,500. Goods delivered to Princeton took six horses to pull the load from Boston or Worcester. The return trip was lighter because it often consisted of braided straw hats made by many local women in their homes. As Princeton's popularity as a summer resort increased by the 1860s, business flourished with the arrival of the wealthy summer guests. Josiah Gregory abandoned his dining room and kitchen to make more space for merchandise. Beginning in September 1866, mail was delivered to the post office in the store by stagecoach. By 1871, it was brought by rail. For some time *c.* 1900, the telephone office was located in the store. Malcolm Chase, beside the mailboxes, owned the store in the 1950s. (Courtesy of the Princeton Historical Society.)

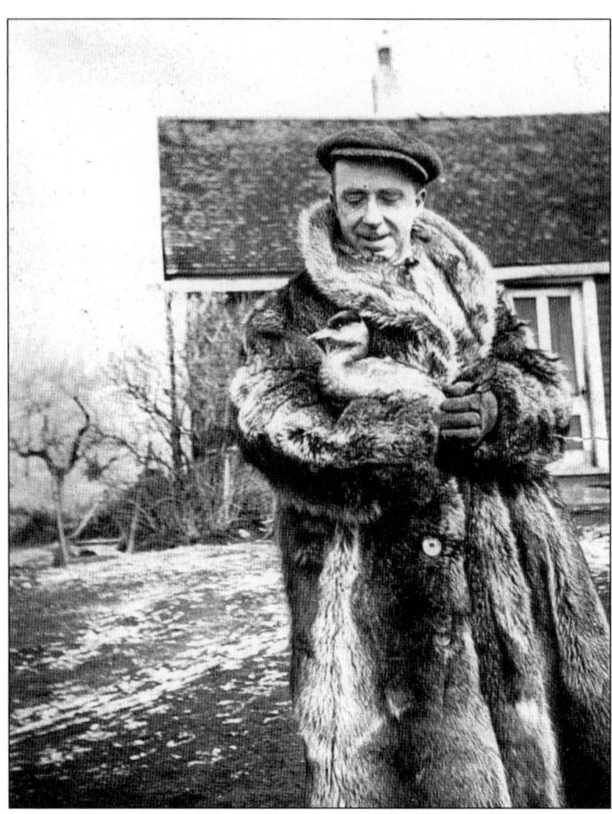

Raymond J. Gregory, postmaster and town clerk, poses in his fur coat with a pet grebe. Gregory was the owner of D.H. Gregory and Company from 1915 until his death in 1942. Credited as an expert in ornithology, he was a charter member of the Forbush Bird Club and was a trustee of the Massachusetts Audubon Society. (Courtesy of the Princeton Historical Society.)

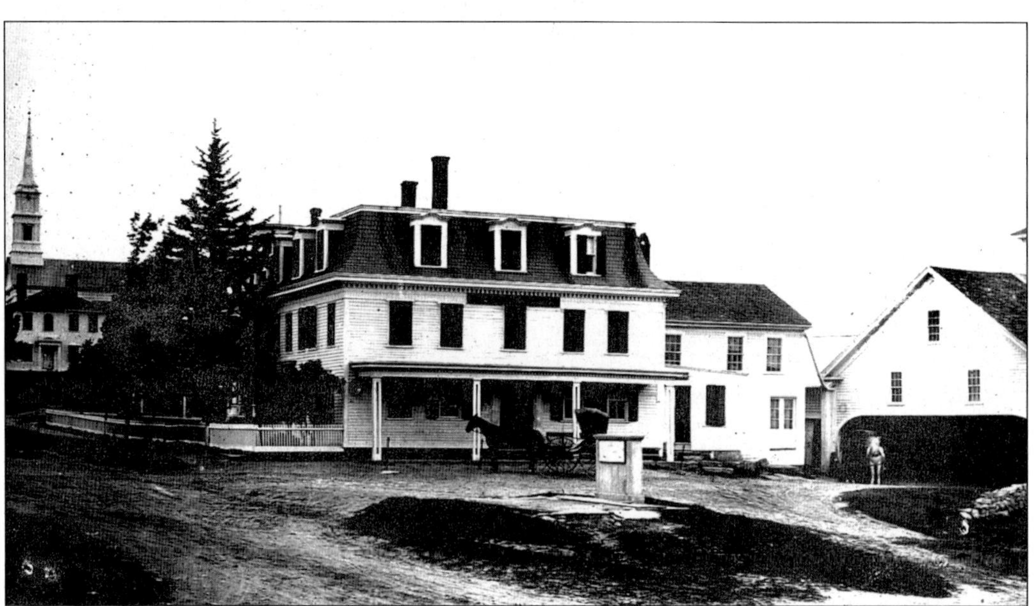

The town hay scales were located on a piece of land in front of the Gregory store at the intersection of Gregory Hill and Mountain Roads. Farmers brought their hay wagons to weigh on this platform scale before selling the hay at market. The hay scales were removed in the 1930s. (Courtesy of Marjorie Ollila.)

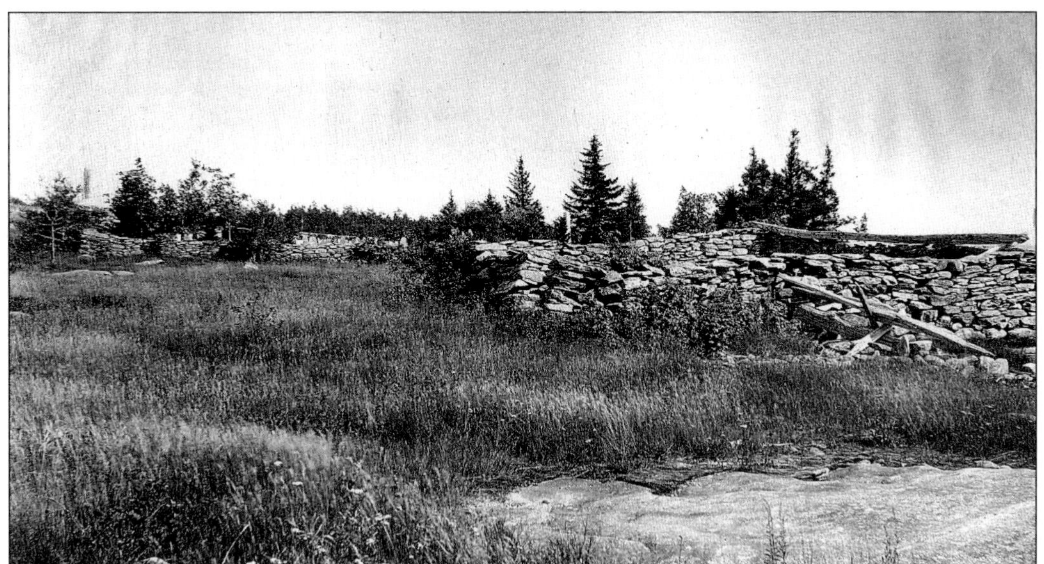

The remnants of the town pound are visible on Mountain Road. As early as 1761, at one of the first town meetings, the warrant articles were to see if the town would build a pound, raise tax money, build a meetinghouse, fix the wages of the assessors, do anything about the roads, and vote whether to let swine run at large. (Courtesy of the Princeton Historical Society.)

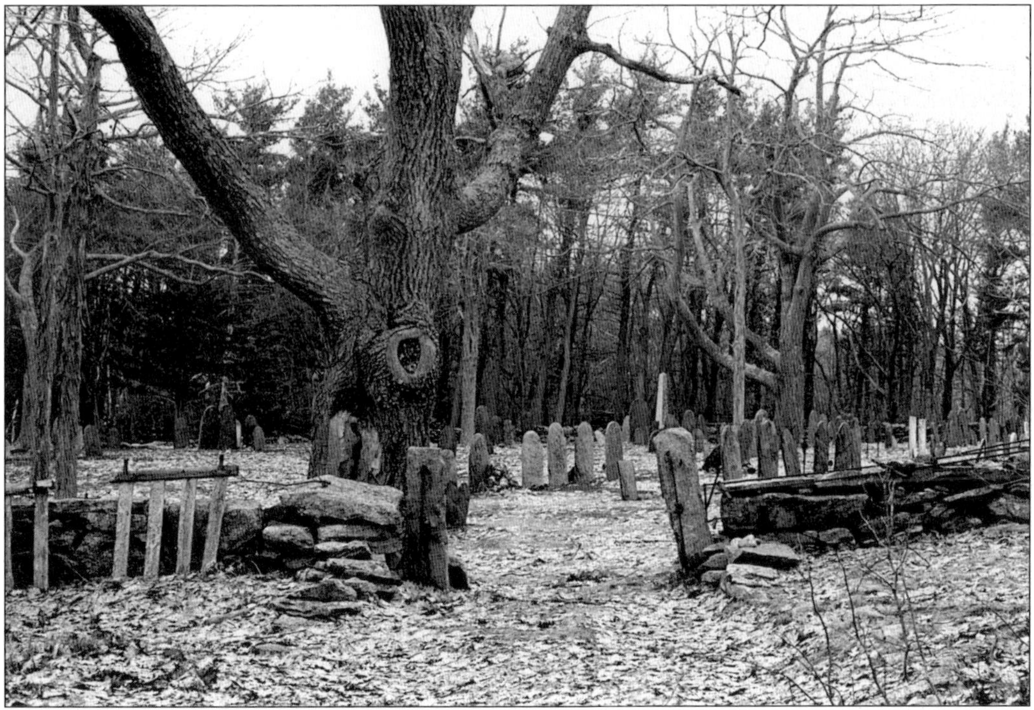

Early burials were either in Rutland or on the farm where the person died. Hon. Moses Gill gave a 20-acre parcel of land to the town in 1765, and from it two and a half acres were reserved for Meetinghouse Cemetery. In 1773, the cemetery was enlarged and a five-foot wall built around it. In the southwest part of the cemetery is the town tomb, where bodies were placed in the winter months. (Courtesy of the Princeton Historical Commission.)

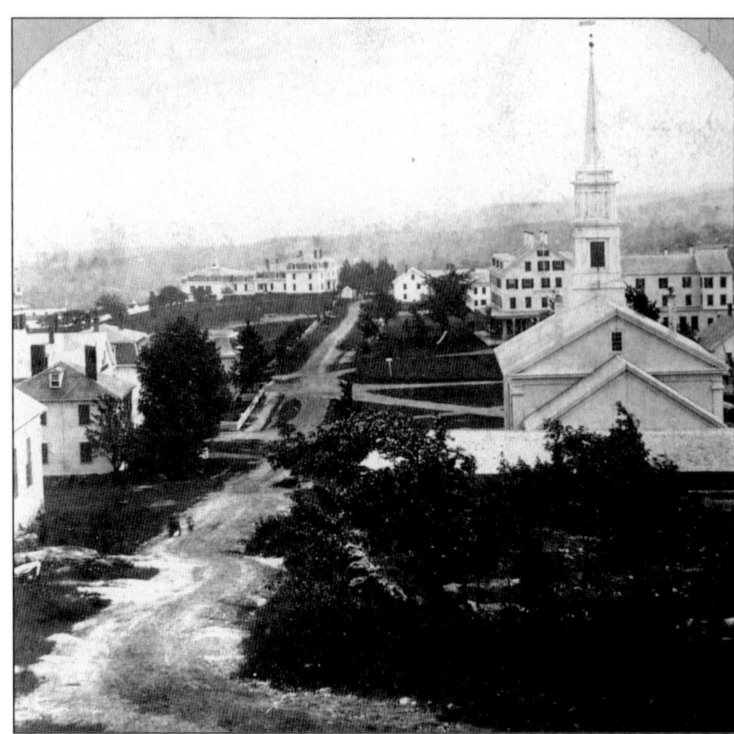

Looking south, this view shows Princeton Center from a steep, winding Mountain Road. The photograph dates from before Boylston Hall (partially seen at the far left) burned in 1883. At the right is the Congregational church, with the horse sheds in the rear. Hillside Farm, home of John Brooks, is seen in the distance as Worcester Road continues out of sight. (Courtesy of Nancy Beaman Flanders.)

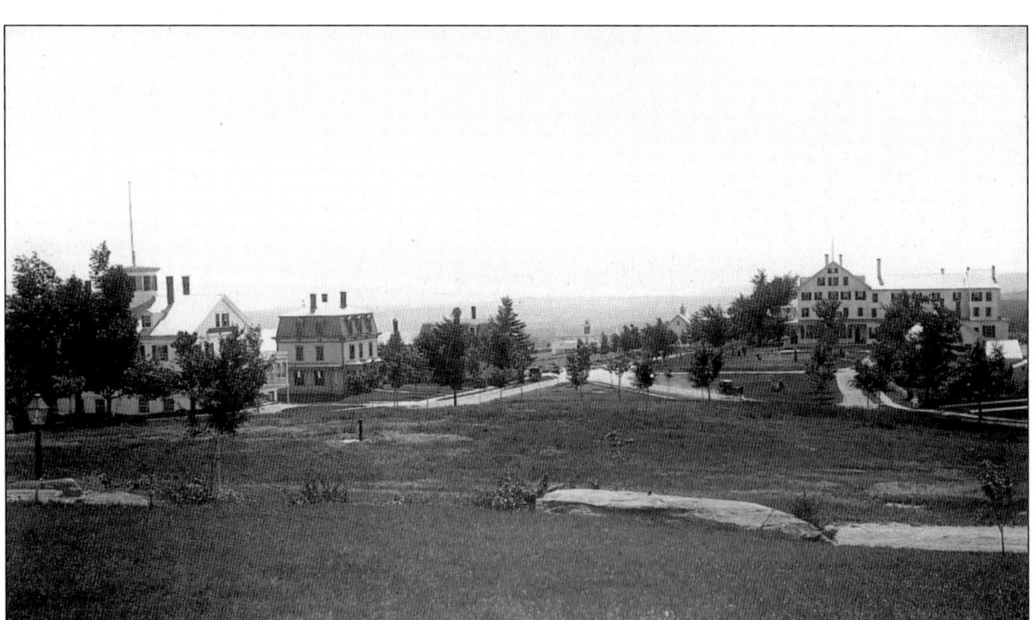

This photograph of the common shows a public water pump located across from Prospect House. The area where the water pump stands coincides with location of the Congregational church and the Rev. Samuel Clarke house before they were moved. The precise earlier locations of the church and the Clarke house were identified in an archaeological survey of the common done in June 2001 by archaeologists from the University of Massachusetts. (Courtesy of the Princeton Historical Society.)

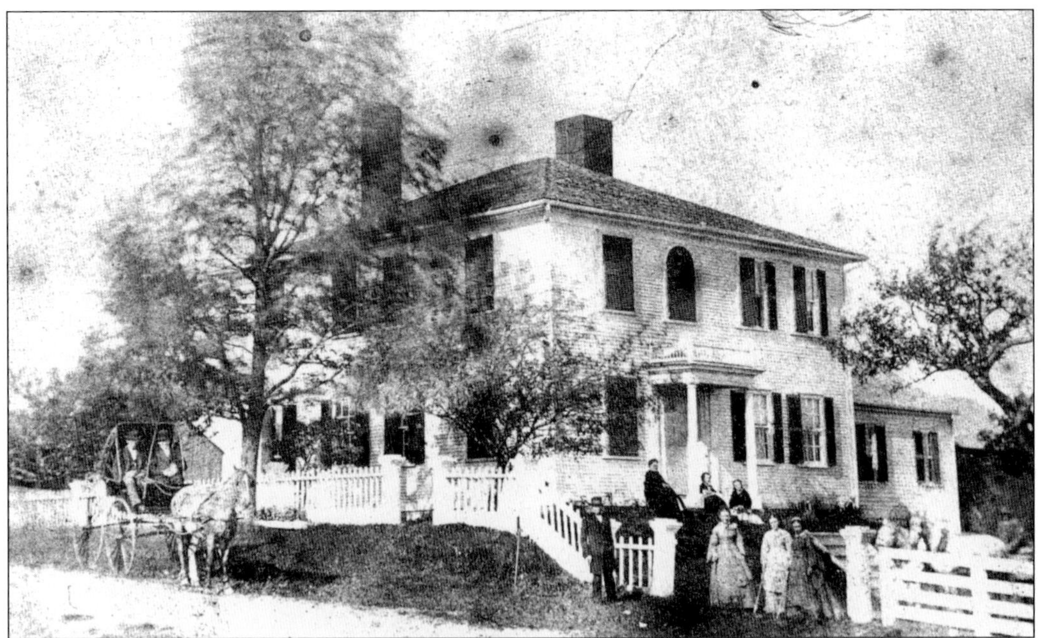

The Rev. Samuel Clarke house is seen after it was moved off the common and across Mountain Road in 1838. Before the separation of church and state in 1833, the town called Reverend Clarke to be the minister. The church claimed it was its right to call the minister and opposed the town. After some time of disagreement and a third split vote, the town proceeded to ordain Reverend Clarke. Phineas Gregory purchased the house in 1845, and it remained in the Gregory family until 1958. (Courtesy of Nancy Beaman Flanders.)

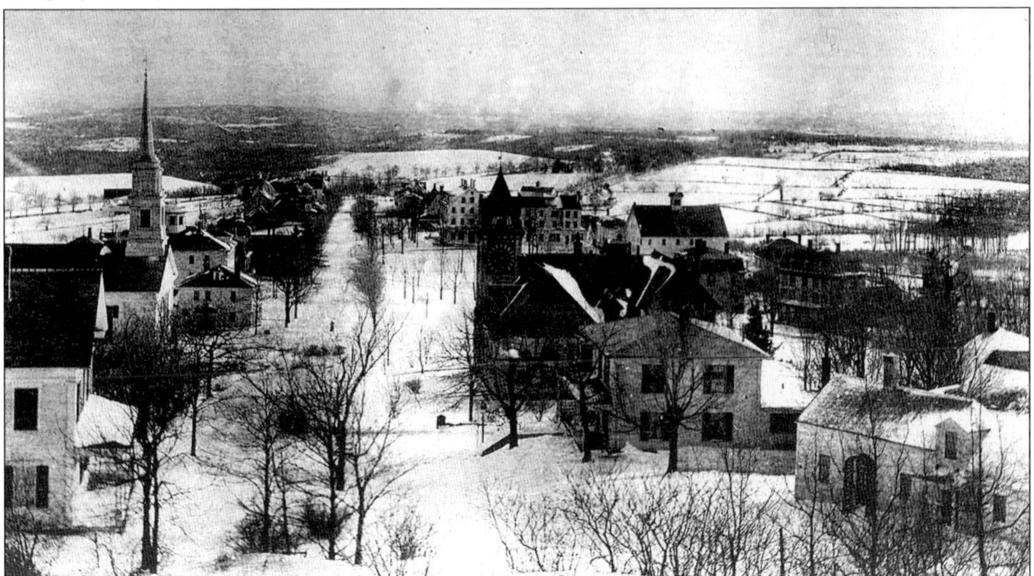

Looking down Mountain Road in the early 1900s, this wintery view shows a snow-covered Princeton Center. The Cape-style house at the lower right belonged to Liberty, Mrs. Charles Washburn's driver. The house below it was Prentice Dolittle's home and livery, where he kept his horses, stagecoaches, and wagons. In the foreground to the left is the Congregational parsonage. (Courtesy of the Princeton Historical Society.)

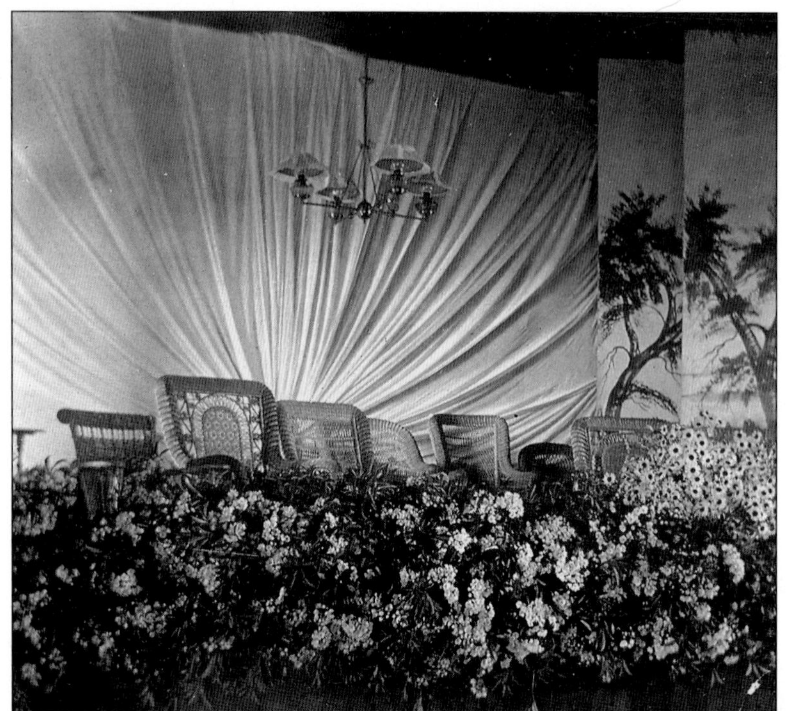

The large meeting room upstairs in Bagg Hall was used for many purposes, including town meetings, graduations, dances, and Grange meetings. In this photograph, the stage is decorated with flowers and a fabric backdrop for an event. Hanging above the stage is a gas lamp with several arms, indicating that the photograph was taken sometime in the early 1900s. (Courtesy of Nancy Beaman Flanders.)

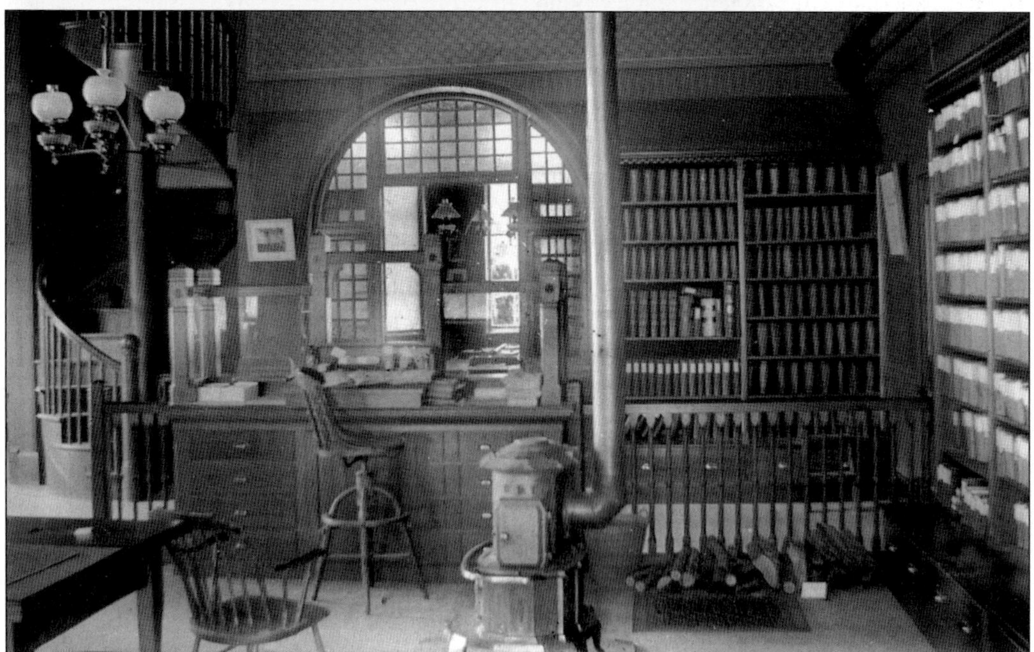

The wood stove in the Goodnow Memorial Building was located near the circulation desk, as can be seen in this late-1800s photograph. A private circulating library was established in Princeton as early as 1790. The Ladies Reading Society and the Princeton Agricultural Society donated most of the books when the new library was completed in 1883. In the early days, only the librarian was allowed to take the books from the shelves. (Courtesy of the Princeton Historical Society and Bruce Dean.)

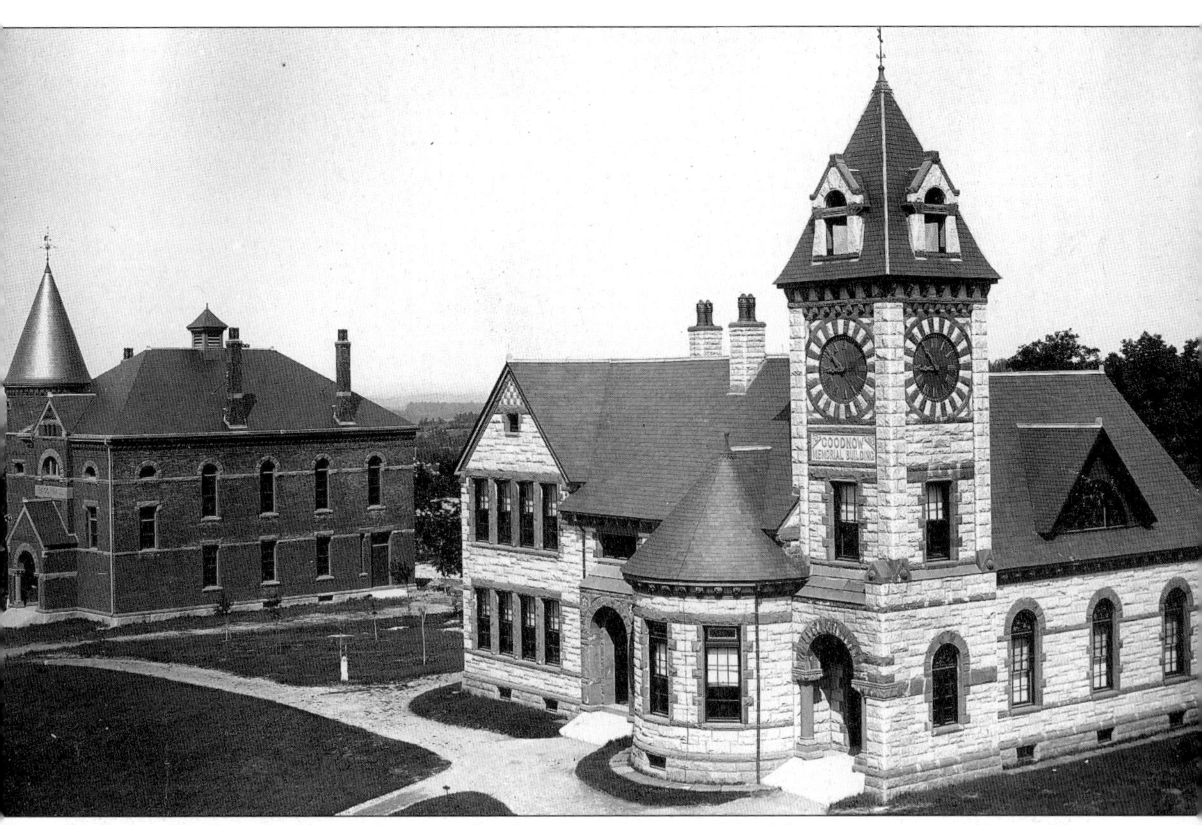

In 1883, Edward Goodnow donated the Goodnow Memorial Building in memory of two of his four wives and his only son. School Districts No. 1 and No. 9 were combined in the building, and school was held for 25 years until it closed in 1906, when the Center School was completed. With a need for more space, renovation of the library began in January 1999 and ended with a rededication ceremony on May 5, 2001. Later that year, the library received a preservation award from the Massachusetts Historical Commission. Next to the Goodnow Memorial Library is Bagg Hall (built in 1884), another building given in part by Edward Goodnow, who donated $3,000 providing the town would raise the remaining $9,000. Town meetings were held in Bagg Hall from March 1886 until the 1970s. Goodnow requested the building be named in memory of two of his wives, daughters of Dr. Bagg, a Princeton physician. Stephen Earle, a noted Worcester architect, designed both buildings. Norcross Brothers of Worcester, known for their exceptional talent in working with stone, were the builders. (Courtesy of the Princeton Historical Society.)

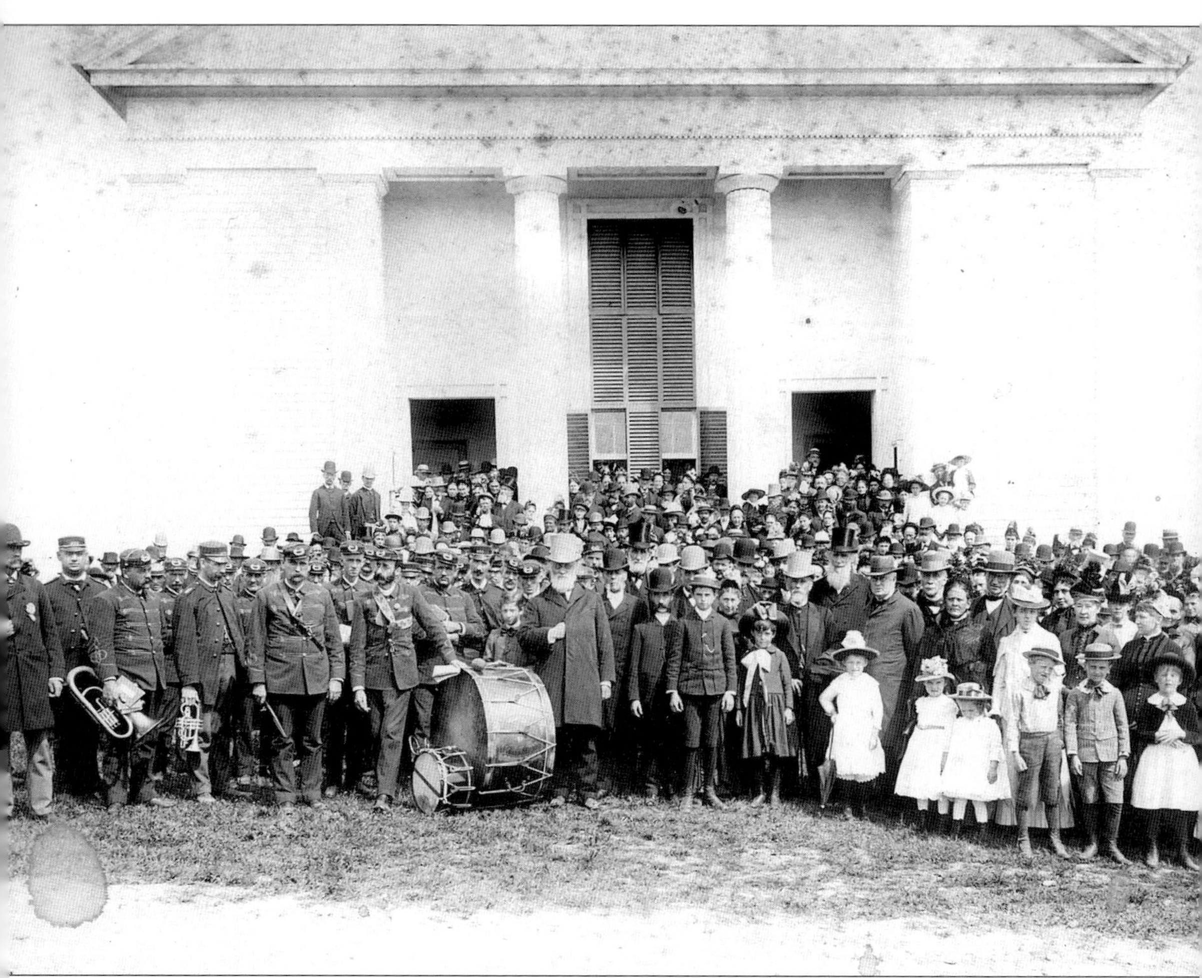

The Goodnow Memorial Building and Bagg Hall were dedicated on September 6, 1887. A grand celebration was held with a procession beginning at 10:00 a.m. from Wachusett House and a service at 10:30 in the First Congregational Church. Dignitaries who attended the ceremony included Edward Goodnow (standing in the center with the light top hat), Hon. Charles Russell, Hon. G.M. Stearns and Mrs. Stearns, the Reverend Dr. Miner, Dr. Nathan Allen, Hon. Thomas Russell, and Hon. George Hoar. The Princeton Cornet Band, established on November 19, 1878, provided music for the occasion. (Courtesy of Princeton Historical Society.)

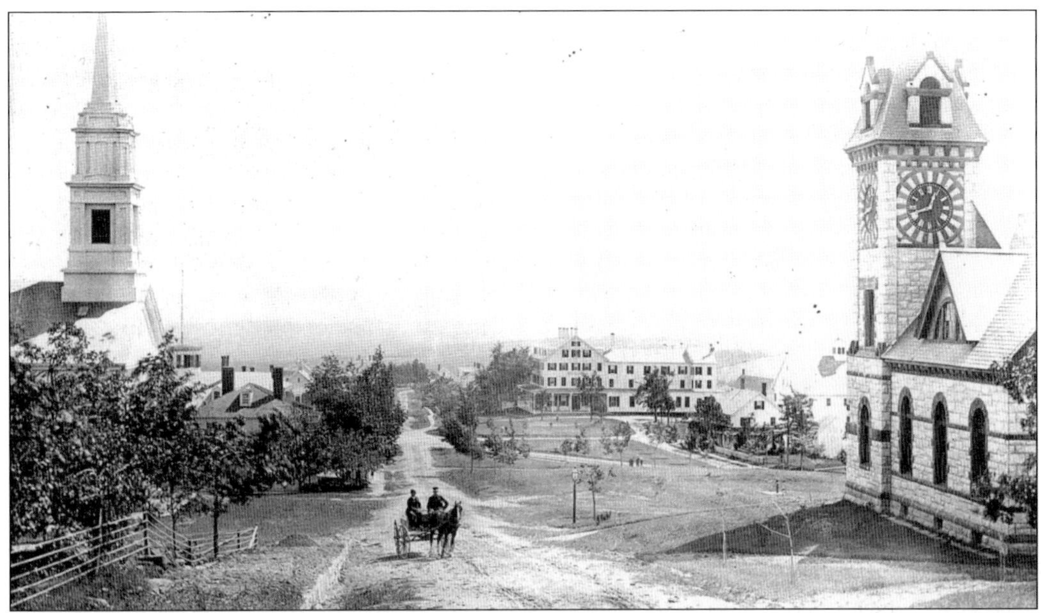

Two people are traveling in a buggy up Mountain Road. In 1903, the town voted to spend $300 for installing and maintaining 70 gas lamps for the center of town and 25 lamps for East Princeton. A gas plant was built behind the Gregory store on Mountain Road, and it furnished the church, the Gregory store, the library, the town hall, and several homes in the center with gas. One of the lamps can be seen to the right of the people in the buggy. (Courtesy of Nancy Beaman Flanders.)

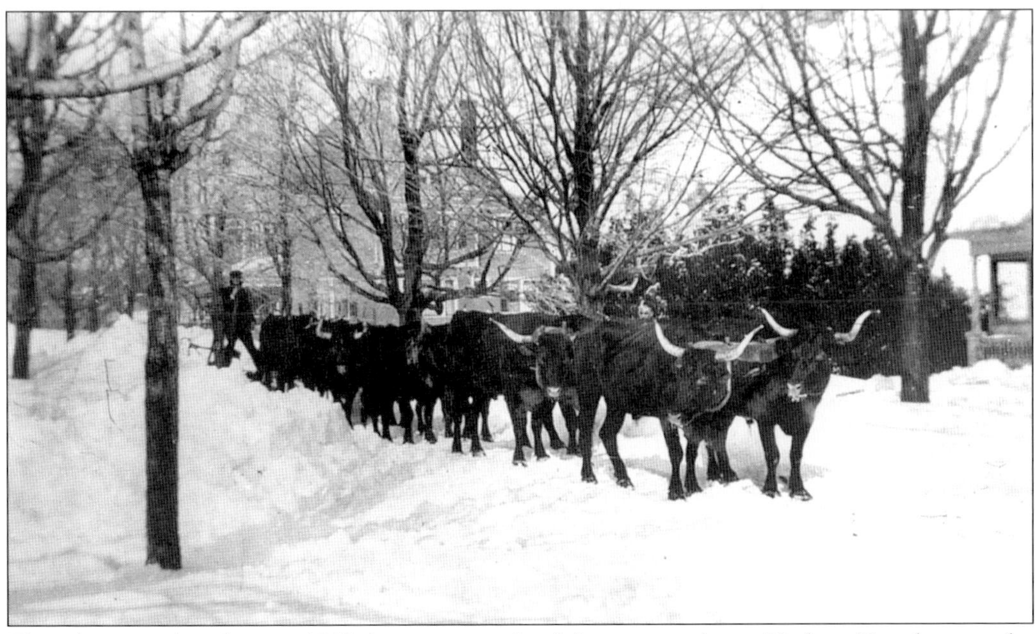

This photograph, taken in 1920 from just south of the center, shows Herbert Houghton and a team of oxen plowing Worcester Road after a snowstorm. (Courtesy of Nancy Beaman Flanders.)

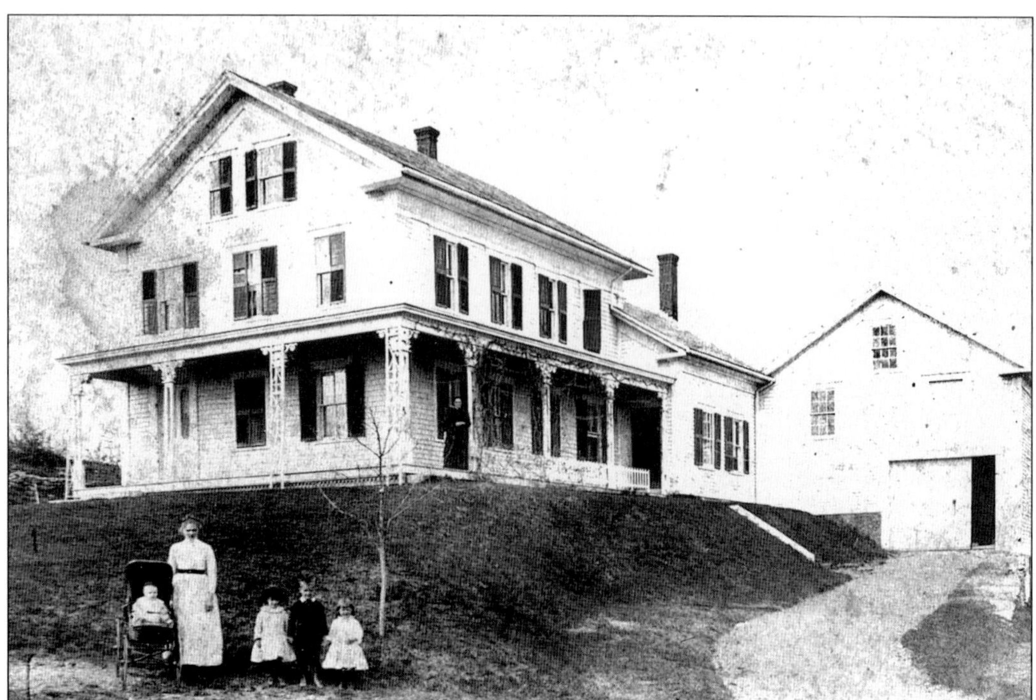

The Greek Revival Congregational church parsonage was built on Mountain Road in 1869 and was home to 14 ministers until the 1980s, when it was sold for use as a private home. This photograph was taken in the late 1800s. (Courtesy of the First Congregational Church.)

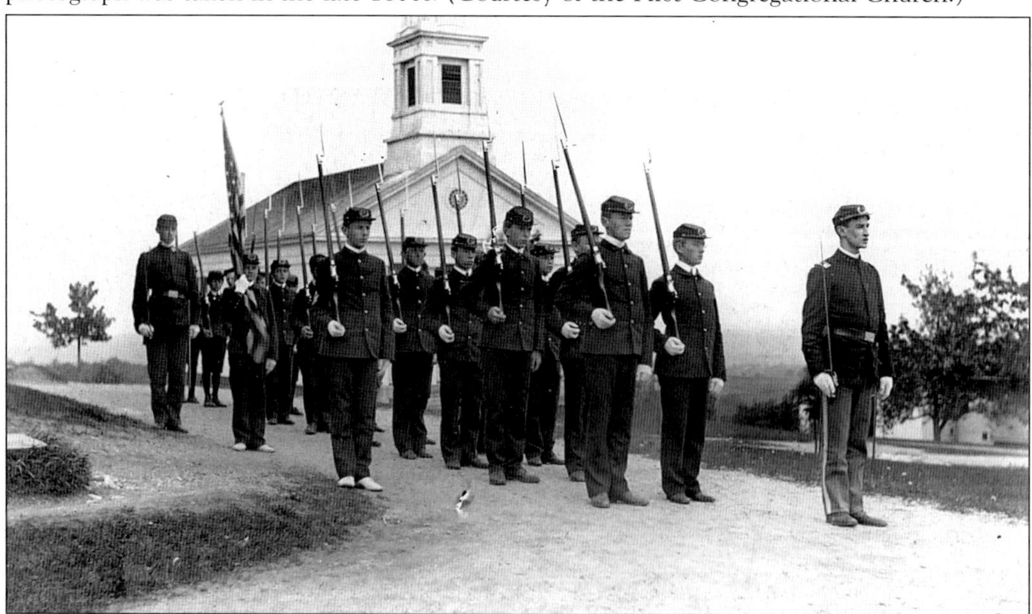

Drill associations began after the Civil War and were linked to local schools. Young cadets over 13 years of age were issued uniforms, and practice drills were held to teach discipline and teamwork. This photograph, taken after 1888, shows the young men practicing in front of the library, with the First Congregational Church in the background. (Courtesy of the Princeton Historical Society.)

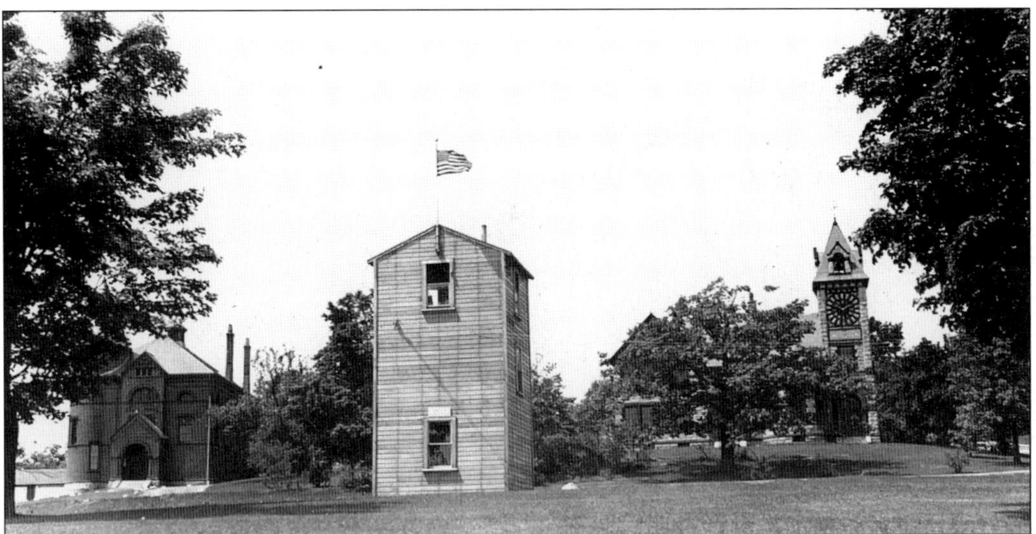

Princeton Common had its own plane-spotting tower during World War II. When it was too foggy for airplane identification on the summit of Wachusett Mountain, people (mostly women and children) would watch the skies for enemy airplanes from this building. Inside was a kerosene heater and a telephone to call Hanscom Air Force Base if a plane was spotted. Known as Fox-101, the three-story building with windows on all sides was torn down after the war. (Courtesy of the Princeton Historical Society.)

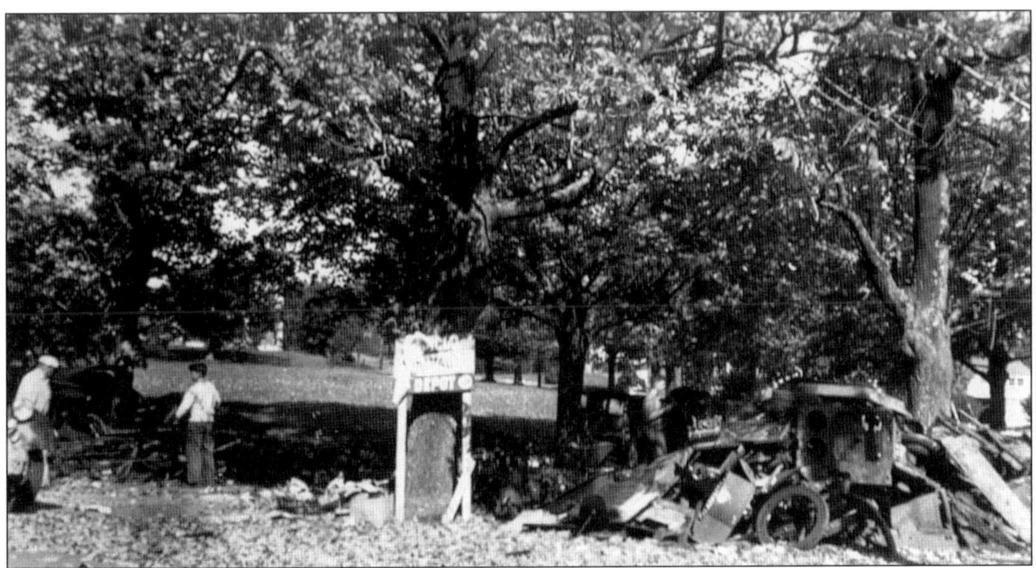

During World War II, Princeton did its share to help. A depot designated for used scrap metal was located on the southern end of the common. The scrap metal was recycled and used to help the war effort. The Goodnow Memorial Library can be seen between the trees in the distance. (Courtesy of the Princeton Historical Society.)

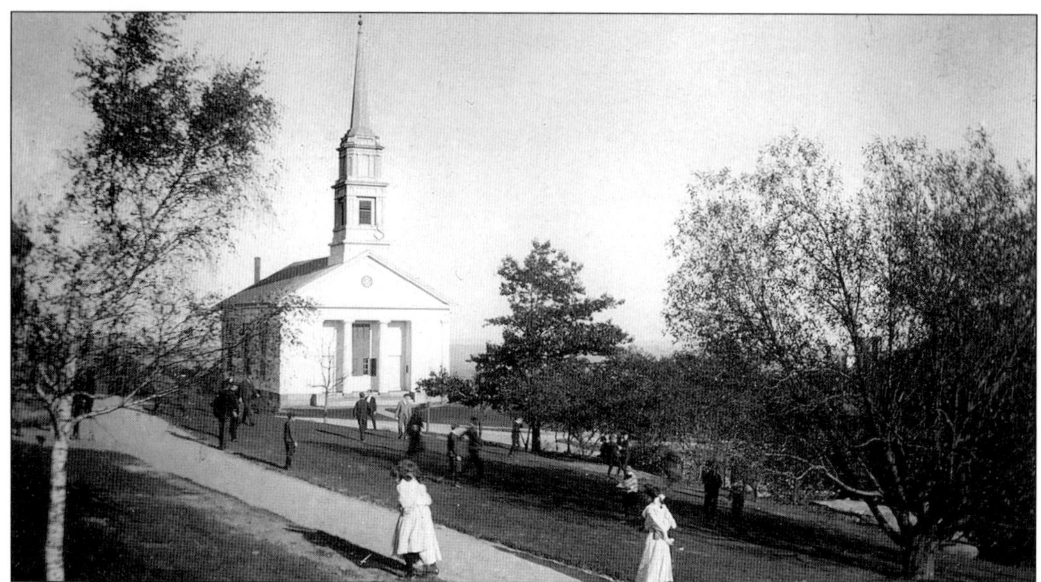

People in this photograph are walking toward the First Congregational Church. The builder of this church may have been Princeton resident David Brooks, who was known to have built 14 meetinghouses. An oculus window in the pediment came from the first meetinghouse and is inscribed with the date 1762. The Paul Revere bell, weighing 874 pounds, was purchased for the second meetinghouse. The church bell was rung as a fire alarm for many years. (Courtesy of the Princeton Historical Society.)

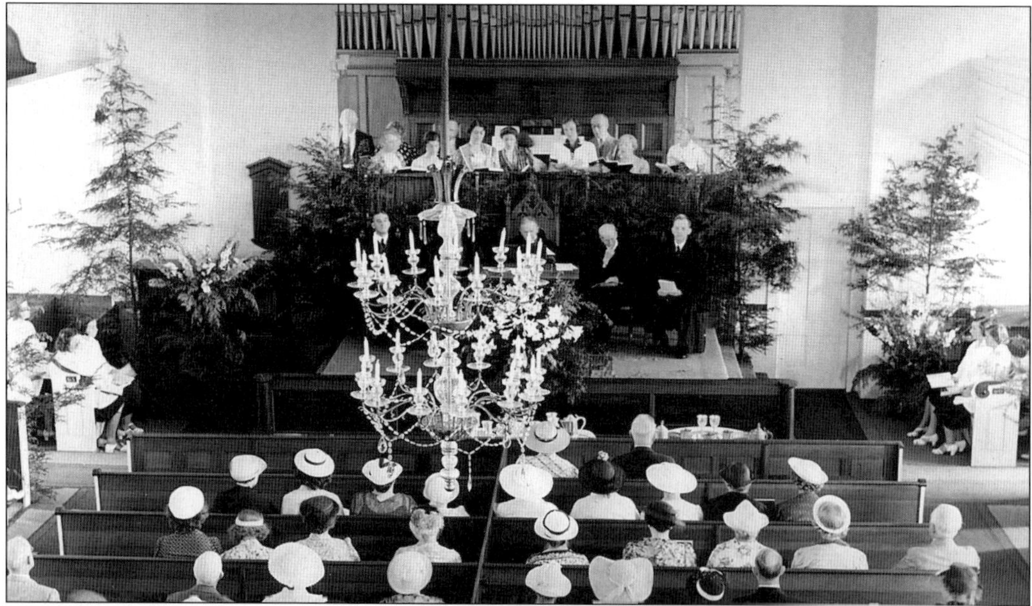

The First Congregational Church held services on July 10, 1938, to commemorate the 100th anniversary of the erection of the third meetinghouse on the common. Shown here, some of the ministers who attended the event include Rev. Charles Peck, Rev. Charles Reeves (former minister, 1906–1917), Rev. Frederic Donaldson (minister of the church), and Dean Philemon Sturges (far right). The others are unidentified. A celebration luncheon was served in Bagg Hall at 1:00. (Courtesy of the Princeton Historical Society.)

This photograph shows the scaffolding still around the new steeple after the construction was finished. The toppling of the steeple occurred exactly 100 years after the church and steeple were built. The 1938 hurricane was responsible for 564 deaths and at least 1,700 injuries in southern New England. A total of 8,900 homes, cottages, and buildings were destroyed, and more than 15,000 were damaged. The strongest sustained wind of 121 miles per hour and a peak gust of 186 miles per hour were recorded at the Blue Hill Observatory. (Courtesy of the Princeton Historical Society.)

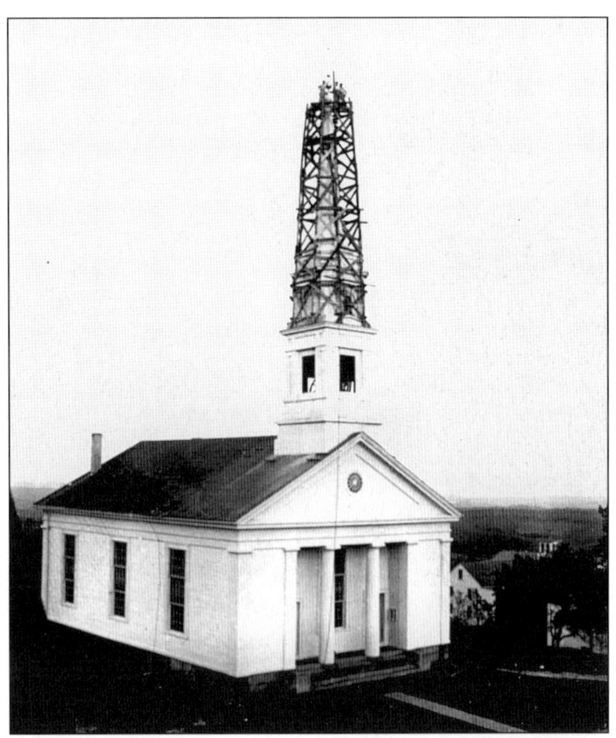

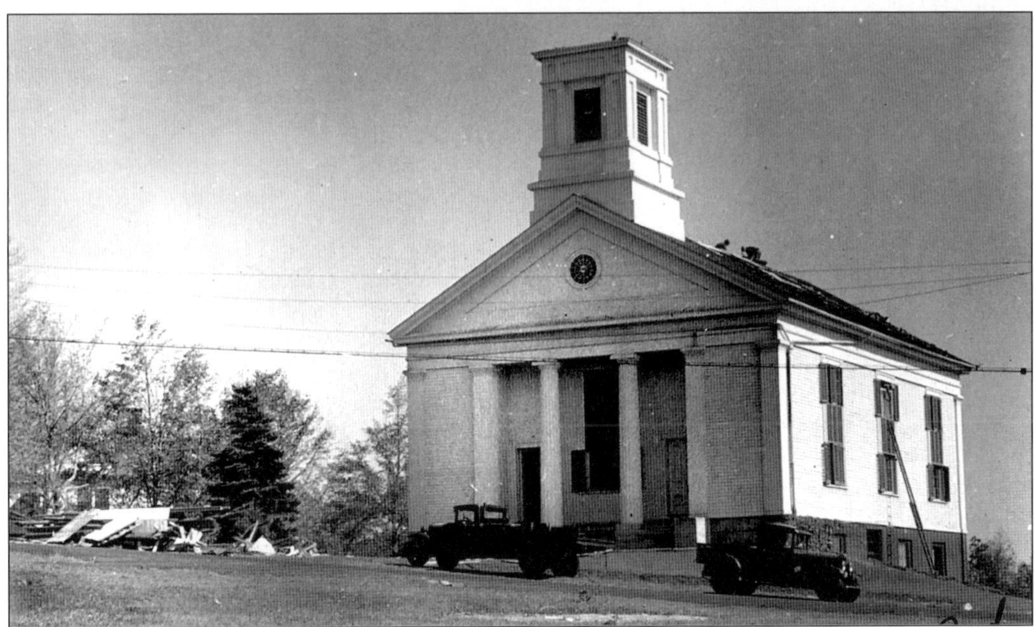

Princeton and other New England towns suffered significant damage on September 21, 1938, when the hurricane came up the coast from Long Island. This photograph, taken shortly after the hurricane, shows two men repairing shingles. Two chimneys on the church were blown over, a large hole was made in the roof, and one of the windows was blown out by the heavy winds. The cost of replacing the steeple was $3,000, and a community-wide campaign to raise money was started. (Courtesy of the Princeton Historical Society.)

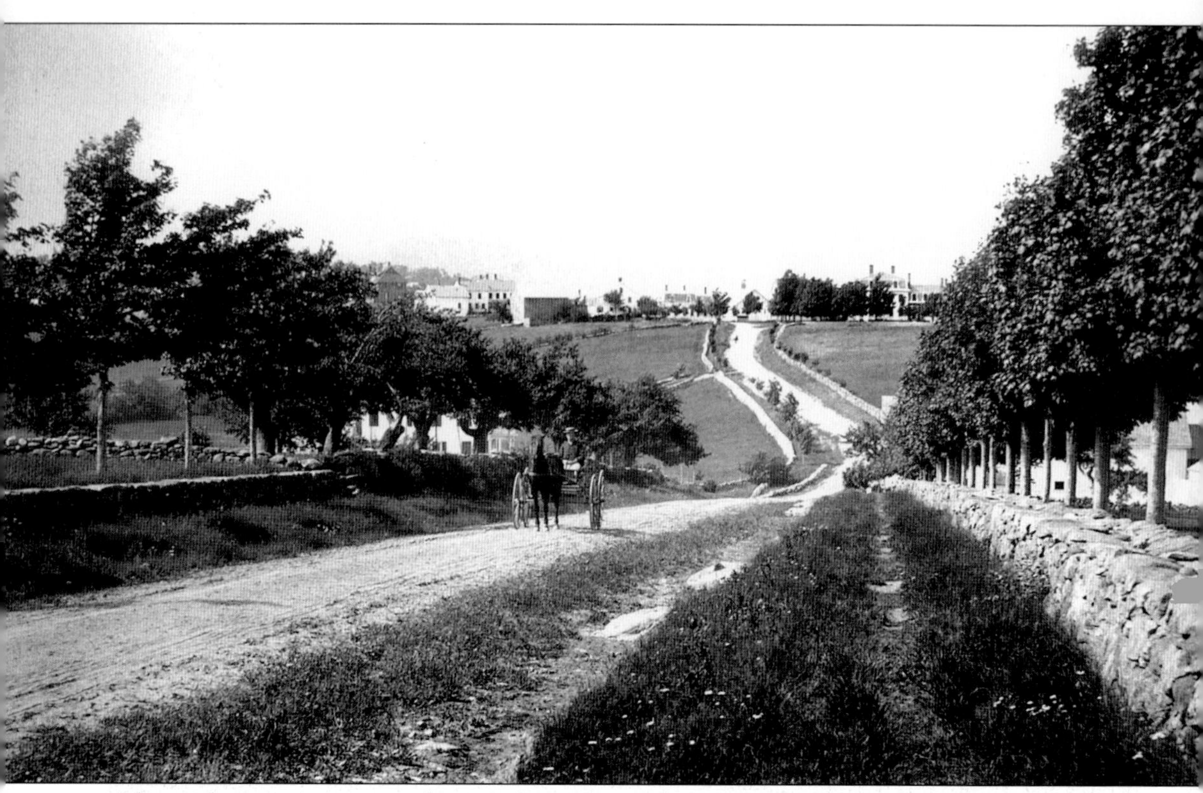

A horse-drawn wagon is traveling south on Worcester Road sometime in the late 1800s. At that time, Worcester and Mountain Roads were known as Wachusett Street. On the hilltop, Wachusett House is on the left, and the Brooks-Goddard house is on the right. John Brooks's estate of several hundred acres reached as far as the center of town and extended to Route 62 on the Sterling Road. Phineas and Algernon Beaman, owners of Wachusett House, planted the maple trees along the road. (Courtesy of the Princeton Historical Society.)

Three
FACTORIES, FARMS, AND FRIENDS

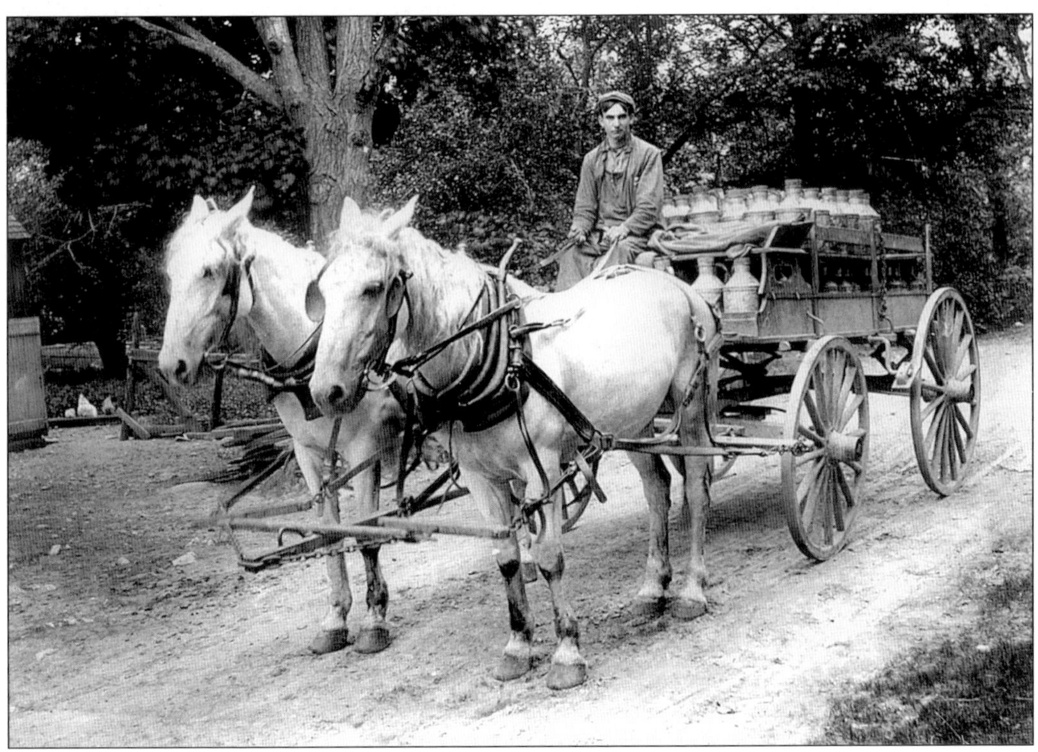

Many people living on the outskirts of town were farmers. Harry Gleason, who lived on Gleason Road, owned about 40 cows and spent all his life dairy farming. Each day, he loaded the milk cans in his wagon and brought them to Pratt's Junction in Sterling, where the milk was shipped to Alden Brothers in Boston for distribution. (Courtesy of Marguerite Gleason.)

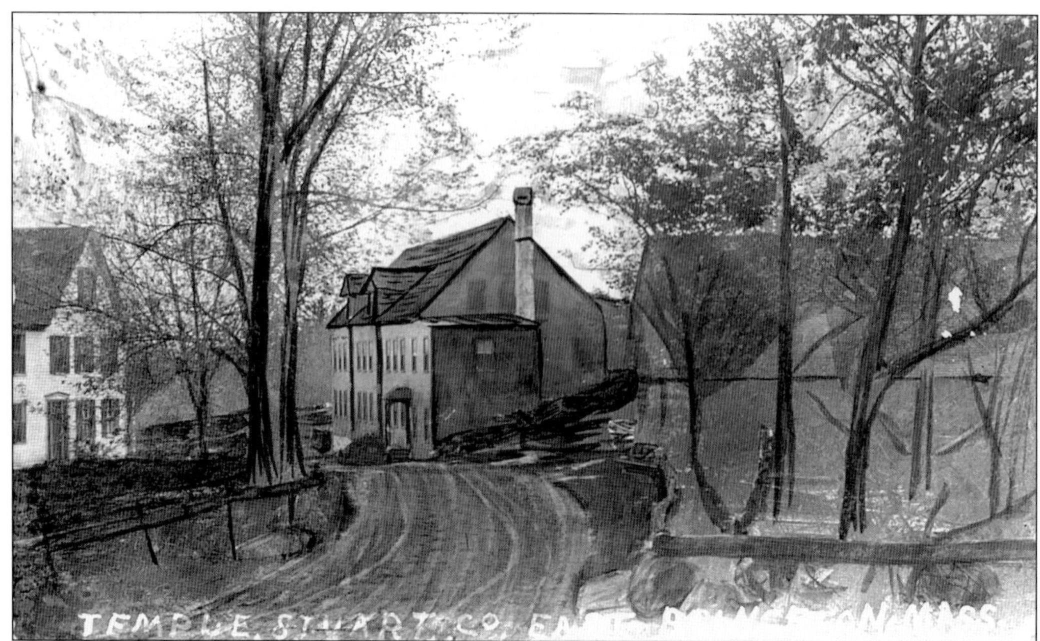

Taken from near the bridge on Gleason Road, this 1907 postcard view shows the Temple-Stuart paint shop on the right and the Temple-Stuart boardinghouse on the left. The paint shop was built in 1899 after an earlier sawmill burned on this site. Temple-Stuart remained in operation until 1910, when fire destroyed the buildings. The company moved its factory to Baldwinville, where it remained until 1990. After Temple-Stuart left East Princeton, the village experienced an economic downturn. (Courtesy of Edith Hubbard.)

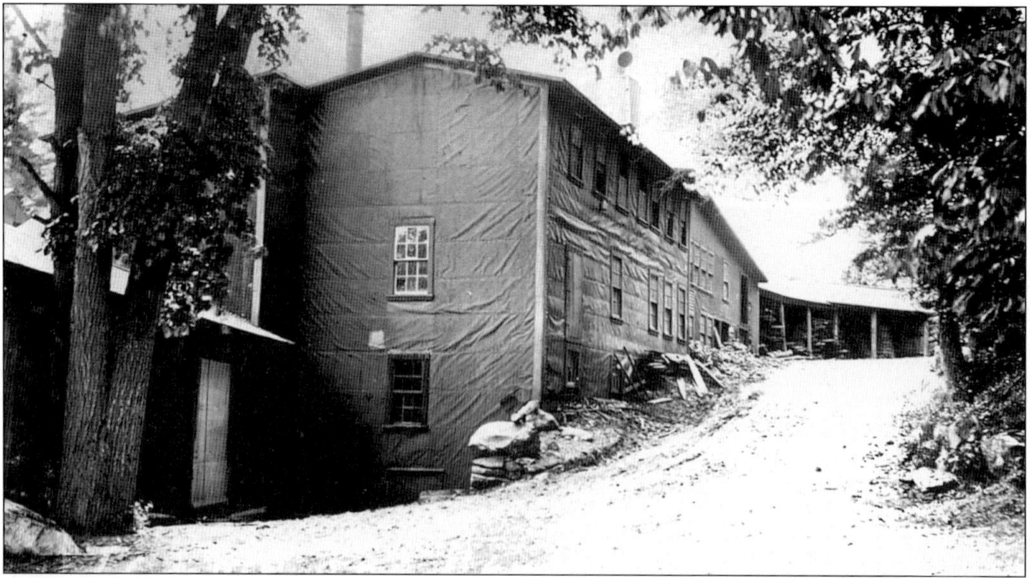

This building (now converted to a home at the intersection of Main Street and Gleason Road) was originally the barn of the Mirick House, at 77 Main Street. It is pictured around the beginning of the 20th century, when Temple-Stuart probably used it for storage. In 1907, Roland Keyes purchased the vacant storage building and opened an automobile paint shop. (Courtesy of Marguerite Gleason.)

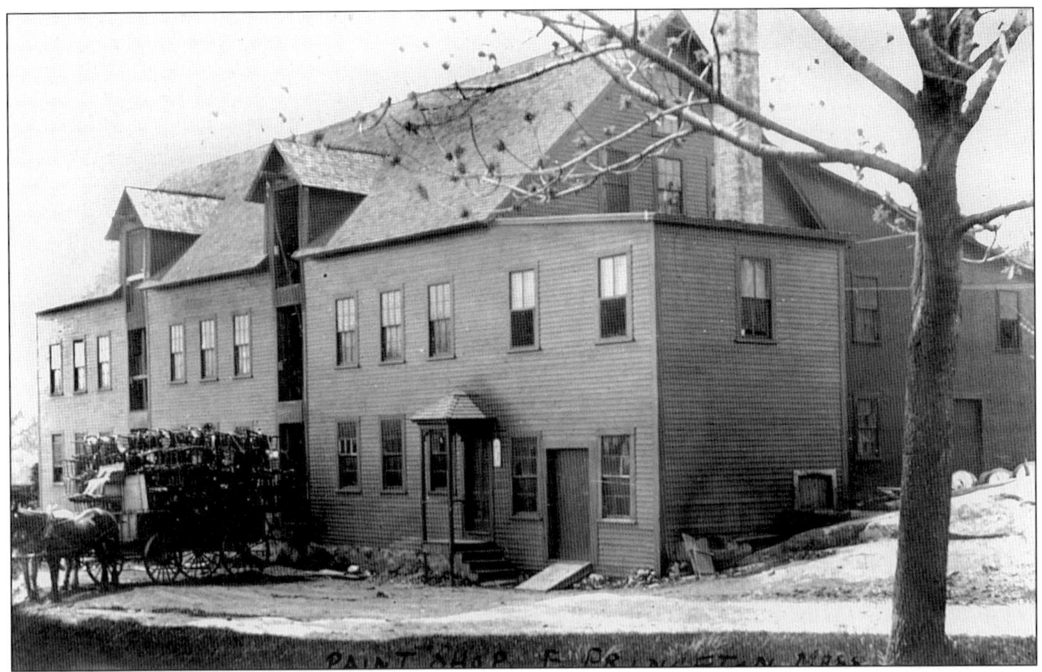

East Princeton thrived during the mid- to late 19th century as a small village where several chair-manufacturing businesses were located. Chair making began possibly in 1841 with Benjamin Stuart and his son Joseph on the west side of the bridge on Gleason Road. In 1904, the business was incorporated as the Temple-Stuart Company. As production increased, the paint shop (shown here) was equipped with large tanks of varnish into which the chairs were dipped, making possible a new era in chair finishing. (Courtesy of Edith Hubbard.)

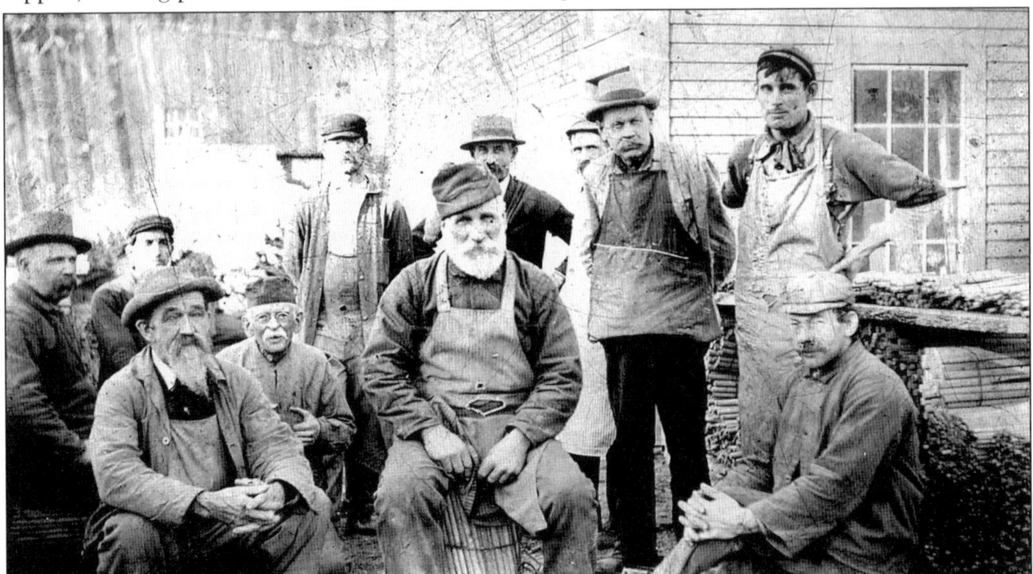

This c. 1900 photograph shows the workers at the Temple-Stuart factory. The men are sitting on bundles of chair stock ready to be turned into spindles for chairs or settees. To the right is more wood ready for turning chair parts. The Stuart Sawmill in Sterling may have supplied the stock for the chairs, thus keeping the cost down. (Courtesy of Edith Hubbard.)

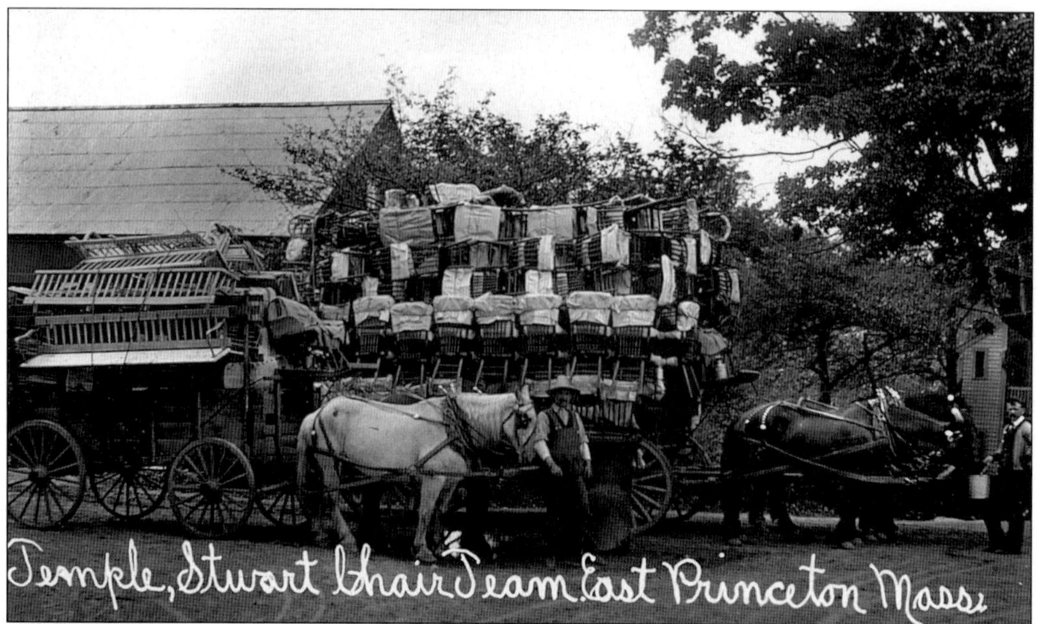

By 1880, with an investment of $7,000, the J.H. Stuart chair factory was operating with 15 men, 3 younger than 15 years of age. It was producing chairs and furniture valued at $30,000 a year, and at one time, as many as eight varieties of chairs were made by the company. The settees in this photograph are similar to the ones in Bagg Hall, the Princeton Center, and the First Congregational Church, and it is possible that the settees in those buildings were made in the East Princeton factory. (Courtesy of Edith Hubbard.)

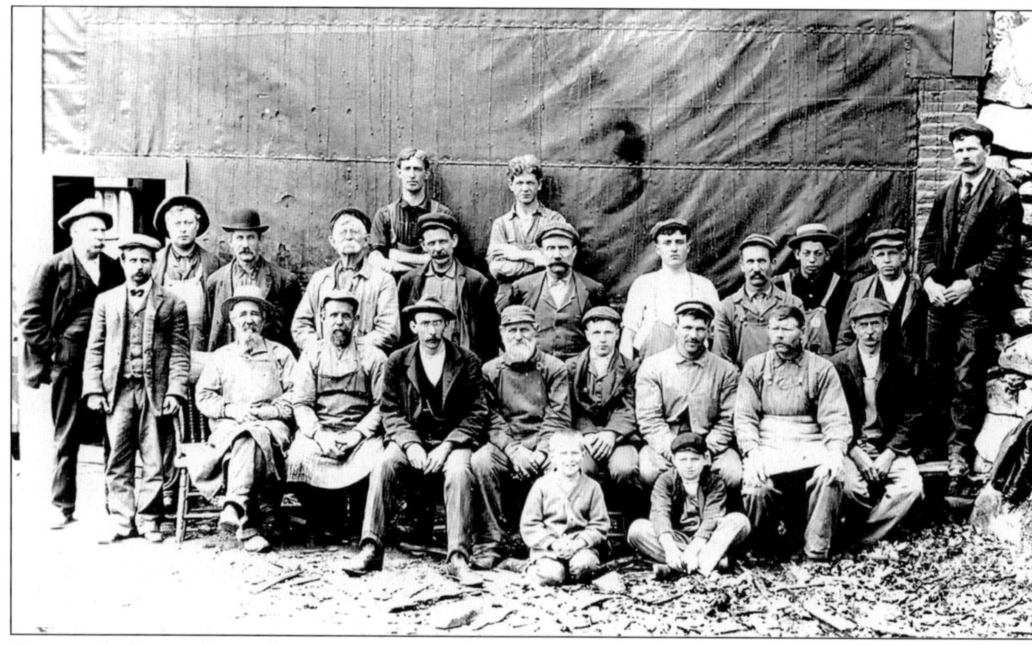

Some of the mill workers are assembled outside the storage building (later, the Keyes automobile paint shop) on Mill Hill. All these men lived and worked in the village. (Courtesy of Donald and Carolyn Slongwhite.)

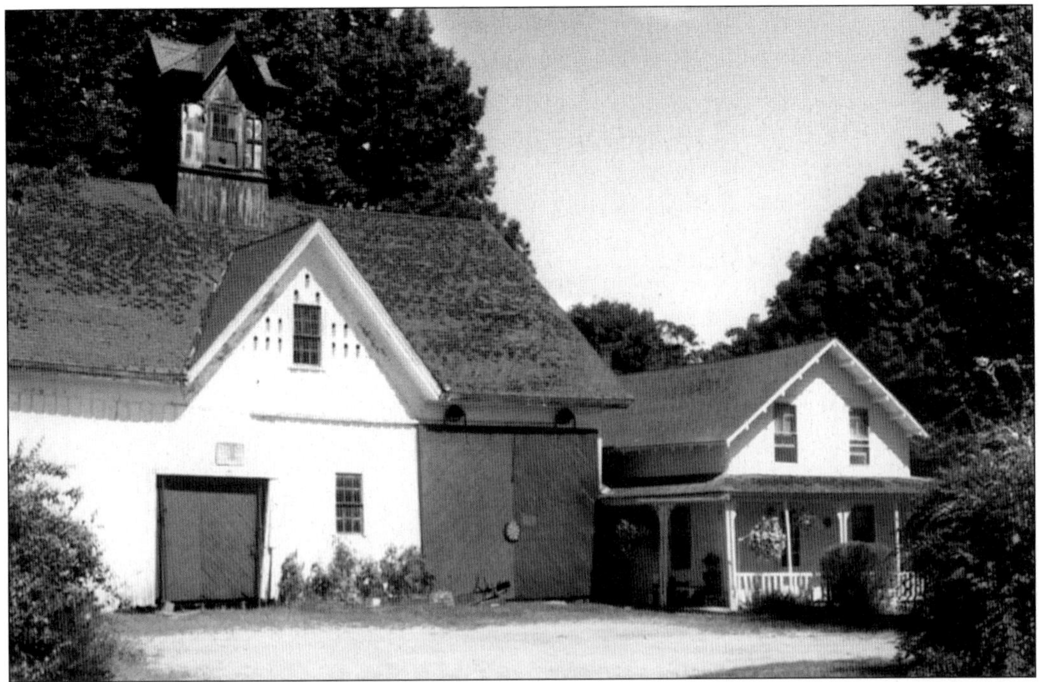

Temple-Stuart chair workers loaded the finished chairs on wagons and brought them to the barn at the corner of Main Street and Leominster Road. The wagons loaded with chairs were stored until the next morning, when they were delivered to the train station in Sterling. To the right of the barn was a store run by the husbands of John Stuart's daughters, Janie and Marion. The Temple-Lamson store began operation as early as the 1850s and closed in the early 1940s.

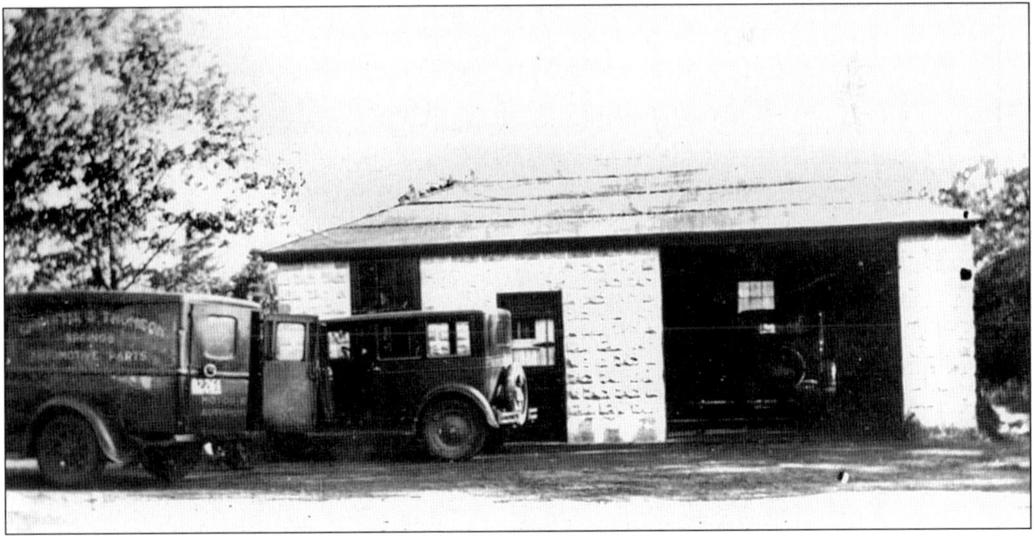

John and Charlie Hubbard operated an automobile-repair garage next to Mechanics Hall in the 1930s. Pictured in front of the garage is a Christie and Thompson auto-parts truck and a Packard. The business began as a one-bay garage and was enlarged with an addition on both sides sometime in the 1940s or 1950s. It now operates as Townline Garage. The fire trucks were stored here until 1984, when a new fire station was built farther north on Route 140. (Courtesy of Clayton Hubbard.)

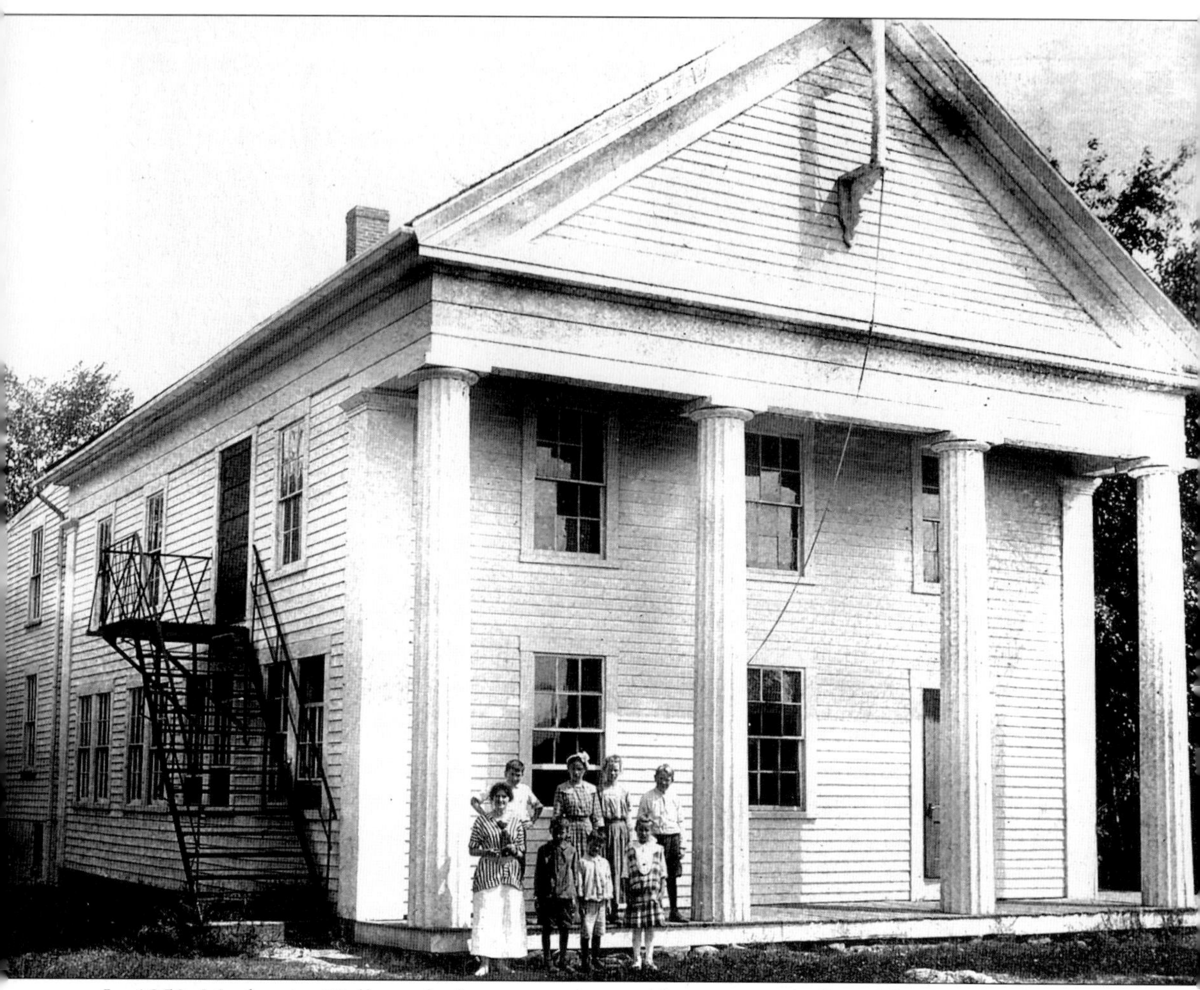

In 1852, Mechanics Hall was built to provide a public meeting hall and larger school facilities for a growing population. The first school in East Princeton, located at the intersection of Routes 31 and 140, was built in 1830 and was replaced in 1843. In this new building, the upstairs was large enough to hold meetings of the Princeton Grange, East Princeton Village Improvement Society, and later the American Legion. The school and branch library were located on the first floor. This c. 1914 photograph shows teacher Theresa McNuttly and her students. From left to right are the following: (front row) John Hubbard, Charlie Hubbard, and Edith Gleason Hubbard; (back row) Charlton Gray, Sara Hubbard Wiggins, Louise Smith, and Warren Whitcomb. The Mechanics Hall District No. 3 School closed in 1945. (Courtesy of Edith Hubbard.)

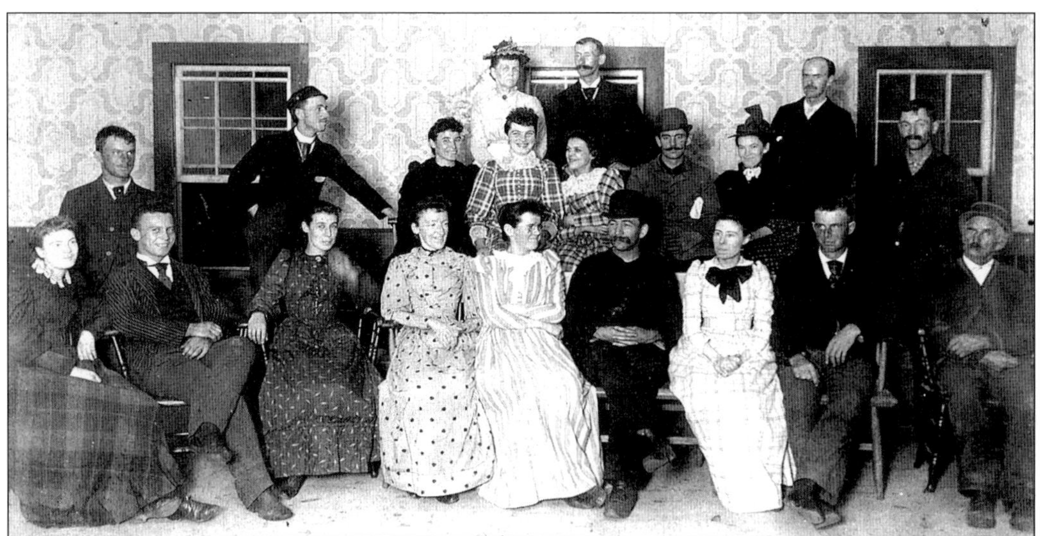

This photograph was taken inside Mechanics Hall. Men and women found a varied social life in the village at the turn of the century. Suppers, dances, and whist parties were held at Mechanics Hall. Sidewalks between Beaman and Leominster Roads provided an opportunity to stroll and meet friends. Band concerts held at the bandstand in front of the Temple-Stuart barn were well attended, and the music was played by East Princeton's band. (Courtesy of Edith Hubbard.)

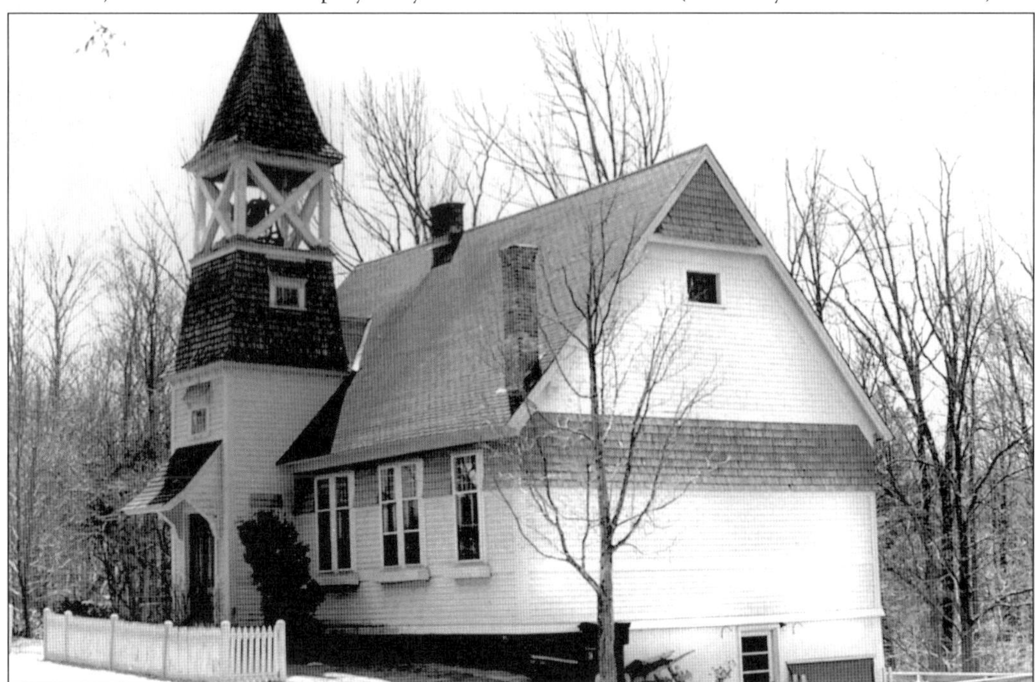

The East Princeton Chapel, built in 1887 by John Fremont Mirick, was an important part of the village. Former chair manufacturer William H. Brown and his wife, Ellen, provided the land for the sum of 1¢. When the chapel opened in 1887, the minister, Rev. Archibald Love, traveled three miles from Princeton Center to hold the service in the chapel at 3:00 p.m. The Ladies Aid Society held suppers once a month. The chapel remained active until June 25, 1960, when it was sold and became a private residence.

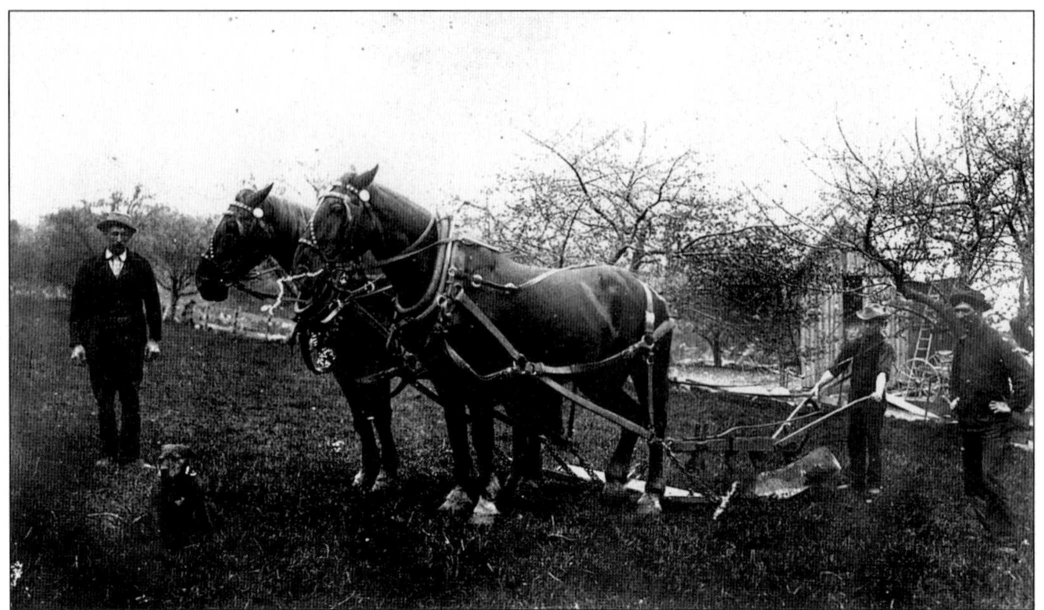

Farming was a difficult occupation. The hilly, rocky soil of Princeton made plowing and planting a tedious and unrewarding job. Strong horses were necessary to furrow the earth. Harry Gleason, who lived all his life in East Princeton Village, is standing at the left. (Courtesy of Edith Hubbard.)

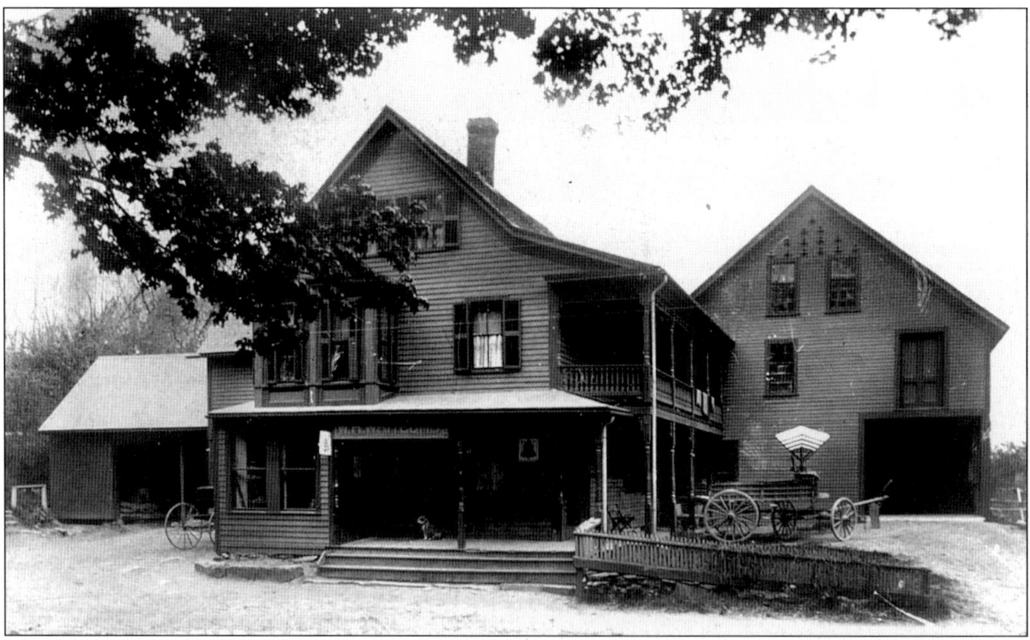

The Union Store, opened in 1848, was probably the first store in the village. Warren Whitcomb became the owner in 1885 and remained in business until 1921. During Whitcomb's ownership, he was both postmaster and proprietor of the store. The post office remained in the store until 1984, when it merged with the post office at the former Gregory store in Princeton Center. The wagon outside the store was used for delivery of goods to the patrons. (Courtesy of Edith Hubbard.)

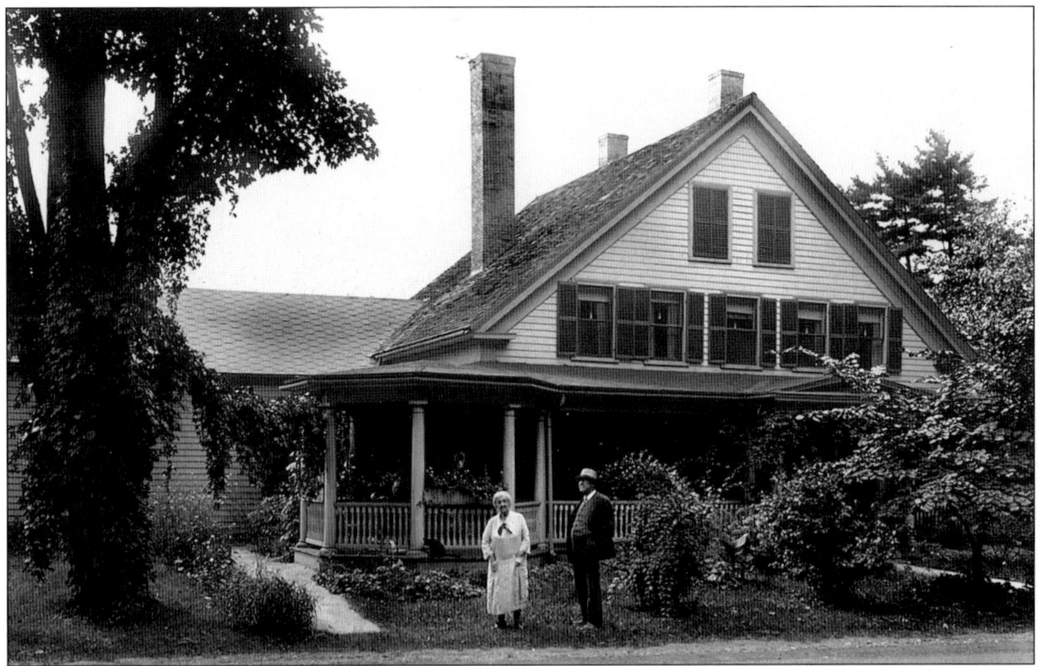

Artist Gamaliel Beaman and his wife, Eileen, are in front of their home at 85 Main Street. This photograph, taken before 1937, shows the house with its late-19th-century wraparound porch that has since been enclosed. (Courtesy of Clayton Hubbard.)

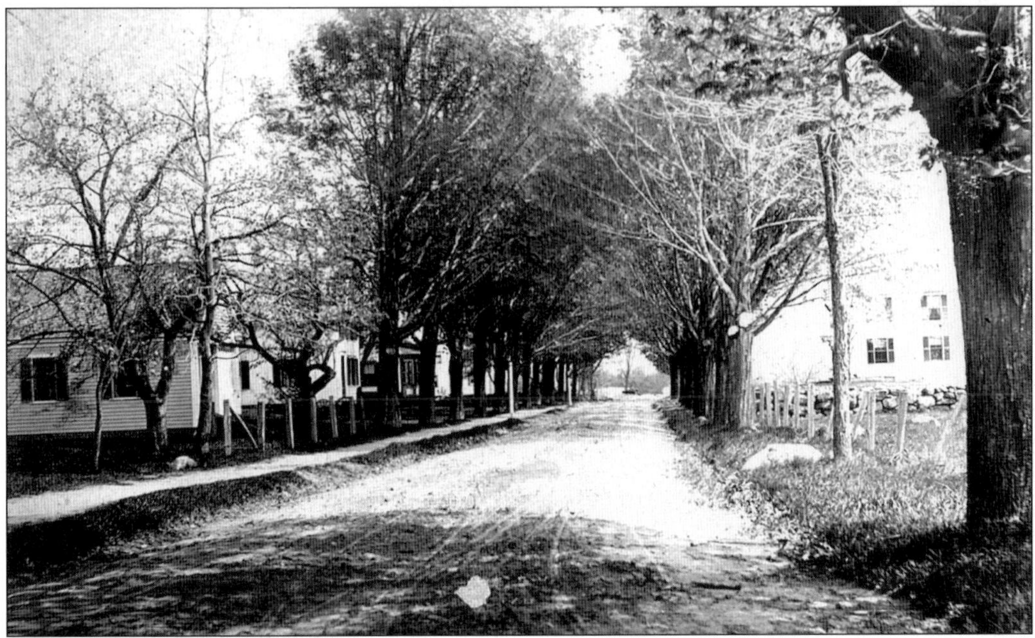

Leominster Road intersects with Main Street in the southern end of East Princeton. The first building on the left is the fire station, which began its role in this community when the town of Princeton voted to supply East Princeton with a pumper truck in 1892. The fire truck was stored here until the mid-20th century. When modern fire trucks became too large to fit in this building, they were kept at Hubbard's Garage on Main Street. (Courtesy of Edith Hubbard.)

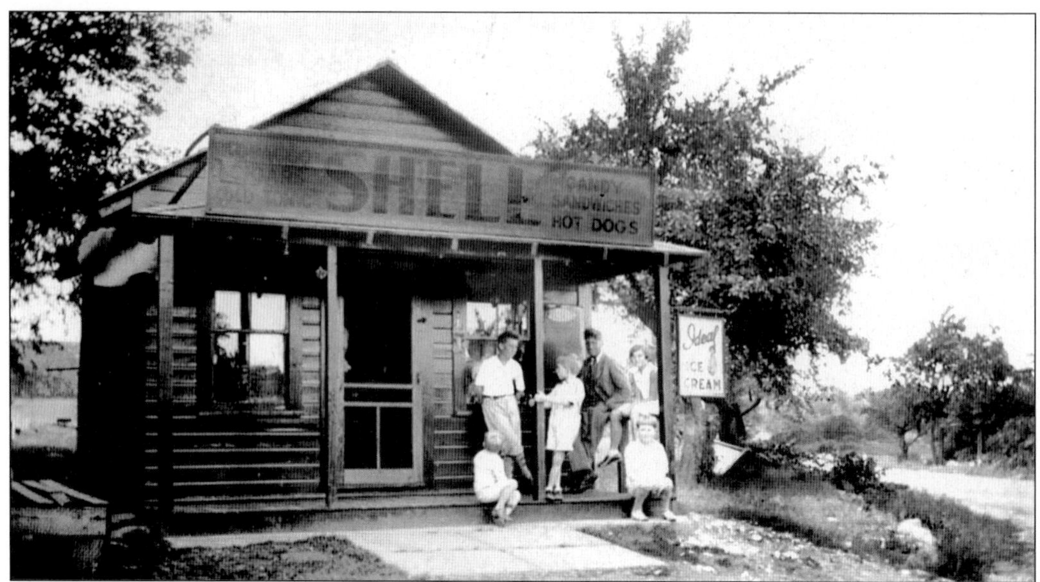

At the intersection of Beaman Road and Route 140, on the site of what may have been East Princeton's earliest school, the Slongwhites owned a Shell gas station and store *c.* 1928. The sign over the front porch of the store advertised tobacco, cigars, cold tonic, candy, sandwiches, and hot dogs. The Slongwhite children are seen on the front porch. In this view looking north, the dirt road to the right is Route 140. (Courtesy of Donald and Carolyn Slongwhite.)

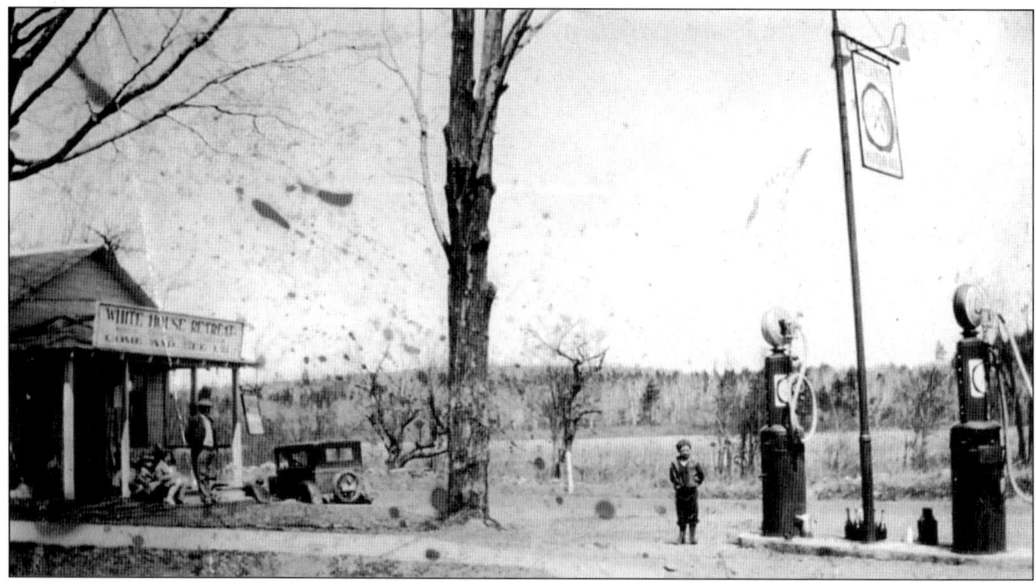

In 1931, Slongwhite's filling station changed the sign over the door, and this time it read, "White House Retreat, Come and See Us." The filling station building, later enlarged, remains today as part of Captain Bob's Restaurant and drive-up ice-cream stand on Route 140. Route 140, then a dirt road, is on the other side of the gas pumps, and beyond it is the swampy area, formerly a pond that powered village chair factories. (Courtesy of Donald and Carolyn Slongwhite.)

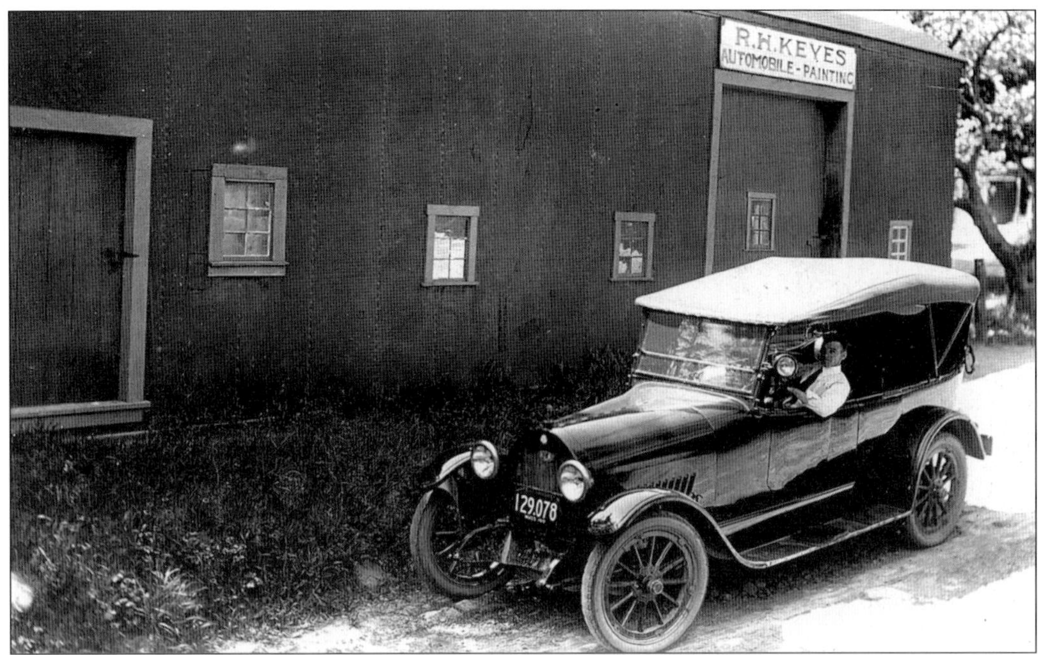

Roland Keyes is pictured in front of his automobile paint shop in his 1919 Dodge convertible. In 1915, Keyes was well known for painting and pinstriping automobiles; he would pinstripe a 1915 Ford for $15. In the 1930s, after 20 years of being in business, Keyes converted his shop into a home for his family and became a mailman. (Courtesy of Edith Hubbard.)

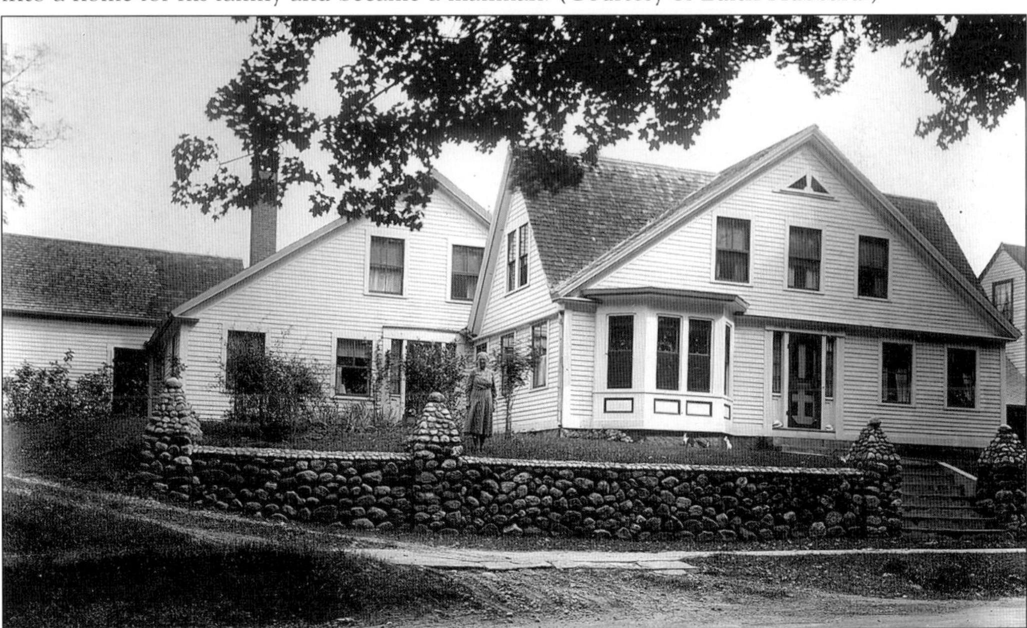

This house on Main Street in East Princeton was built by John Temple between 1857 and 1870 and may have housed two families or chair factory workers. Temple, a chair factory owner, was a partner with Benjamin Stuart of New York City in 1894. He was also co-owner of the Temple-Lamson store, on the corner of Leominster Road and Main Street, in 1898. (Courtesy of Clayton Hubbard.)

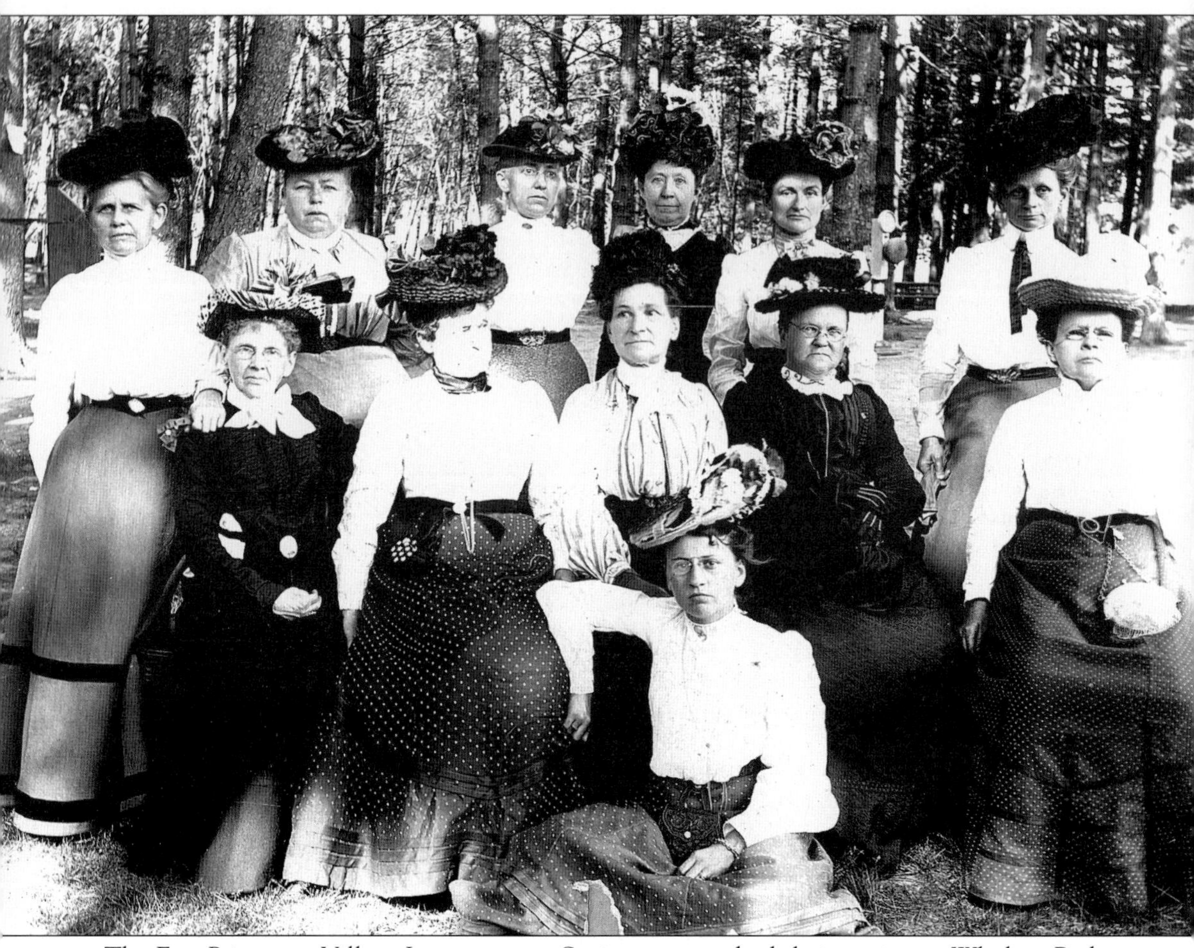

The East Princeton Village Improvement Society women had their outing at Whalom Park, a recreational area in nearby Lunenburg. Wives of the factory and store owners, these women played a part in making the village a better place to live in the late 19th and early 20th centuries. The society was responsible for seeing that sidewalks were constructed along Main Street and, in 1903, was instrumental in having 25 gas streetlights installed. The East Princeton Village Improvement Society remained active until the 1980s. The woman sitting in front is unidentified. The others are, from left to right, as follows: (front row) Marion Lampson, Mary ?, unidentified, Nell Stuart, and Janie Temple; (back row) Rosie Reed, Sarah Ross, unidentified, unidentified, Anna Whitcomb, and Agnes Stuart. (Courtesy of Edith Hubbard.)

Four
SUMMER SANCTUARIES

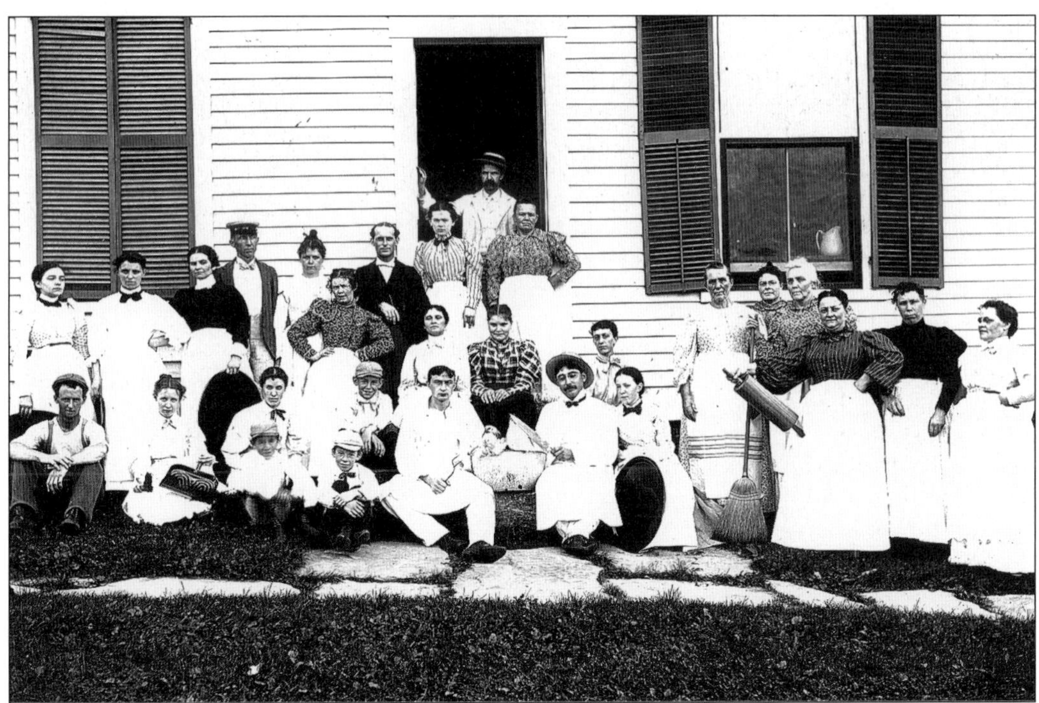

A large staff was required to run a hotel that accommodated up to 200 guests. Standing by the side door of Wachusett House in 1893 are employees of Algernon and Harry Beaman. Some of the staff is pictured with implements of their occupations: a rolling pin, a broom, a dustpan, and trays. The man seated in front on the left has a fork, and the man on the right has a butcher knife. (Courtesy of Nancy Beaman Flanders.)

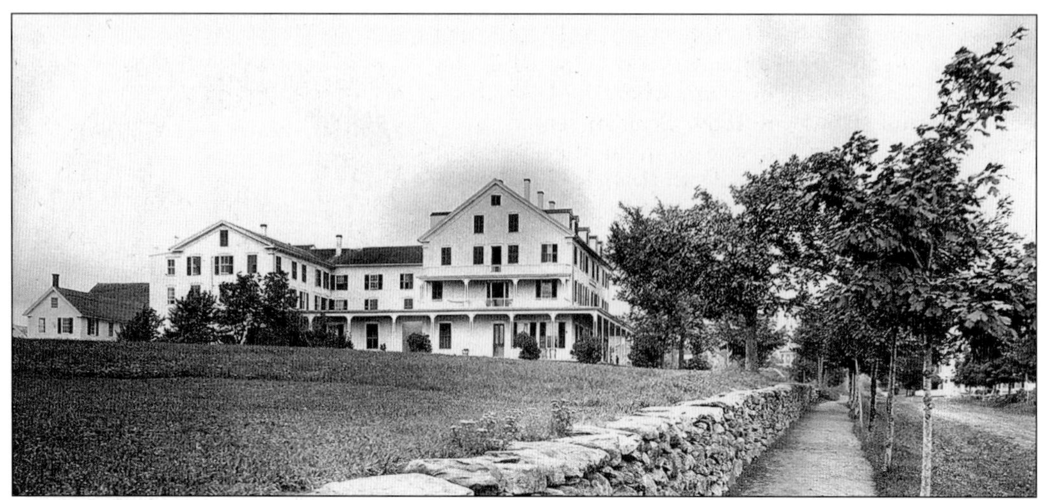

Wachusett House was located at the southern end of Princeton Common on what is now Dingman Park. The view above, taken before 1910, looks north and shows Wachusett House from Worcester Road. Below, the hotel is seen from Princeton Common in a view looking south. Wachusett House was purchased by Phineas Beaman in 1859 and, over the years, was enlarged until it had 65 rooms. A third story was added when the hotel was raised in 1869. A bowling alley and a laundry were built in 1861, and a large barn was constructed in 1864. In 1904, there was one bathtub, located on the ground floor, and the key to it was available at the front desk. As a boy, Harry Beaman remembered seeing sponges hanging from almost every window sill. When the wind blew them away, the bellboys were sent to chase them. (Courtesy of the Princeton Historical Society.)

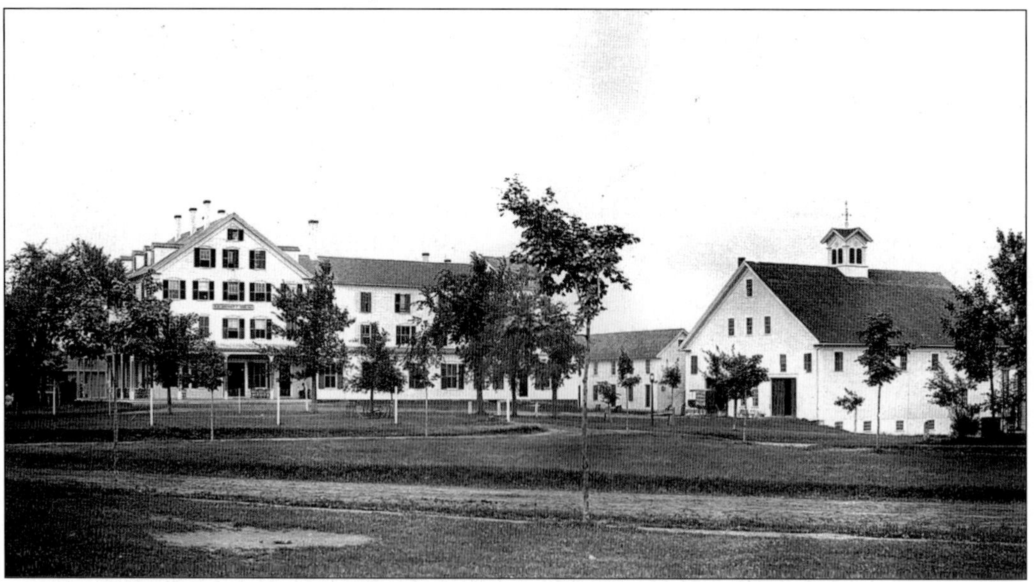

Phineas Beaman, born in Princeton in January 1819, purchased Wachusett House in 1860. In 1882, he purchased Wachusett Mountain, where he built the second Summit House in 1884. Beaman served in various town offices and one term in the state legislature. At the time of his death (March 1894), his two sons, Harry C. and Algernon T. Beaman, were associated with him in the ownership of Wachusett House and the Summit House. (Courtesy of Nancy Beaman Flanders.)

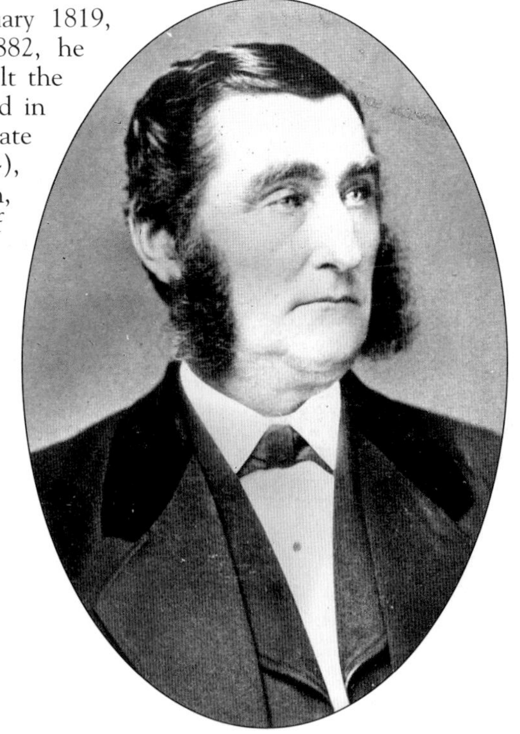

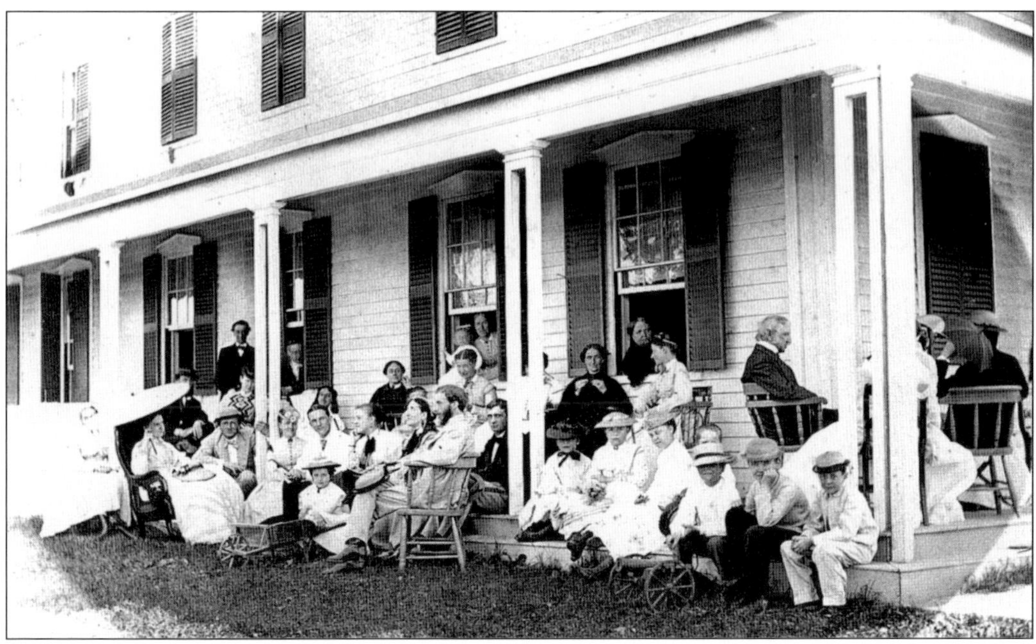

Guests gather on the south piazza of Wachusett House in 1864. Porches, symbols of hospitality, were an important part of hotel life in the 19th and 20th centuries. Guests were able to socialize and enjoy the healthy air in an outdoor environment. Harry Beaman was quoted as saying, "People did not need amusement when they came to Princeton. They came for a healthful rest and were content to relax." (Courtesy of Nancy Beaman Flanders.)

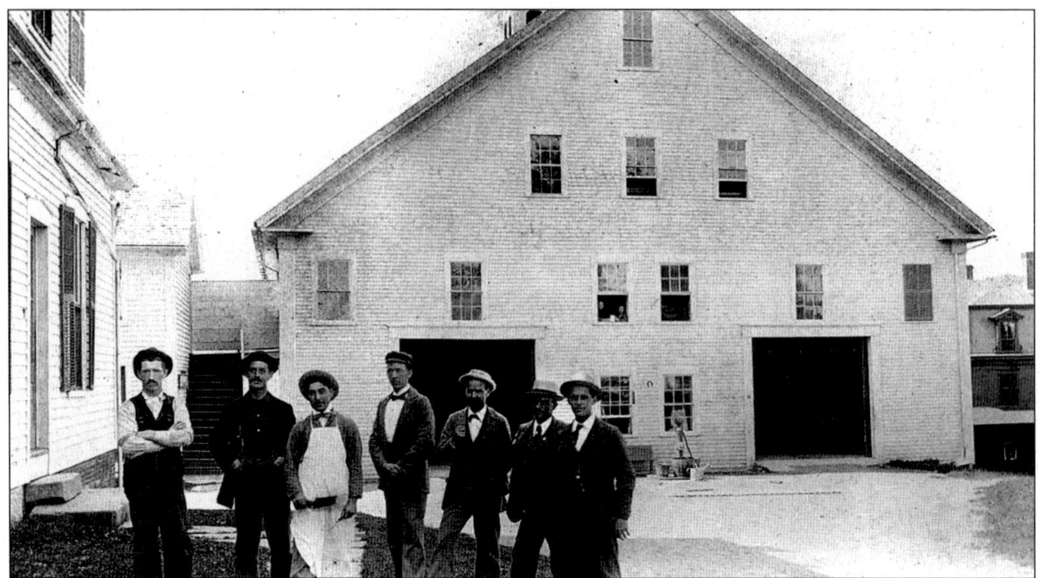

A photograph taken before 1910 shows some of the staff in front of the large barn at Wachusett House. Dances were held on the second floor of the barn. Guests from other hotels were invited to the dances, and ice cream, sponge cake, and lemonade were served. To the left is Wachusett Cottage, on Boylston Avenue. (Courtesy of Edith Hubbard.)

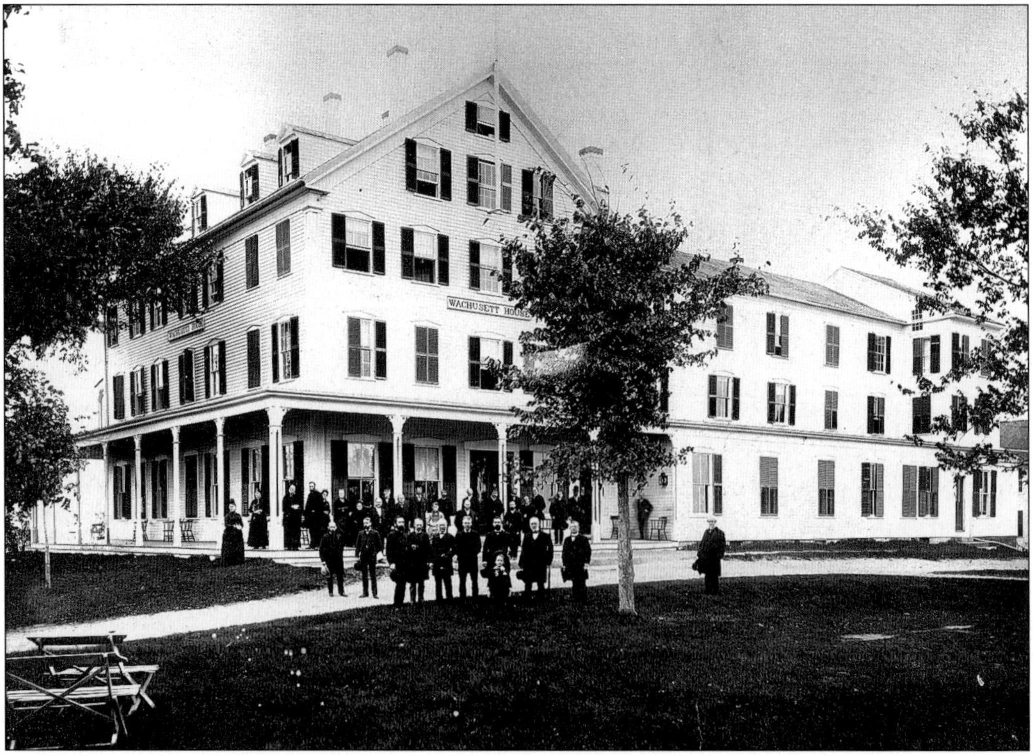

Standing in front of Wachusett House in the late 1800s, people appear dressed ready to attend a special event. The dressy appearance of the men, with top hats and long coats, and women, with dark dresses, suggests that it was not an ordinary day. (Courtesy of Judith Chandler Chute.)

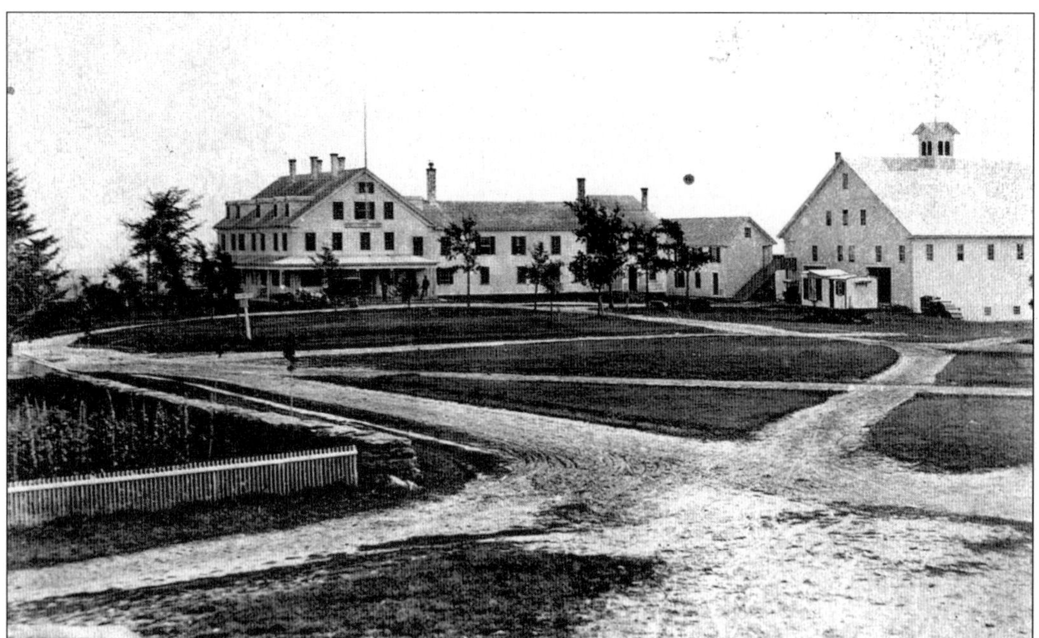

In this photograph taken before 1869, a photographer's studio is seen in front of the barn at Wachusett House. Photography was in its infancy and photographers were eager to photograph scenes of everyday life. At the southern end of the common, in the foreground, is a small garden protected by a fence and stone wall. (Courtesy Judith Chandler Chute.)

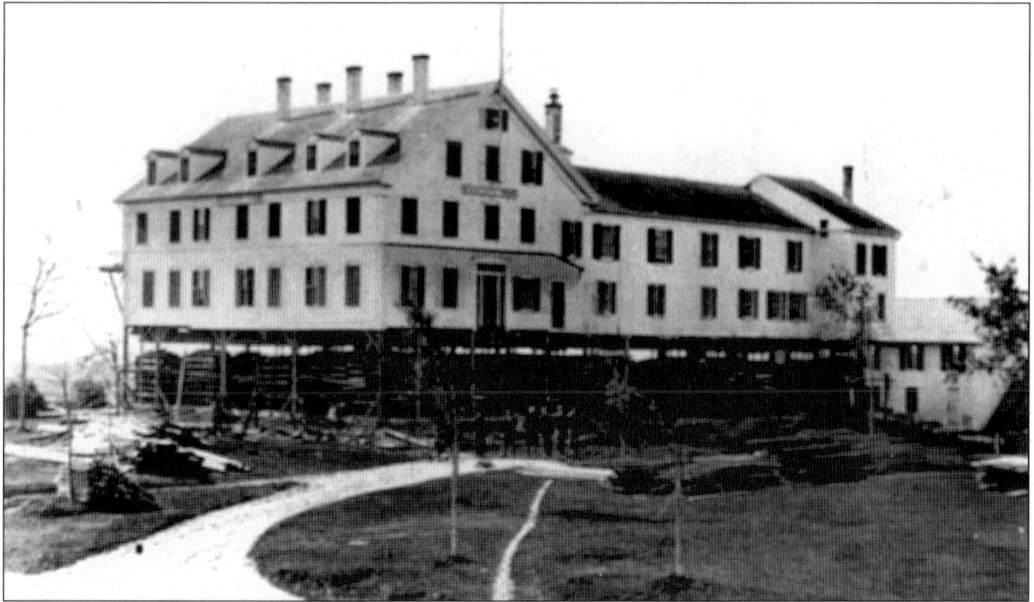

In the winter of 1869–1870, Phineas Beaman enlarged Wachusett House, adding a new ground floor by using cribbing and manual screw jacks. In March, there was a storm and only one chimney was lost after men spent the day bracing the building. While the building was being raised, Beaman and his wife continued to live there, and oral history relates that she did not leave the hotel for three months while the building was being renovated. (Courtesy of Nancy Beaman Flanders.)

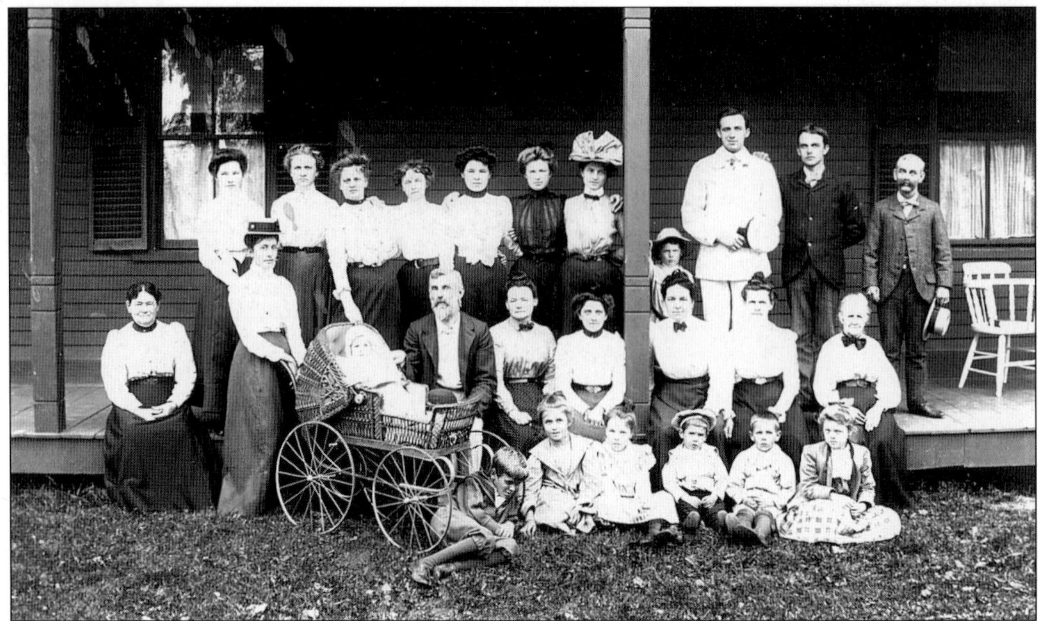

The Wachusett House staff poses on the porch of Wachusett Cottage in 1901. The children seated in front were guests at the hotel. Algernon Beaman, owner of Wachusett House, is sitting near John Beaman, his nephew, in the carriage. (Courtesy of Nancy Beaman Flanders.)

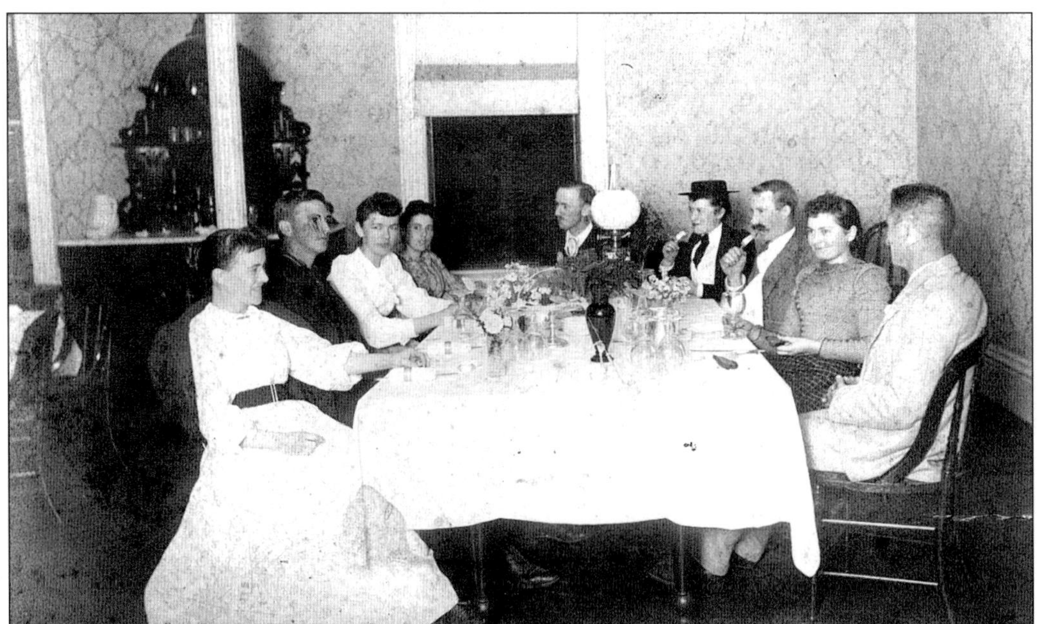

In this 1888 view, young people are gathered around a table in the small dining room at Wachusett House. They may have been planning their evening, which could have included bowling tenpins, playing cards in the parlors, reading quietly by kerosene lamps, singing hymns around the piano, or going to a Saturday night dance at either Mountain House or Wachusett House. (Courtesy of Judith Chandler Chute.)

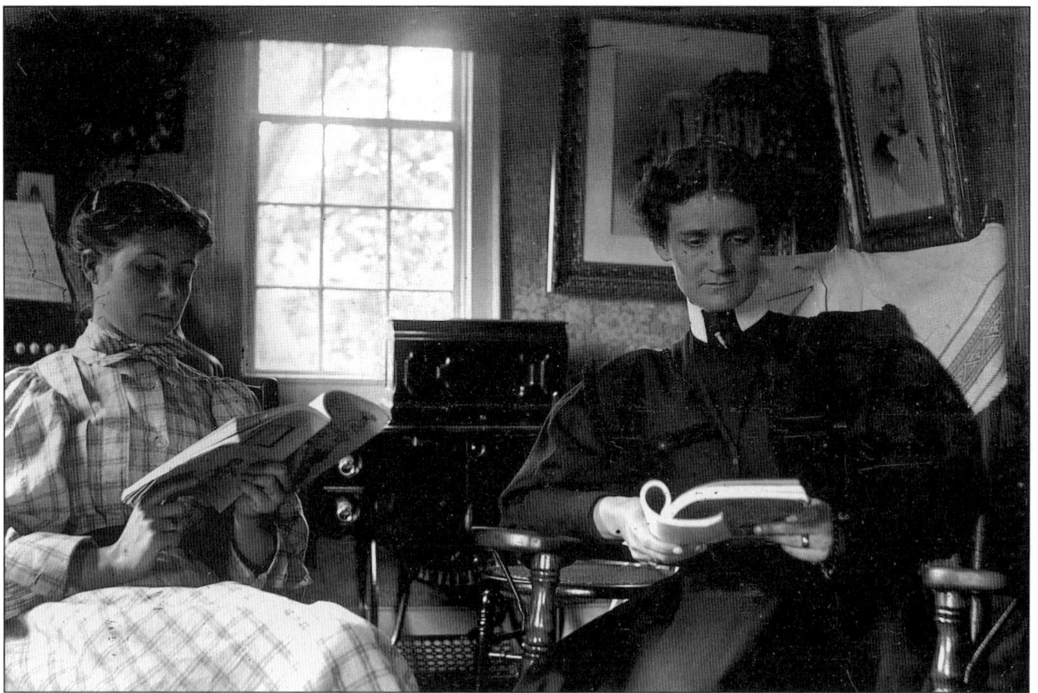

This photograph made from a glass negative shows two unidentified women reading in one of the rooms at Wachusett House in the late 1800s. A parlor organ is behind the young woman at the left. In the center, in front of the window, is a sewing machine. (Courtesy of the Princeton Historical Society and Bruce Dean.)

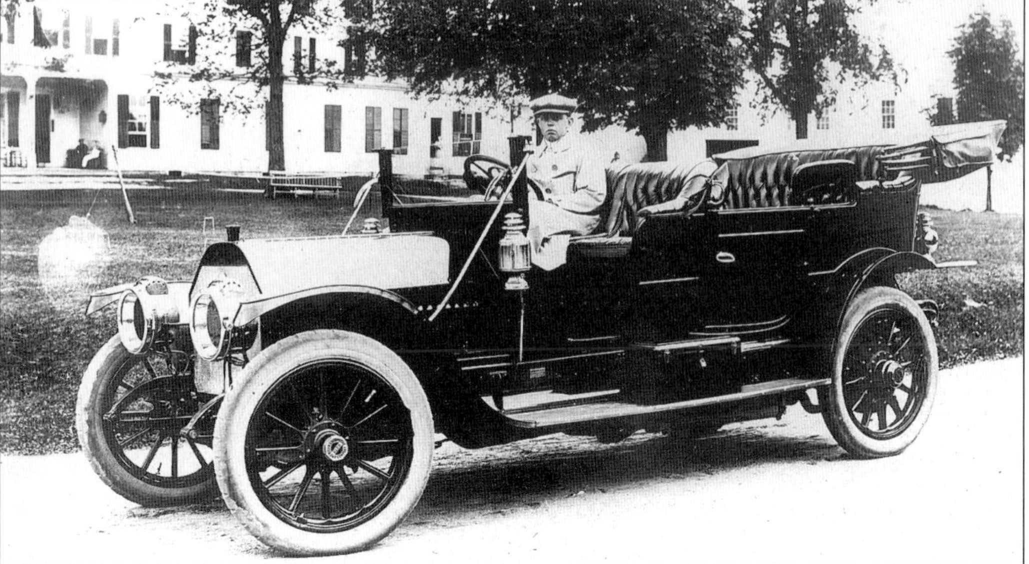

A young man is sitting in an American Locomotive motorcar in front of Wachusett House before 1910. The first Alco was built in Providence, Rhode Island, in 1906. In 1908, a bigger and better car was made. It took 19 months to build each one, and all types of body styles were available, as well as chassis from custom coach builders. Only the wealthy could afford an Alco, with prices ranging between $6,000 and $7,500. (Courtesy of Edith Hubbard.)

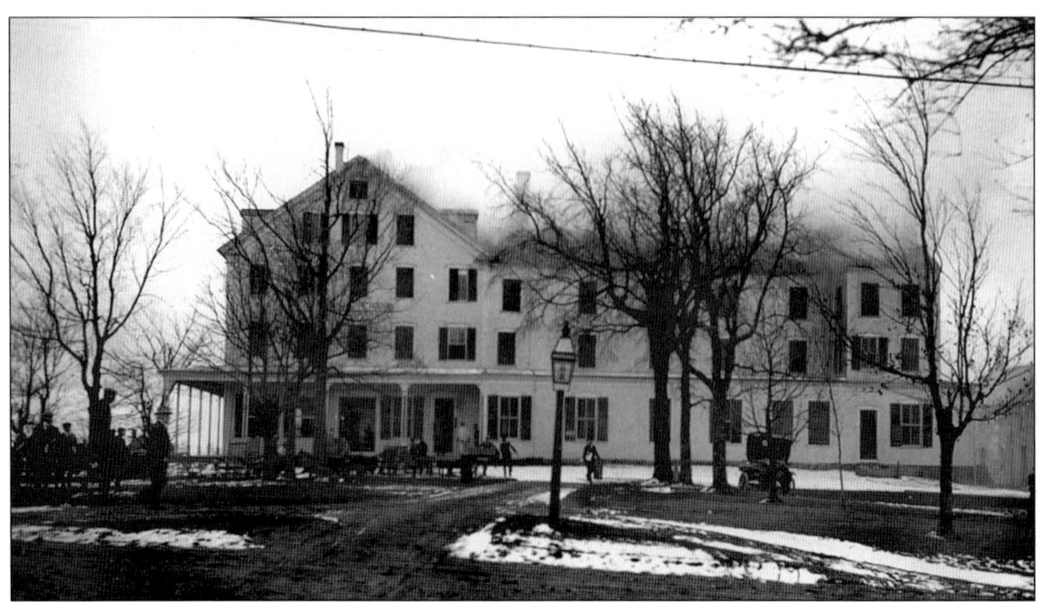

The roof of Wachusett House was ablaze at 9:30 a.m. on November 28, 1910. When the above photograph was taken, it was 9:45. Stanley Haley ran to the church to ring the bell to call the fire department. By 10:45, as the blaze progressed, furniture was moved to the lawn with the hope that something could be saved. *Evening Gazette* reporters rushed to the scene, and details of the fire were telegraphed to Worcester from the Western Union Telegraph office at Brooks Station two miles away. The fire caused an estimated $30,000 in damages. Business had declined over the past years, and the hotel was never rebuilt. (Courtesy of the Princeton Historical Society.)

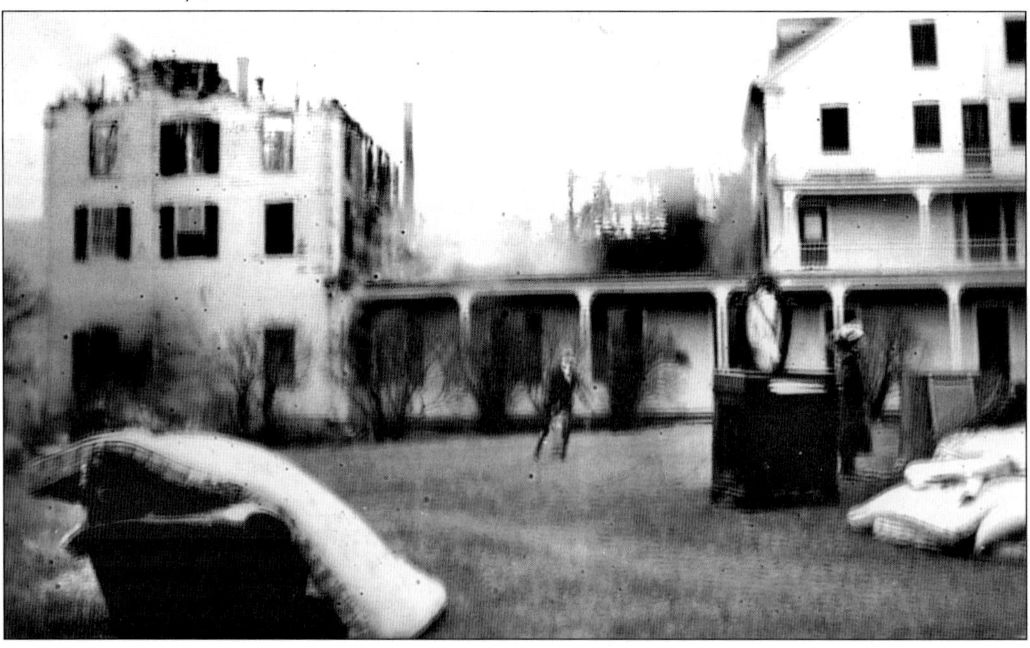

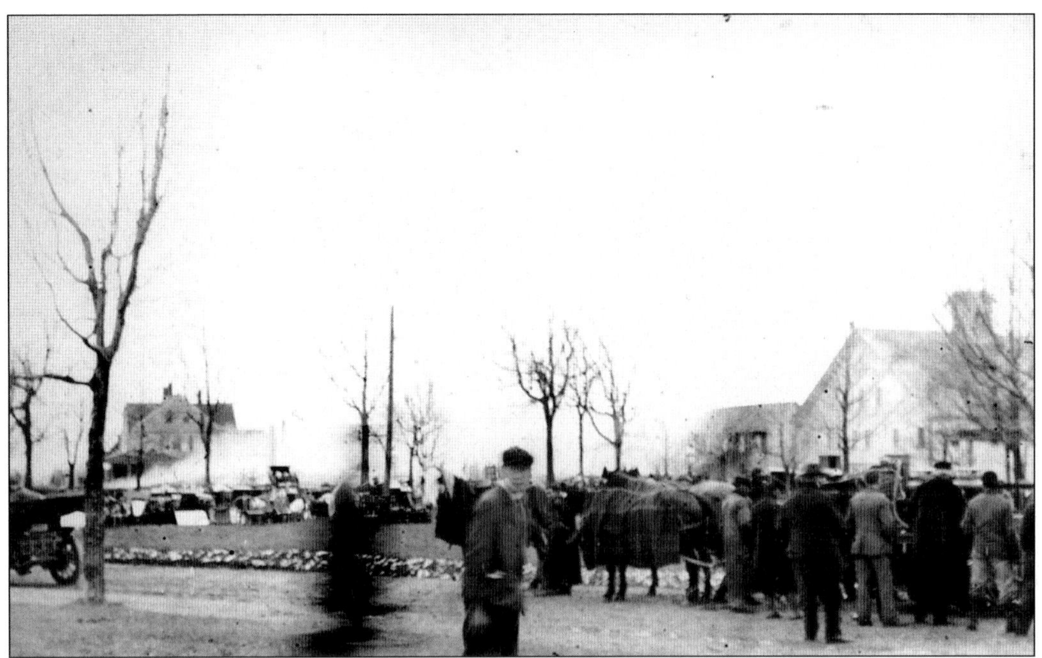

In the photograph above, taken at 12:30 p.m., the hotel and adjoining laundry have burned to the ground. In the distance to the left is the home of Harry Beaman, owner of Wachusett House. As the Wachusett House fire burned, telephone service was cut off and rumors were circulating that other buildings nearby were burning. There was little water to fight the fire because there had been a drought that summer, but with an easterly wind and the determination of the firefighters, more was saved than anticipated. The photograph below was taken the day after the fire. (Courtesy of the Princeton Historical Society.)

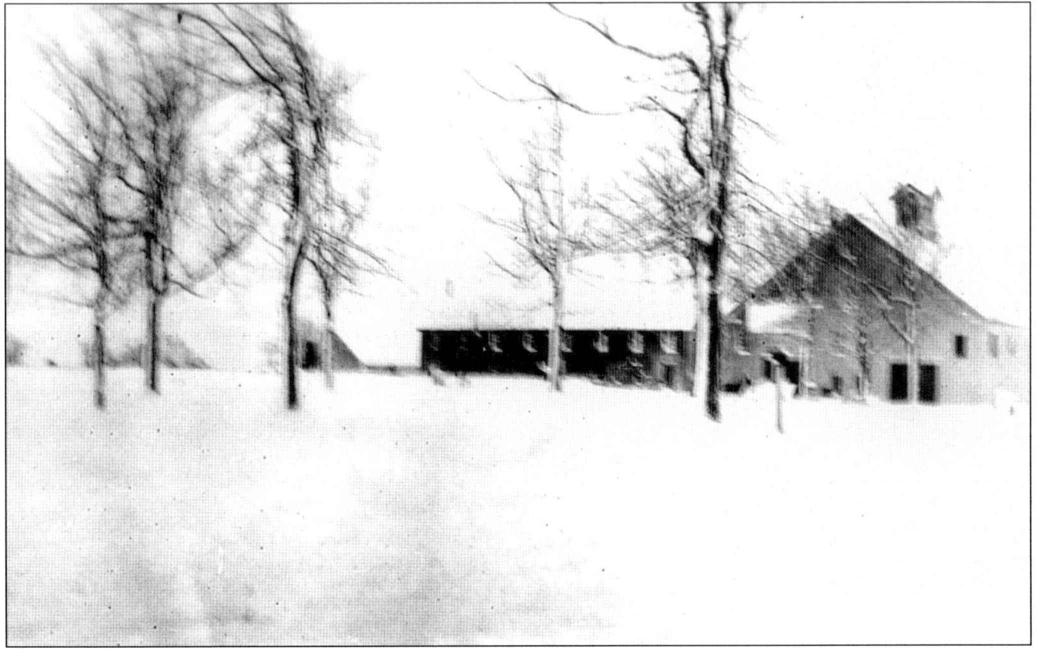

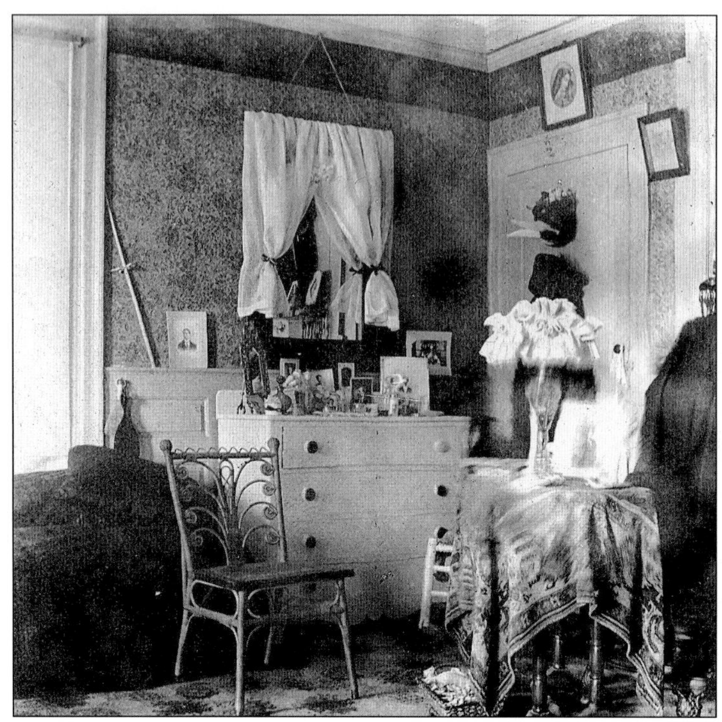

This photograph, taken on June 24, 1899, at Wachusett Cottage, is titled "The Palatial Residence of Harriet." The room was that of Harriet Beaman, daughter of the hotel owner, Algernon Beaman. (Courtesy of Nancy Beaman Flanders.)

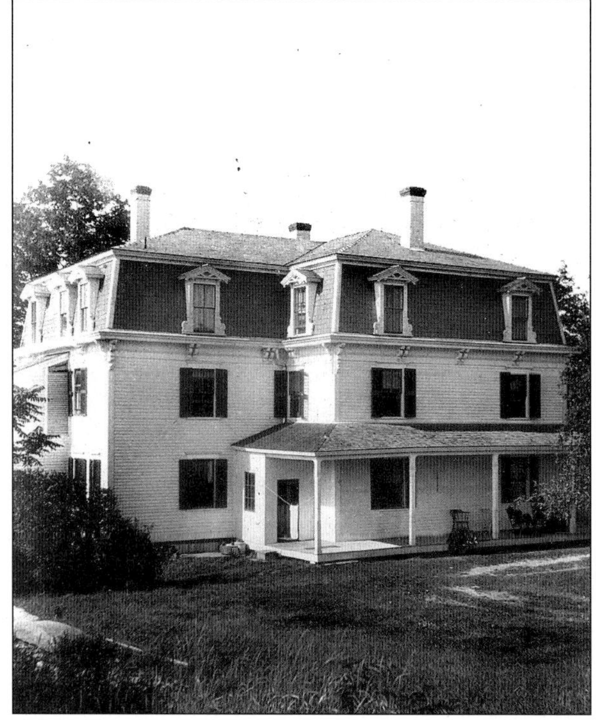

John Brooks built the first hotel on the Wachusett House site in 1822 and named it Wachusett House. In 1847, the building was moved to its present location, 7 Boylston Avenue, and sold to Phineas Beaman and Son. When Beaman remodeled it in 1883, he replaced the hip roof with a mansard roof and added a wing and a porch. After the remodeling, it accommodated 20 people and was known as the Annex or Wachusett Cottage. This photograph shows the back of the building. (Courtesy of Nancy Beaman Flanders.)

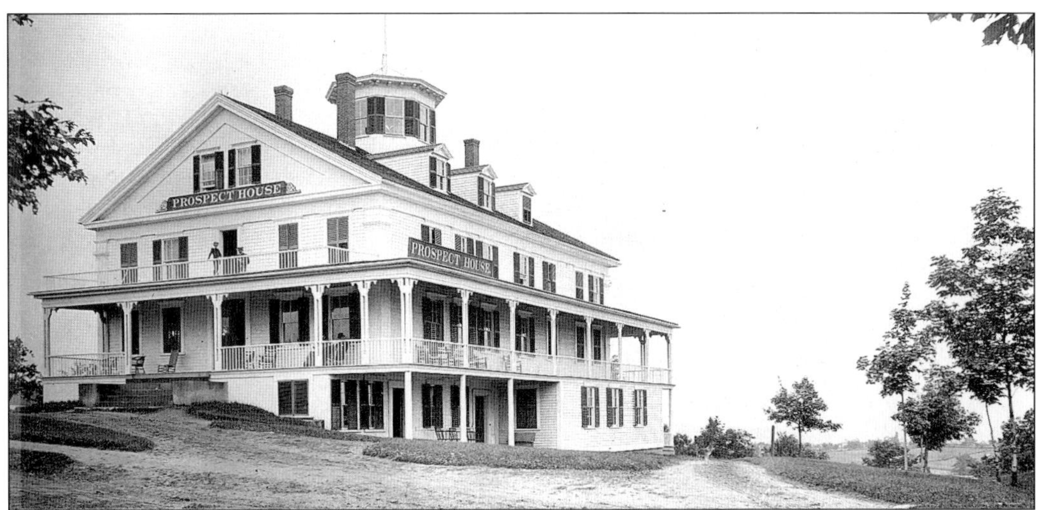

The Baptist church was built in 1840 and faced the common. It was sold to Wilkes Roper in 1860, when he converted it to a hotel and named it Prospect House for its view of Boston Harbor. In 1874, it was sold to George Bliss, who made an addition to the barn and enlarged the dining room. The hotel then accommodated 75 people. At Prospect House, the room rate was $8 to $15 for the week, which included board. (Courtesy of the Princeton Historical Society.)

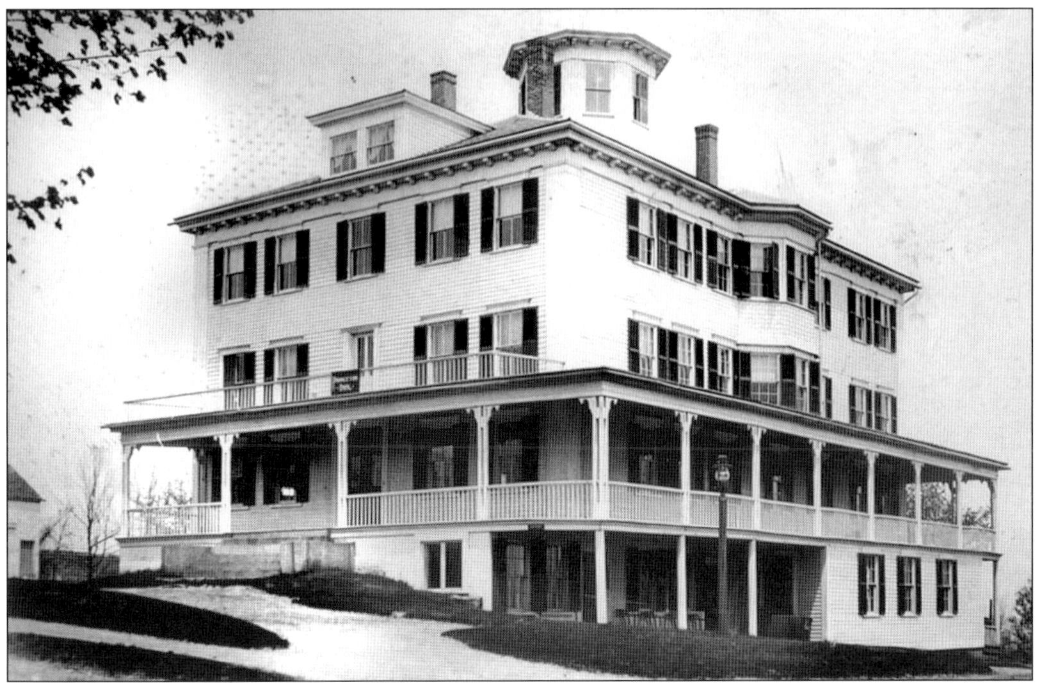

On October 15, 1923, at the end of the season, the Princeton Inn (formerly Prospect House) burned, and the fire nearly spread to the houses on either side. Blankets were nailed to the sides of the two adjacent Gregory houses and were kept wet. The two houses and barn were saved by the quick action of the men from the four towns who fought the fire. The loss from the Princeton Inn blaze was estimated to be $50,000. (Courtesy of the Princeton Historical Society.)

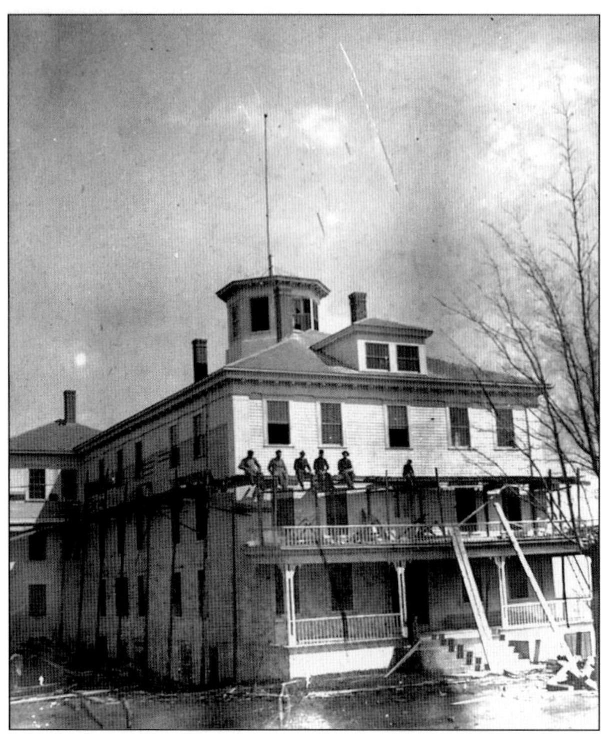

This photograph, made from a glass negative, shows workers sitting on scaffolding as they work on Prospect House. Wayland Davis leased the property in 1883 and remained the proprietor for 18 years. In 1895, during his time of proprietorship, Davis added a story to the house. With earlier additions, the hotel now accommodated 100 or more guests. Harry Beaman purchased the Princeton Inn in 1913. (Courtesy of the Princeton Historical Society.)

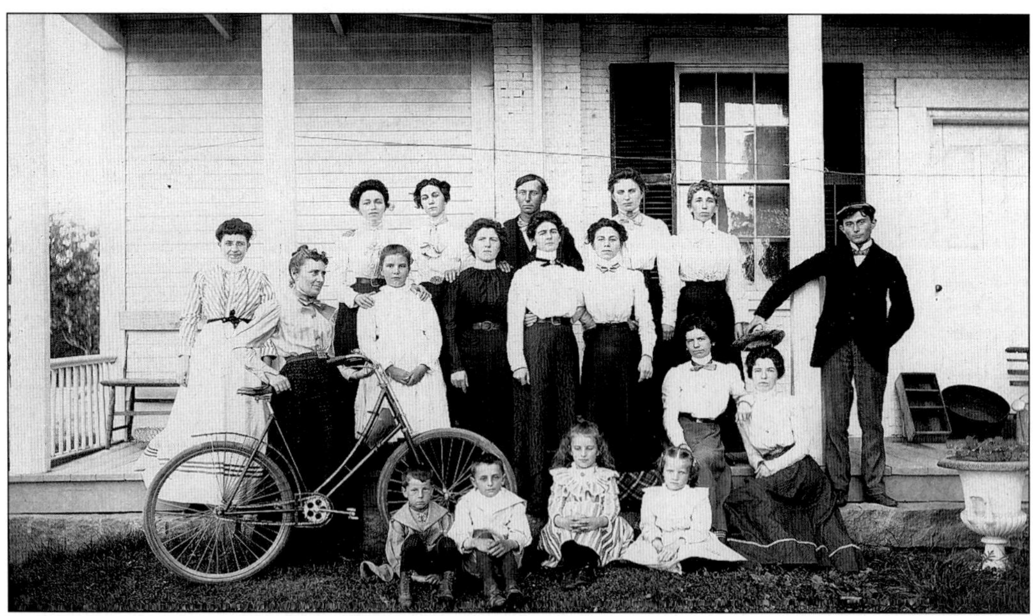

The employees of Prospect House are shown on the steps. The hotel was known for its excellent food and clean rooms. It also boasted a good stable, livery, and boarding of horses. A staff member is seen with a bicycle, a popular item in the 1890s. There were few level roads in town on which to ride, and Wayland Davis, owner of Prospect House, would take people in a hay wagon to East Princeton, where they could enjoy riding on a level road. (Courtesy of the Princeton Historical Society.)

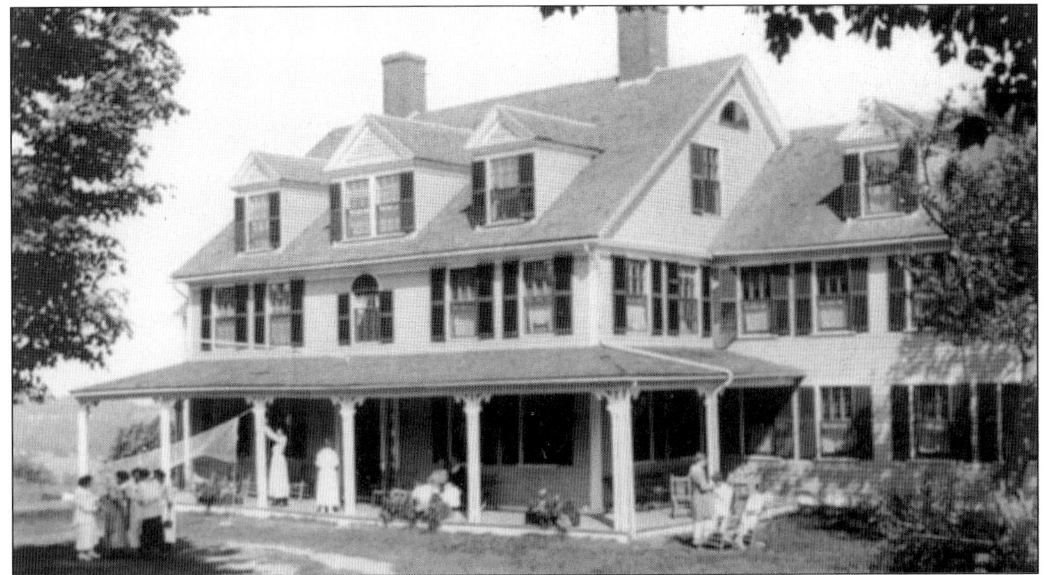

Capt. Benjamin Harrington built this as his home in 1835. Wilkes Roper purchased it *c.* 1870. He added the wings and established a hotel known as Summer House. In the summer of 1890, Roper rented the house to M. Josephine Allen of Boston for use as a "vacation home for working girls." That fall, she purchased the house, barn, 10 acres of land, and furnishings for $3,800. Allen named the property Fernside, and for nearly 100 years, it operated as a vacation house for women. (Courtesy of the Princeton Historical Society.)

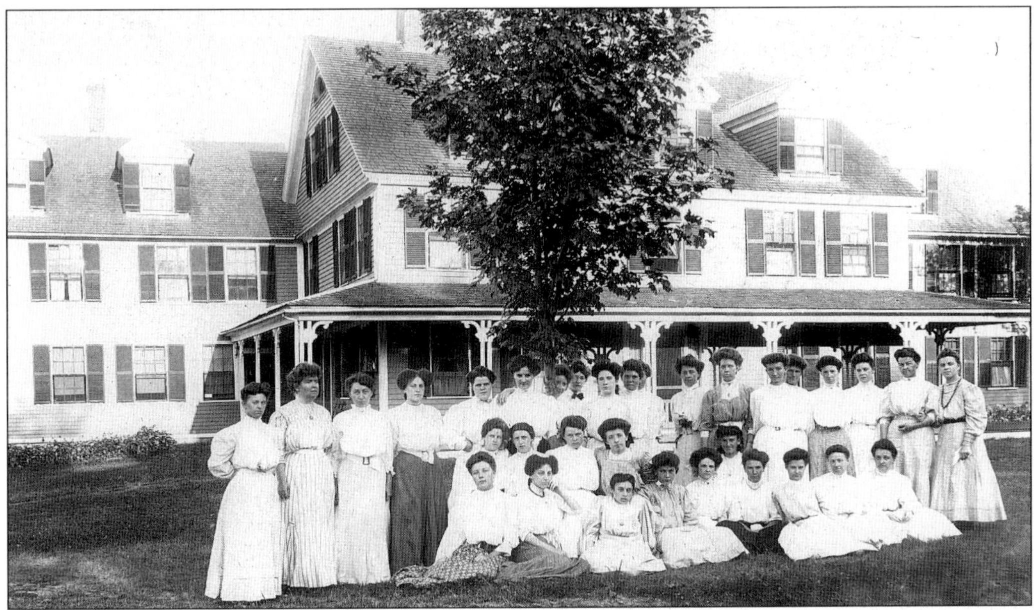

This photograph of women at Fernside was taken in the late 1800s. The daily routine started with the rising bell at 7:00 a.m. After breakfast, an excursion to Wachusett Mountain, a trip to the village post office, or picking berries were the events of the morning. Lunch was served, and in the afternoon the girls could write, rest in their rooms, or lie in hammocks under the apple trees. After dinner at 6:00, the evenings were filled with entertainment. (Courtesy of Fernside Inn.)

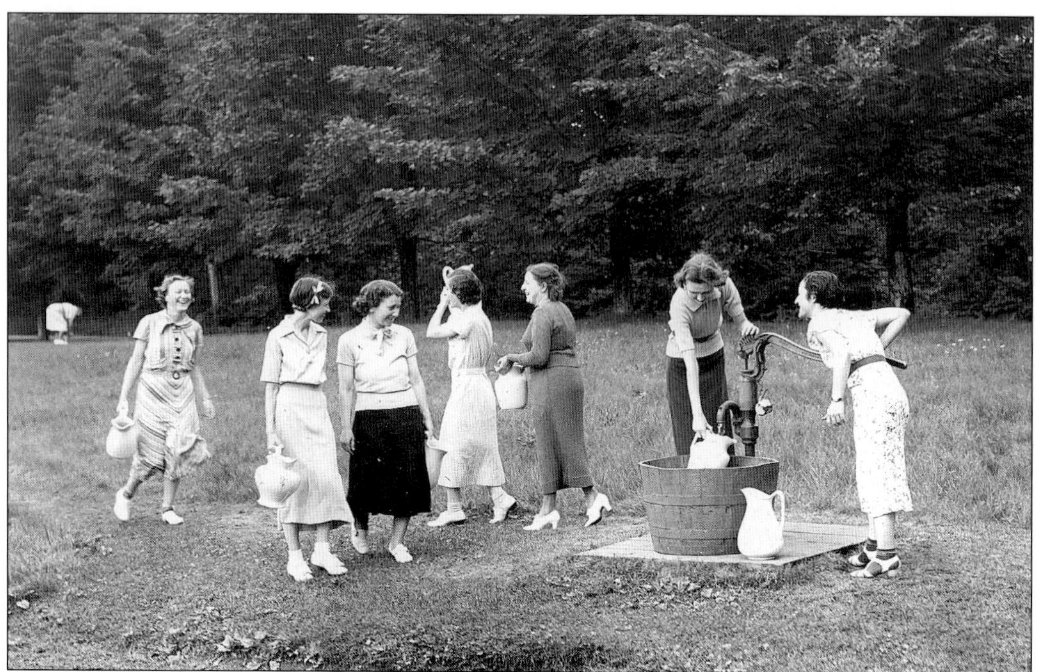

Fernside made an appeal for funds that would help purchase an artesian well, pump, and plumbing that cost $2,500 in 1939. This photograph, titled "The Pitcher Parade," shows guests getting water for their washbowls in the days before plumbing was installed. It was used as part of the brochure that told about Fernside, which made available a vacation in the country to city dwelling "business girls from seventeen to seventy." (Courtesy of the Princeton Historical Society.)

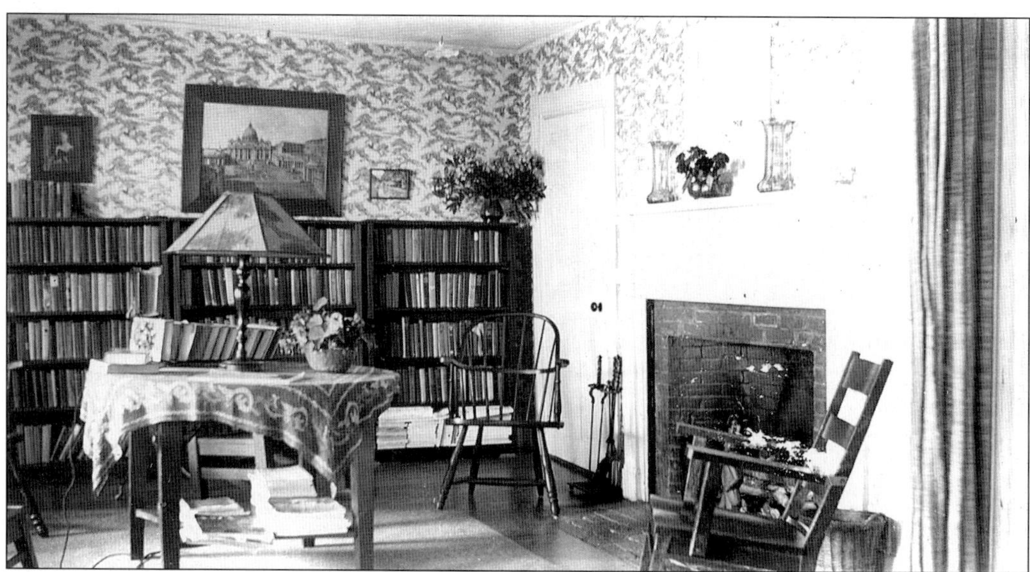

The interior of Fernside was comfortable and spacious. There was a reading room with books available for the guests and, adjacent to it, a music room where the older guests could watch the dancing, games, and charades or could hear the girls playing the piano and singing. (Courtesy of the Princeton Historical Society.)

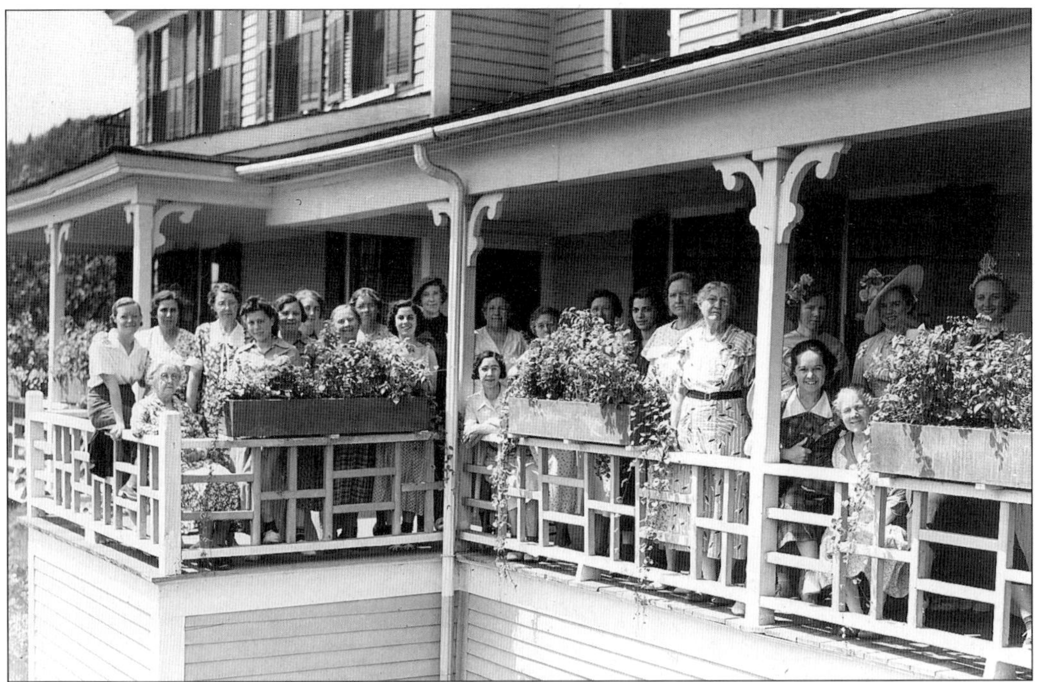

Fernside was originally established to make vacations at a mountain resort available to working women who would not have been able to afford them otherwise. A 1939 brochure noted, "Fernside attracts new friends each year and retains old ones. Since 1890, more than 5,000 girls and women have benefited from vacations at Fernside. It has become a tradition, passed on from mother to daughter." (Courtesy of the Princeton Historical Society.)

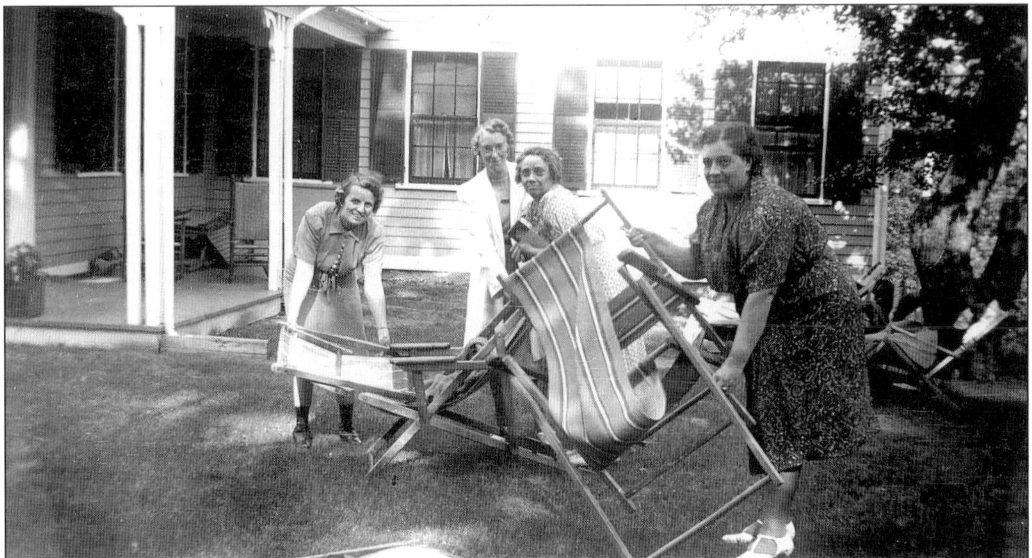

Over the years, Fernside lost its attraction, as the lifestyles of young women changed and as the automobile made a broader range of vacation possibilities available to the American public. Fernside opened for its final summer in 1988. Over the years, the cost remained affordable for most women. In 1890, a week's stay cost $3. By the 1980s, room and board cost $70 a week. (Courtesy of the Princeton Historical Society.)

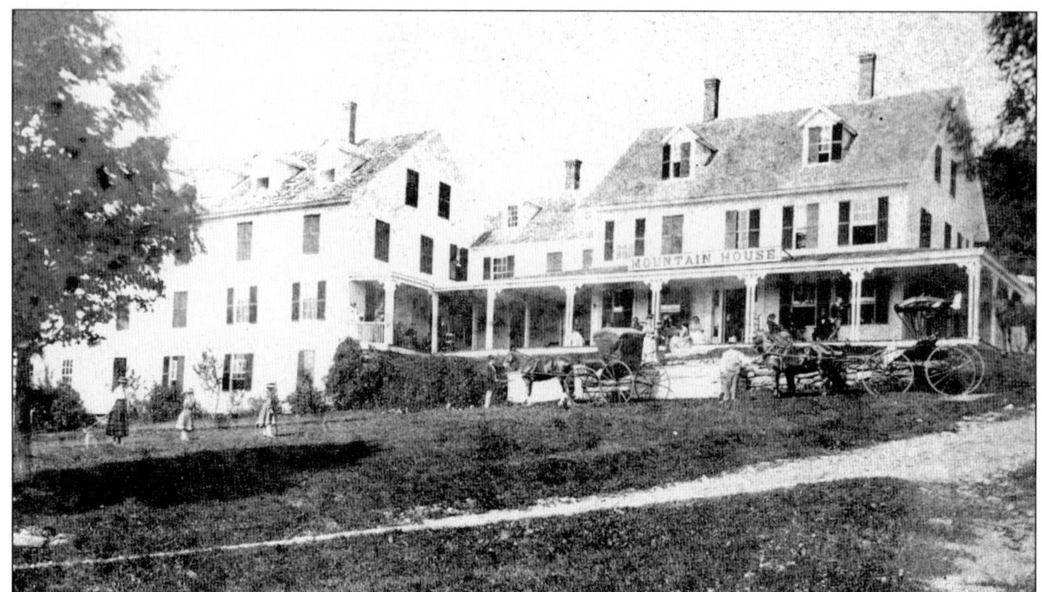

Mountain House began as a hotel in 1859. In the photograph above, Mountain House is seen before an addition to the main house was built in 1880. Samuel and Moses Bullard, the owners of Mountain House, felt a certain amount of rivalry with other hotels in the center of town and wanted to avoid having their guests see the other establishments. They initiated construction of the continuation of Allen Hill Road so their coach could travel from Princeton Depot and bypass the center of town. For many years, there was a summer post office at Mountain House. The hotel met its fate in 1914, when flames swept through it. The bowling alley across the road was spared and was later known as the Bowling Alley Tea Room. The photograph below, taken after 1880, shows Mountain House (center) from a distance. The Grand View House is on the left, and the bowling alley is on the right. (Courtesy of the Princeton Historical Society.)

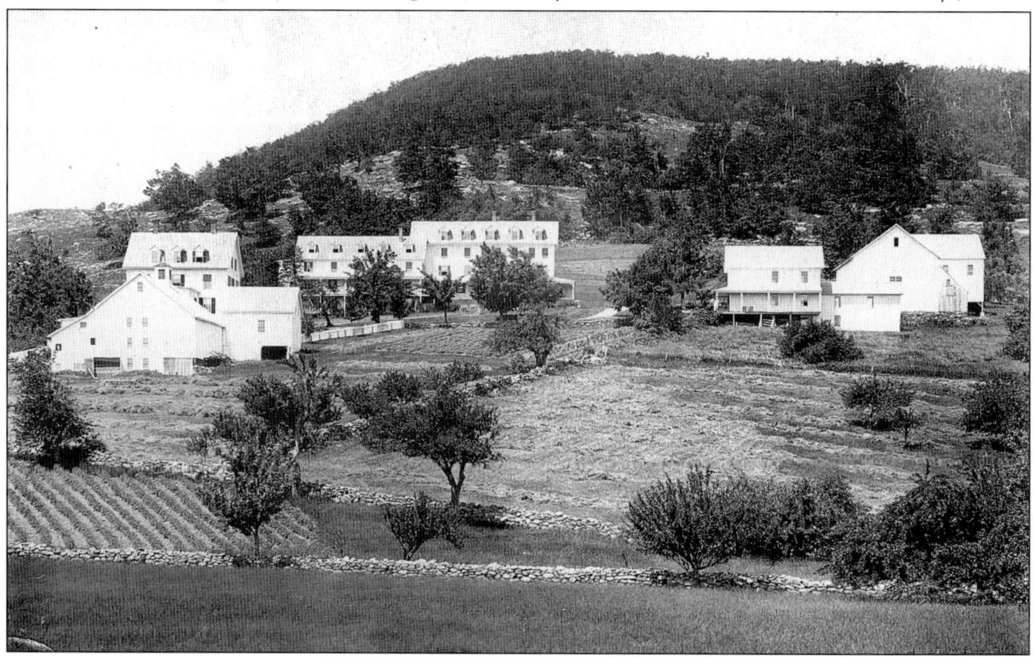

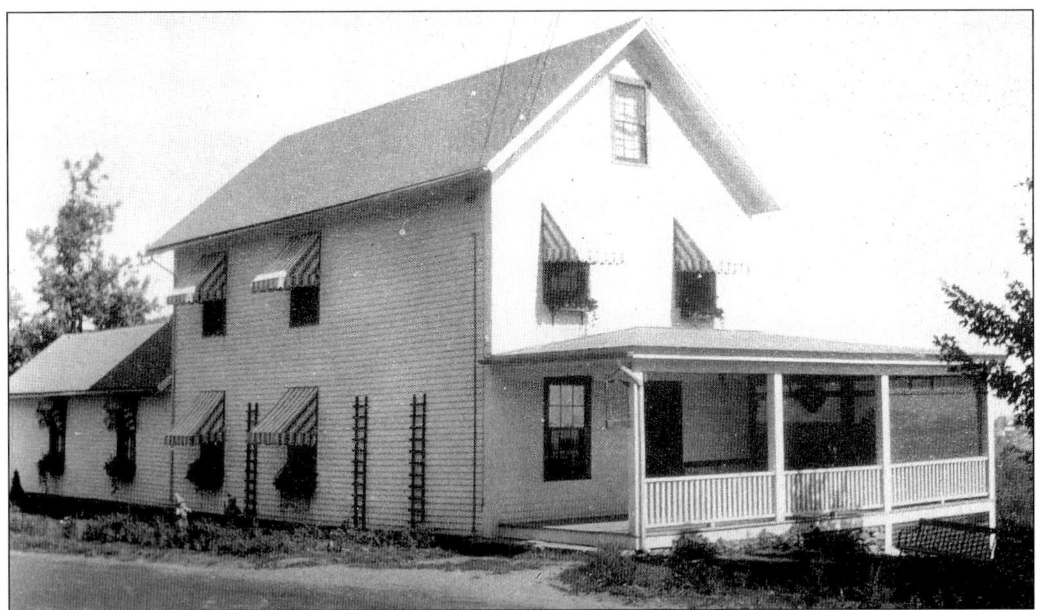

Across Mountain Road from Mountain House was a bowling alley associated with the hotel. When Mountain House burned in 1914, the bowling alley was spared. Ina Needham purchased the property in 1924, and she and her daughter opened a tearoom there. A couple of years later, Christine Mason purchased the restaurant. For almost 40 years, she served dinners during the summer at the Bowling Alley Tea Room. (Courtesy of Calista and Russell Vickery.)

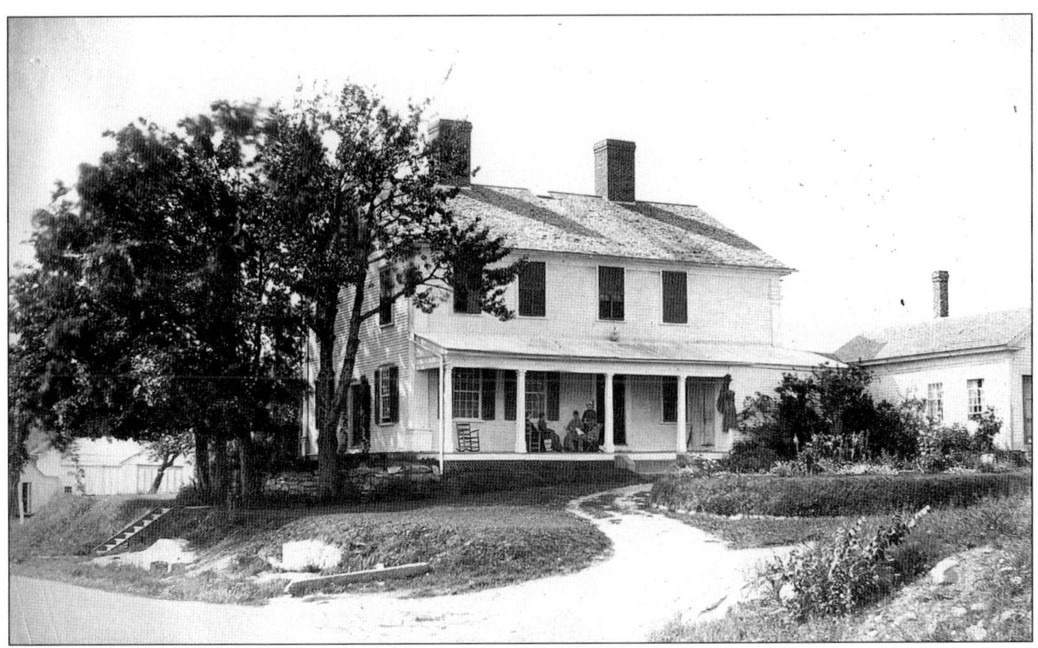

Grimes Cottage was located at the corner of Hubbardston and Allen Hill Roads. Deacon Edwin Grimes purchased the property in 1853 and opened it to summer boarders in 1869. The house had 15 to 20 rooms with a view of Rutland from the porch. (Courtesy of the Princeton Historical Society.)

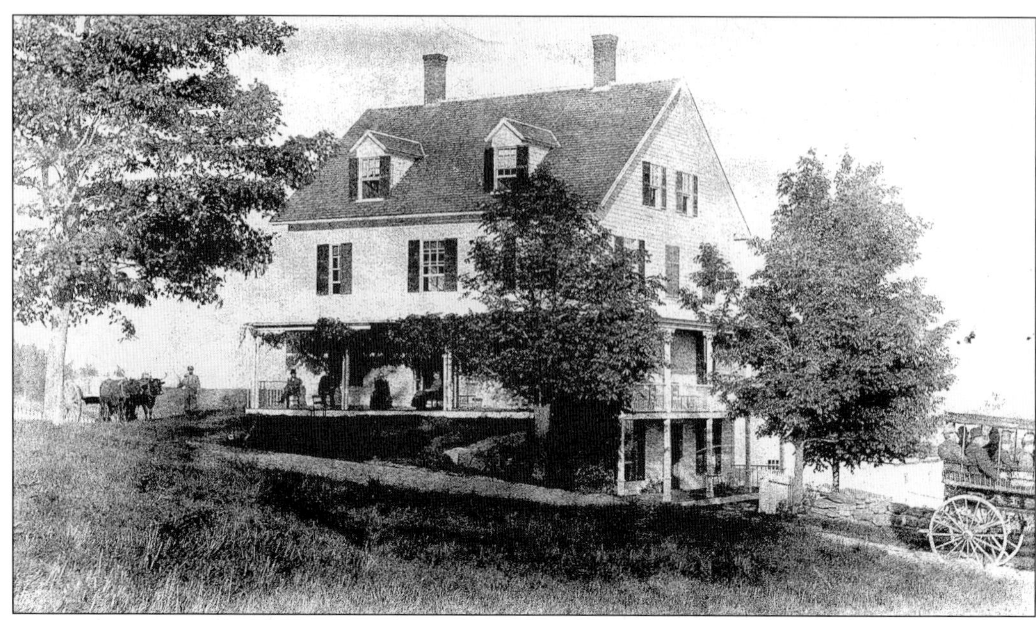

On the easterly side of Mountain Road across from the Mountain House Hotel was the Grand View House, which was enlarged and remodeled several times. The Grand View Cottage is shown above before William Howe remodeled it in 1893. Below is the Grand View after two additions and shortly before it burned. At the refurbished hotel, the parlors had fireplaces and rooms for 100 guests. It boasted the very best sanitary appointments of any hotel in Princeton. Pure running spring water, both hot and cold, with bathrooms on every floor, made it especially attractive to visitors. The beds were advertised as having the best hair mattresses and patent springs. A large farm supplied fresh vegetables and berries daily, and the dairy produced butter, cream, and milk. The hotel burned in September 1899. (Courtesy of the Princeton Historical Society.)

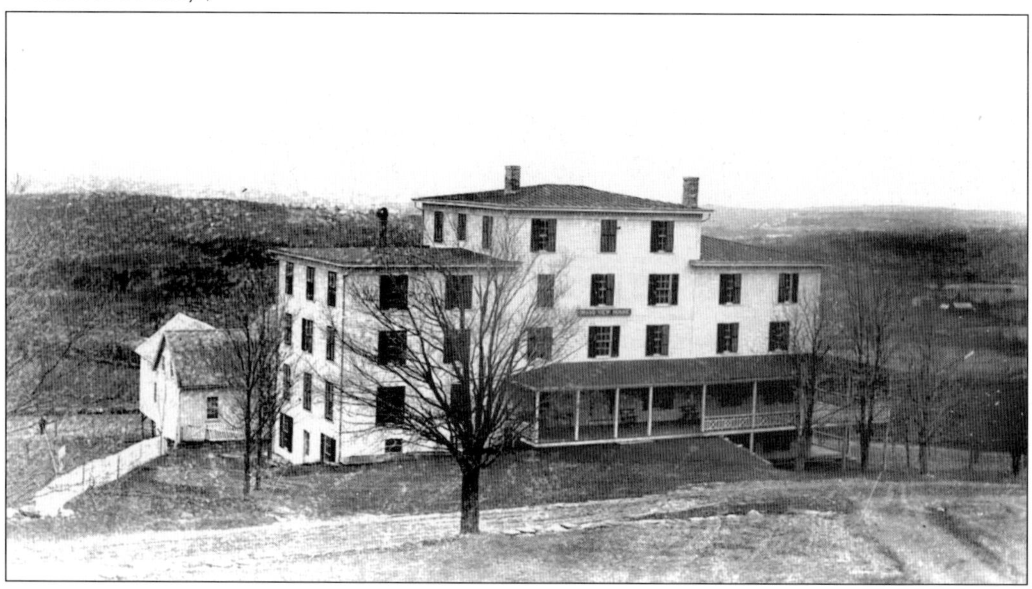

Clara Padgham, the owner of Woodland Cottage, rented throughout the school season to teachers who found that living at this house enabled them to get to school in the winter when it snowed. The interior of Woodland Cottage (shown here) was comfortable and provided a homelike atmosphere for guests staying there. There was a barbershop in the basement, and the barn adjacent to the house provided lodging in the summer for the hired help. (Courtesy of Ann and J.P. Flatt.)

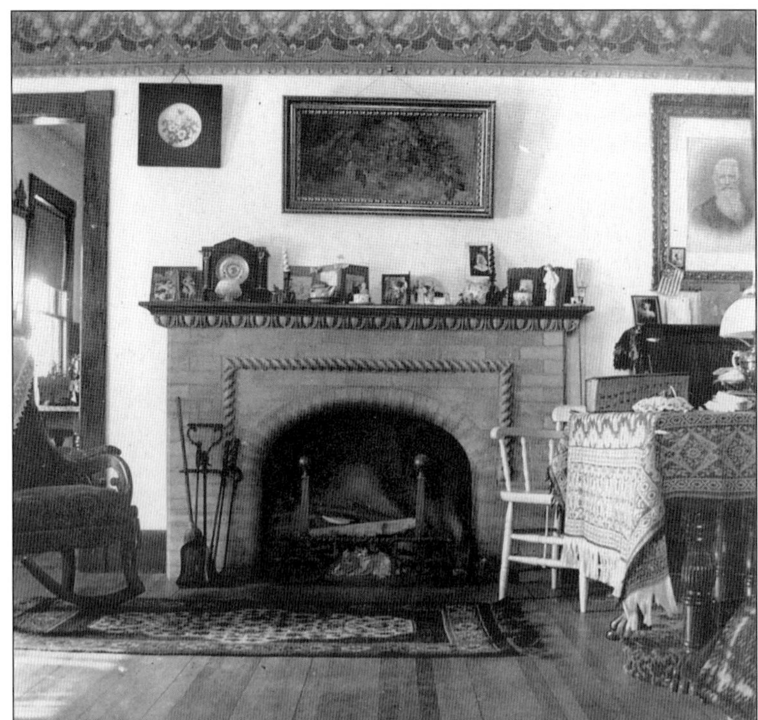

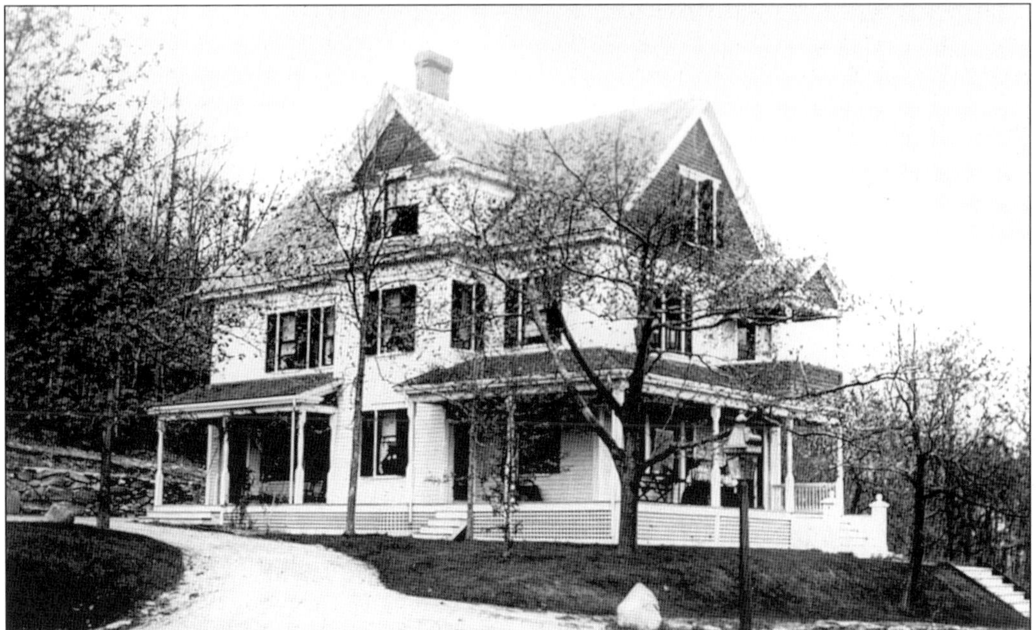

Woodland Cottage, now a private home on Prospect Street, opened as a boardinghouse *c.* 1905 with accommodations for 10 to 12 guests. In the early part of the century, a view of Boston Harbor and the customs house was part of the attraction of staying here. There was a serious fire in the house many years ago when lightning struck, and the hook-and-ladder truck was not tall enough to reach the attic. Charred timbers are still visible on the third floor. (Courtesy of the Princeton Historical Society.)

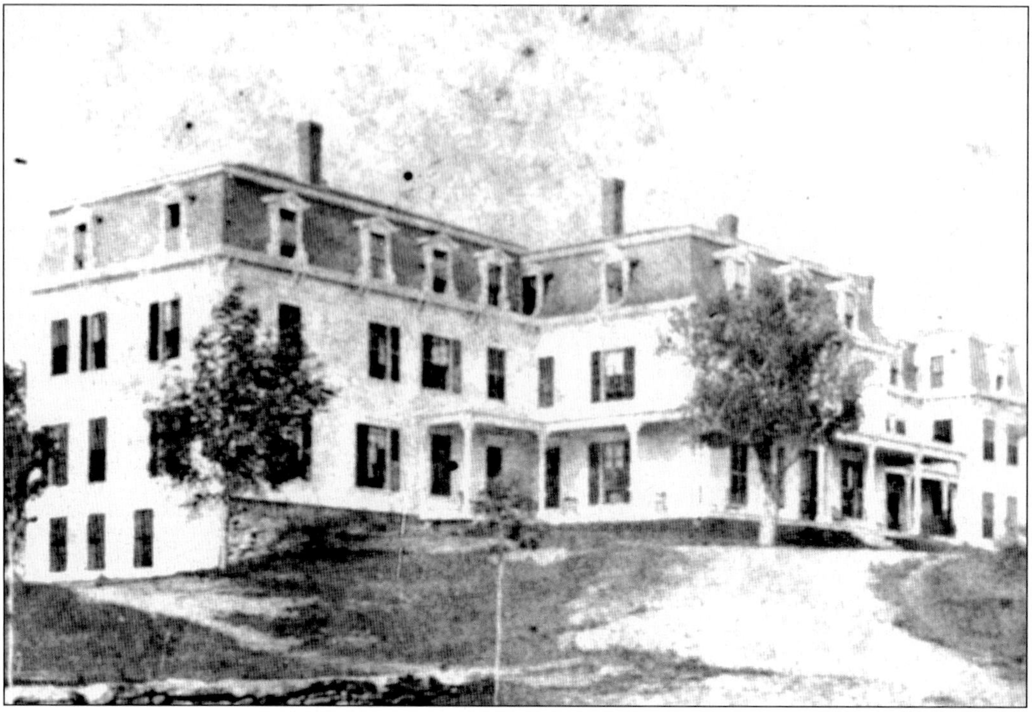

In the view above, dating from before 1912, Mount Pleasant House is shown before it was divided. It is shown below as a private home. Situated on 150 acres on Goodnow Road, it opened as a hotel in 1868. By 1875, it was enlarged to accommodate 40 to 60 guests. In the spring of 1912, Edward and Harry Whitney of Worcester purchased the property, divided the house in two, and moved half to an adjoining lot. Helen Hunt Jackson, who was often a guest, wrote an article in 1876 for *Scribner's* magazine about the pristine beauty of Princeton. (Courtesy of the Princeton Historical Society.)

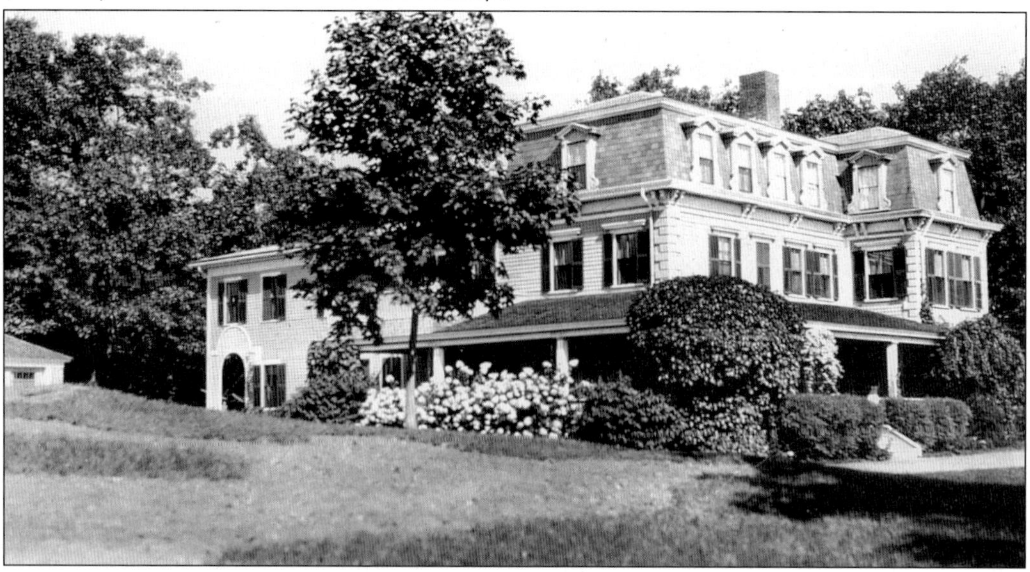

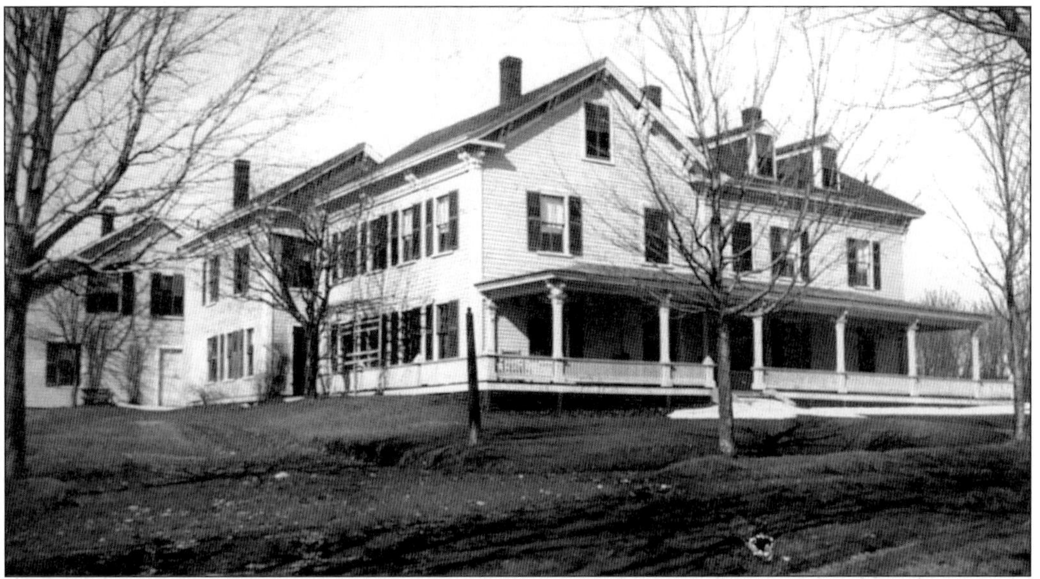

Howard House, on Worcester Road, was built in 1868 by Deacon Nelson Howard, a skilled carpenter and mason. It was later enlarged to accommodate 40 or more guests. After Howard stopped taking guests, he rented rooms to accommodate the overflow of the center hotels. Howard retired in 1889; the house was demolished in 1961. (Courtesy of the Princeton Historical Society.)

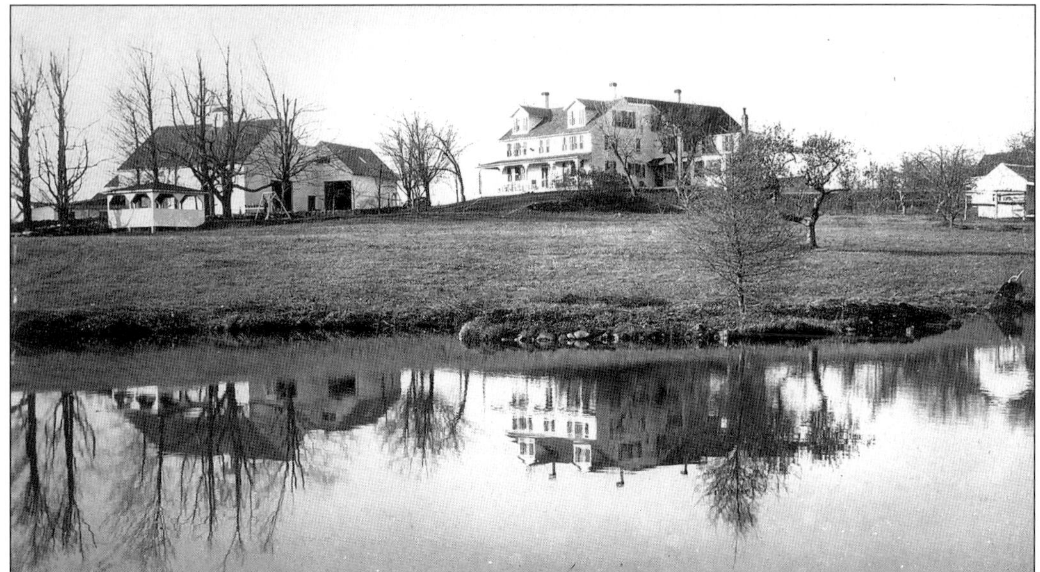

Harrington Farm opened in 1882 as a summer boardinghouse under the ownership of Almira Harrington and her son Joseph. Families were welcome and Joseph would set up cots in the rooms so families were able to stay together. Harrington Farm accommodated up to 30 guests, but if it became too crowded, Joseph set up tents in the fields where people could sleep under the stars. (Courtesy of the Stimson family.)

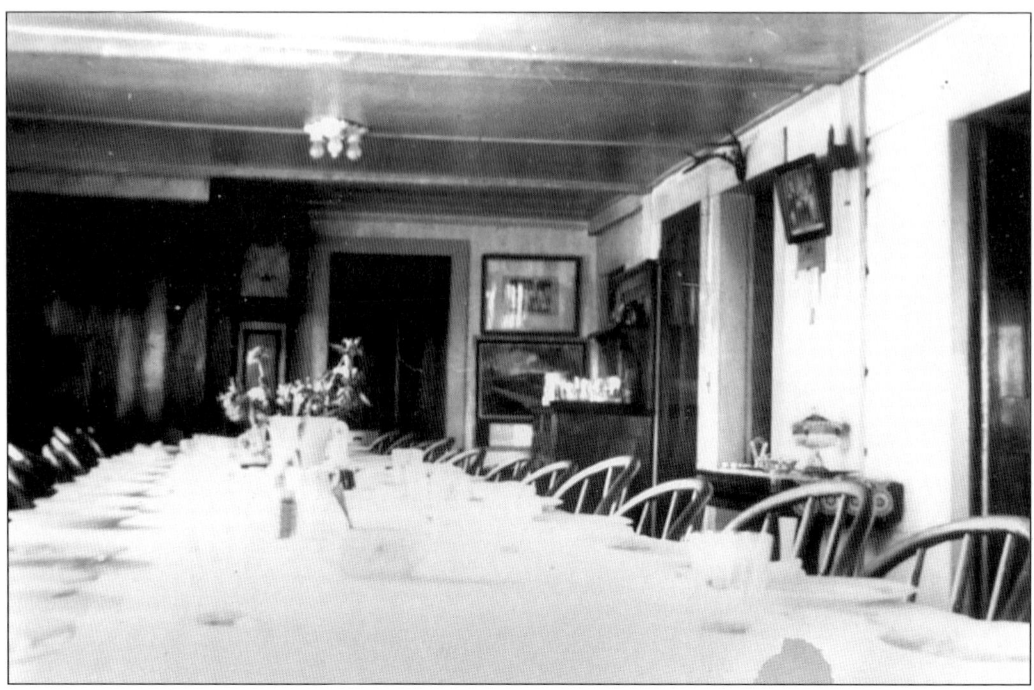

When it was dinnertime, a large bell was rung to announce dinner was being served. The meal was served family style at Harrington Farm, with as many as three long tables pushed together with a seating capacity for 34 people. Turkey dinners and the bounty of the land provided delicious home-cooked meals. This tradition continued into the 1970s. (Courtesy of Harrington Farm.)

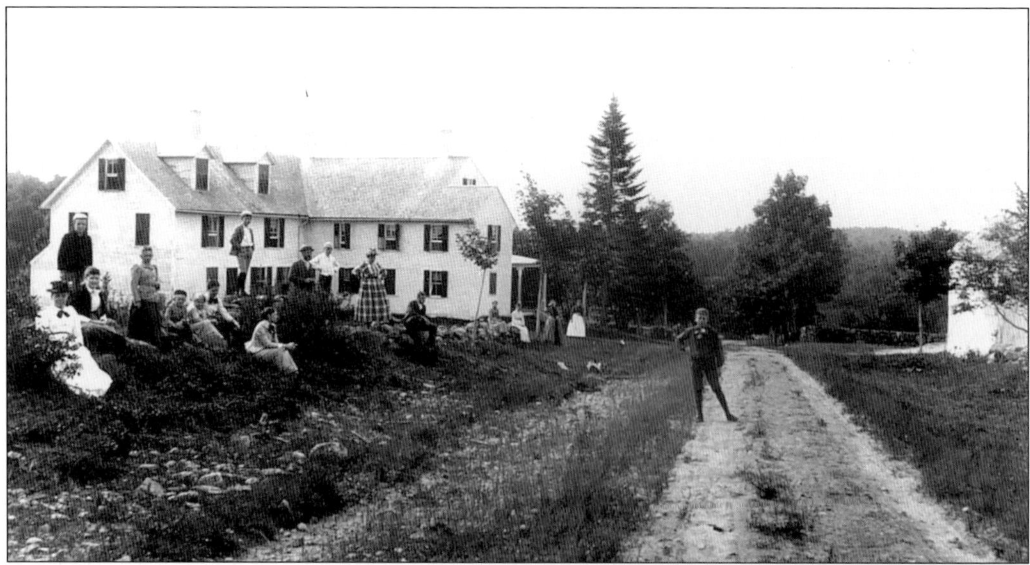

This late-1800s photograph shows guests gathered at Harrington Farm. The young man is standing in Westminster Road. Lansford Harrington, a Civil War veteran, purchased Harrington Farm in 1864. After his death, his wife, Almira, and son Joseph continued to run the business. Another son, Francis, was a well-known fire spotter on Wachusett Mountain in the mid-1900s. (Courtesy of Harrington Farm.)

Five

As We Grew

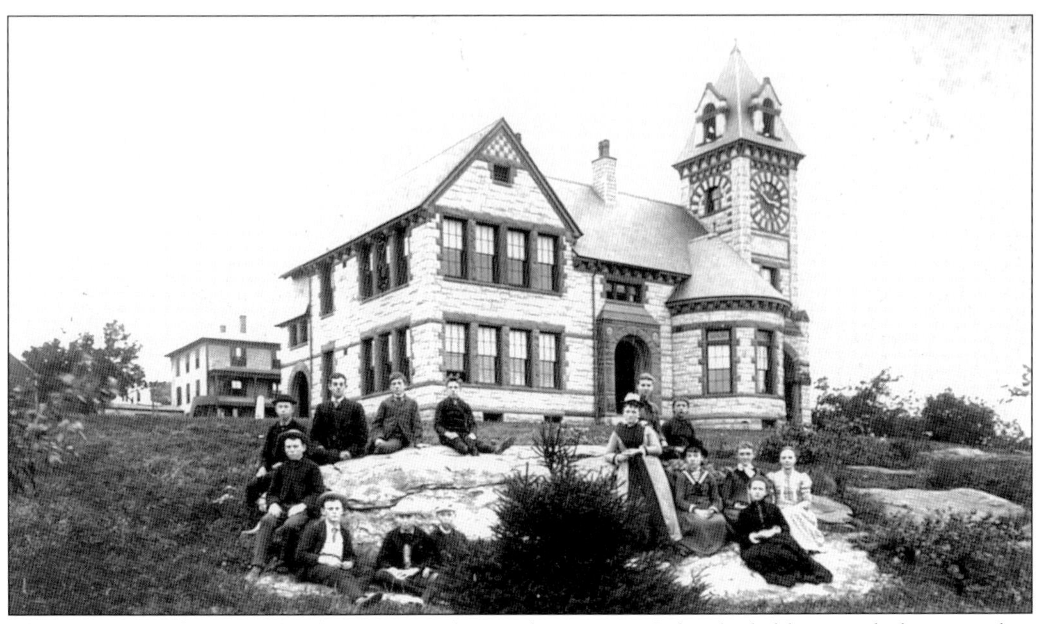

This photograph from the late 1800s shows the Upper School children and their teacher outside the Goodnow Memorial Building. The first high-school graduation from the Goodnow Memorial Building was in 1892 with a graduating class of four girls. (Courtesy of Marjorie Ollila.)

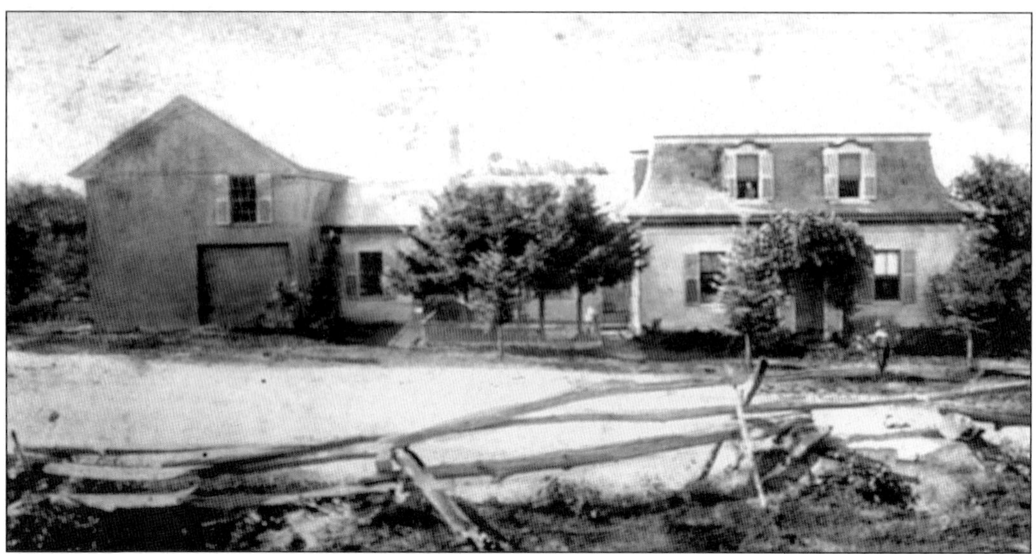

The first schoolhouse was built in 1774, and it burned in 1789. A new school was immediately built to replace it. John Stratton purchased the school in 1834, and a team of oxen moved it in two days to Hubbardston Road, where it was converted into a private residence. It was later purchased by Dr. Joseph West and named the Snuggery. This photograph, taken in 1885, shows the schoolhouse on the right with a later addition of a mansard roof. (Courtesy of Henry and Joyce Rettstadt.)

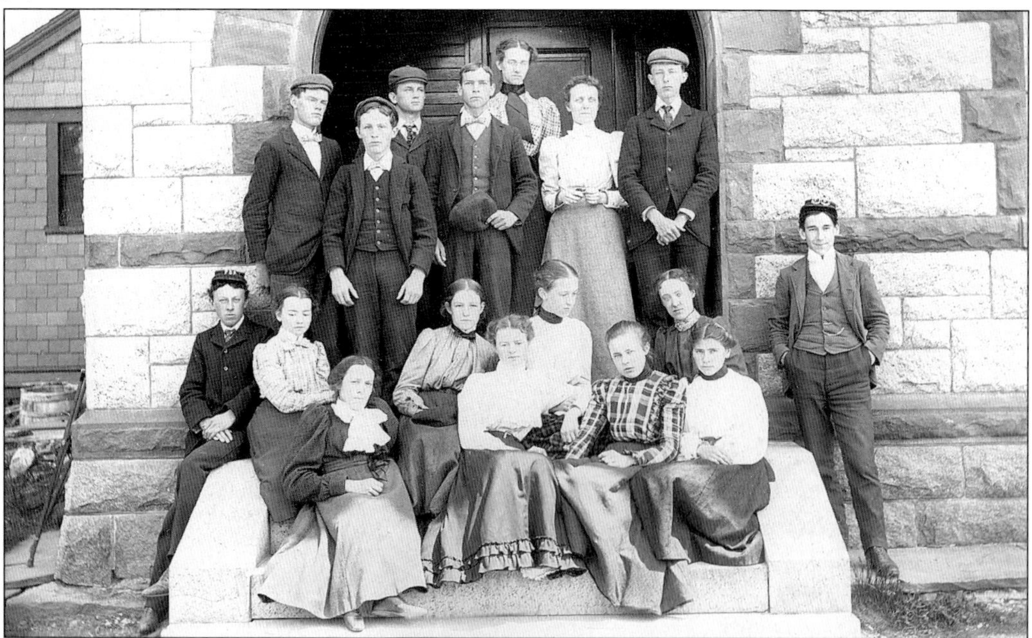

A picture from 1901 shows the students of the Upper School assembled on the side steps of the Goodnow Memorial Building. By 1901, new courses had been added to the simple courses of arithmetic and grammar taught in the early days of school. Some of the new courses included geography, history, nature study, drawing, vocal music, and sewing. The high-school courses included algebra, civil government, literature, physics, Latin, and French. (Courtesy of the Princeton Historical Society.)

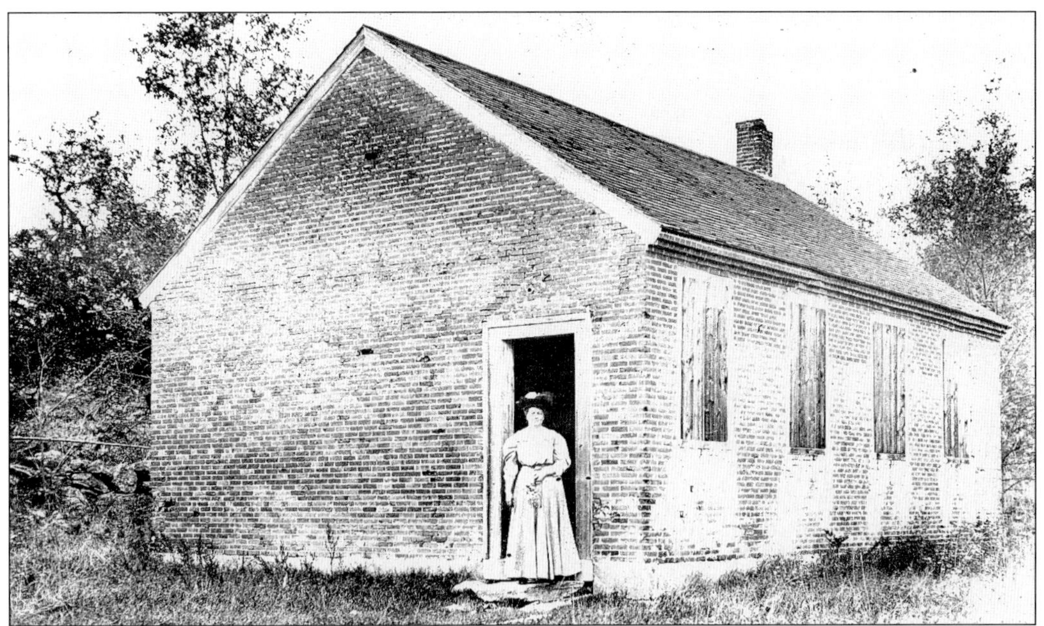

Schoolhouse No. 2 was a wooden structure originally built on Mirick Road near the stone house. After the schoolhouse burned in 1837, classes were held in the basement of the house. The new schoolhouse was constructed of brick and built on the corner of Gregory and Mirick Roads. By 1838–1840, all the wooden schoolhouses had been replaced with brick except Schoolhouses No. 2 and No. 7. Schoolhouse No. 2 was razed in 1920. (Courtesy of the Princeton Historical Society.)

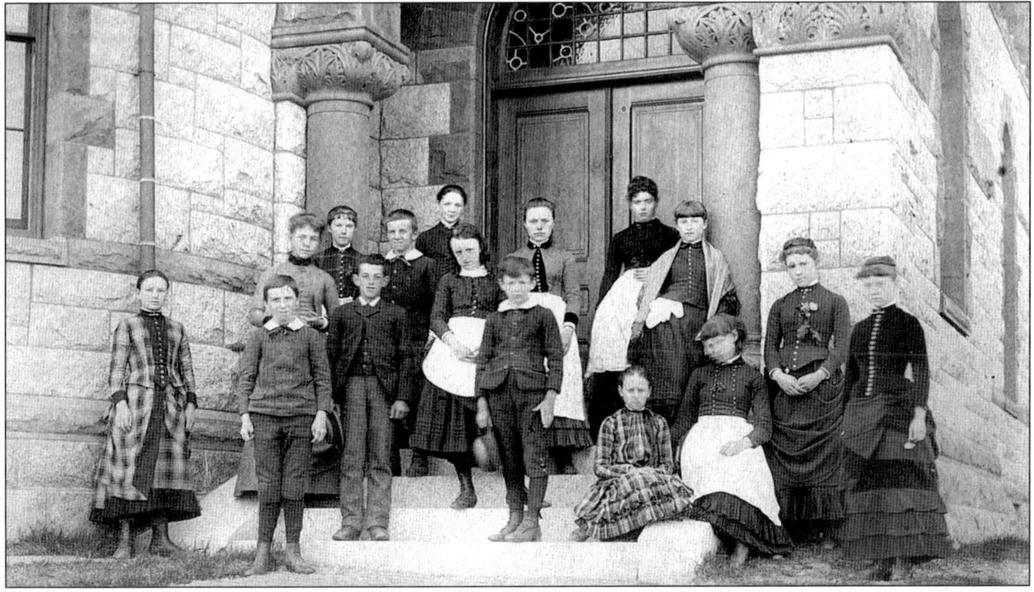

The students from the Upper School are standing on the steps of the Goodnow Memorial Building in 1886. From left to right are the following: (front row) Kate Wilder, R.J. Gregory, Fred Bryant, Edna Skinner, Milton Smith, Harriet Beaman, Jennie ?, Alice Howard, and Lizzie Pratt; (back row) Priscilla Whiton, Mabel Howard, Hermes Heywood, Ella Gately, Mary Brooks, Sadie Smith, and Isabel Davis. (Courtesy of the Princeton Historical Society.)

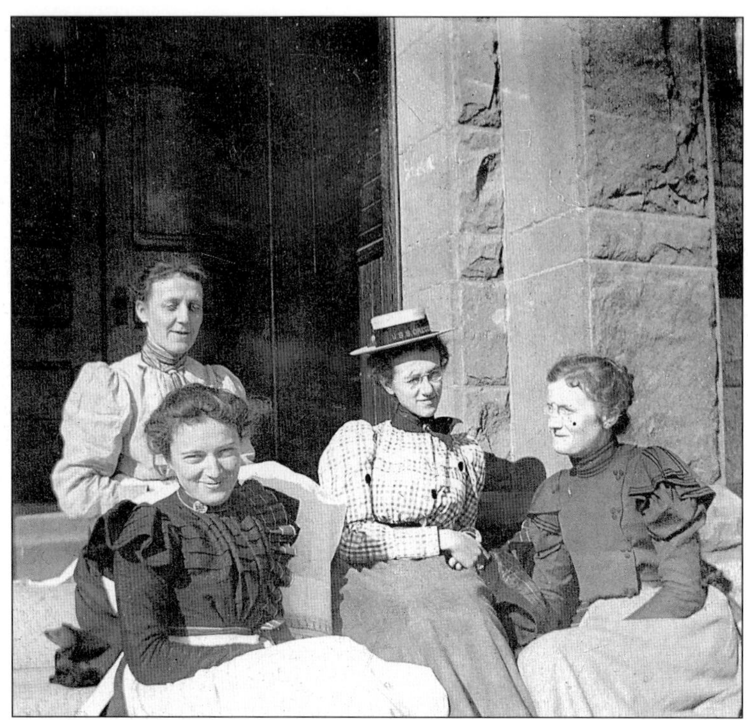

Four Princeton teachers are sitting on the steps of the Goodnow Memorial Building in 1901. Wearing the straw hat is Harriet E. Beaman. The others are Anna Mason, Maud Doolittle, and Julia Bennett. (Courtesy of the Princeton Historical Society.)

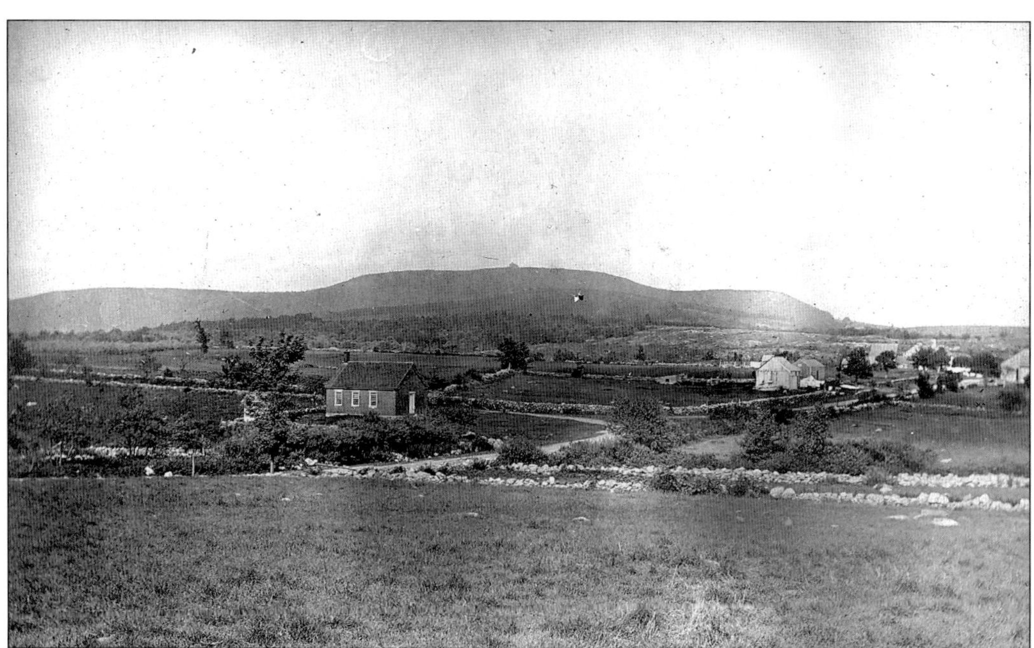

Schoolhouse No. 8, located at the corner of Thompson and Rhodes Roads, was built *c.* 1833. There were 10 school districts in Princeton from 1837 to 1840, and most of the one-room schoolhouses cost $100 each to build. This school was abandoned in 1921, when students attended the Center School, and it is now a private residence. (Courtesy of the Princeton Historical Society.)

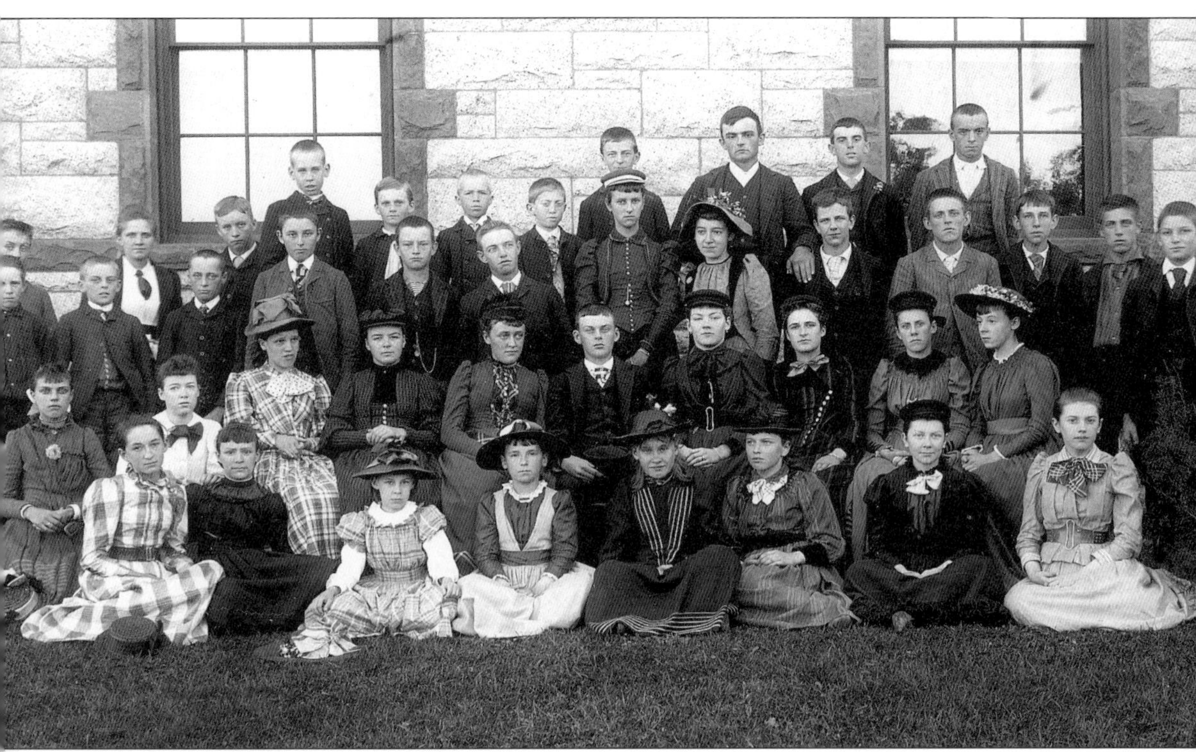

The school picture of September 1891 shows the children assembled beside the Goodnow Memorial Building. From left to right are the following: (first row) Alice Weaks, Bertha Roper, Gertrude West, Louise Gregory, Mable Elliot, Maude Dolittle, Lena Whitcomb, and Jennie Thompson; (second row) Amanda Stanton, Mamie Lanpher, Della Hubbard, Carrie Gregory, Alice Gill, Eddie Mason, Mary Keyes, Florence Joslin, Bertha Matthews, Grace West, and Charlie Putnam; (third row) Henry Skinner, Harry Mason, John Davis, Earnest Morgan, Harry Sweet, Carroll Barber, Harriet Beaman, Josie West, George Ross, Eugene Roper, Thomas Sprowl, and Willie White; (fourth row) Charlie Nelson, Alice Coffin (teacher), Harry Ball, George Richardson, Walter Mirick, Herbert Richardson, Roy Muzzy, Victor Muzzy, Edward Beaman, Charlie Thompson, and Earnest Young. (Courtesy of the Princeton Historical Society.)

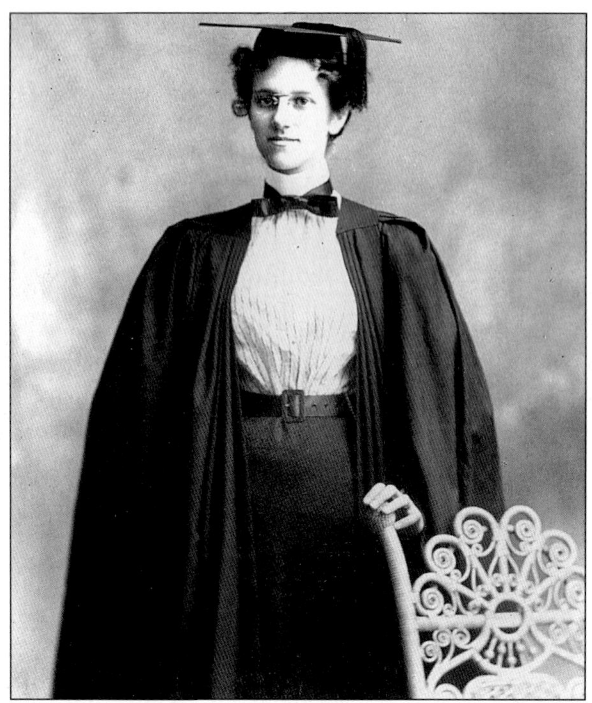

Harriet Beaman graduated from Mount Holyoke College in 1897. She is shown here in her mortarboard and gown upon graduation from college. After graduating, she taught in the Sterling and Princeton schools and later became the principal at the Princeton Center School. (Courtesy of Nancy Beaman Flanders.)

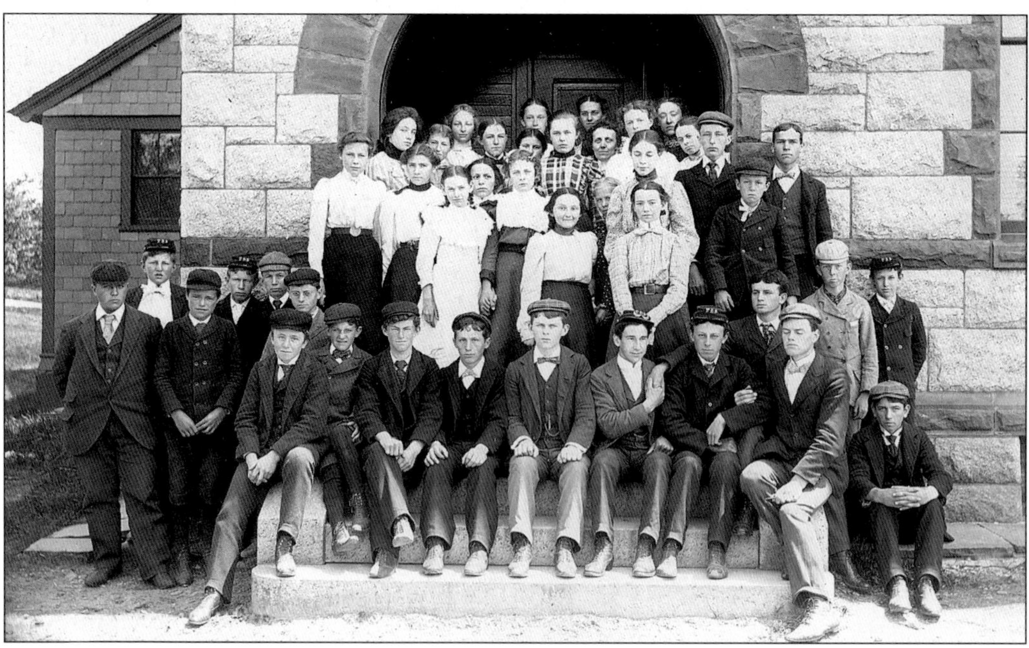

Students of the Princeton Upper School are assembled in 1899 at the rear entrance of the Goodnow Memorial Building. The teachers were Harriet Beaman (in the back) and Anna Mason. The first graduation from the three-year high school was in 1891. Until 1942, Princeton had only three years of high school, and to receive a diploma, the students were tuitioned to larger schools in the area for the fourth year. (Courtesy of Nancy Beaman Flanders.)

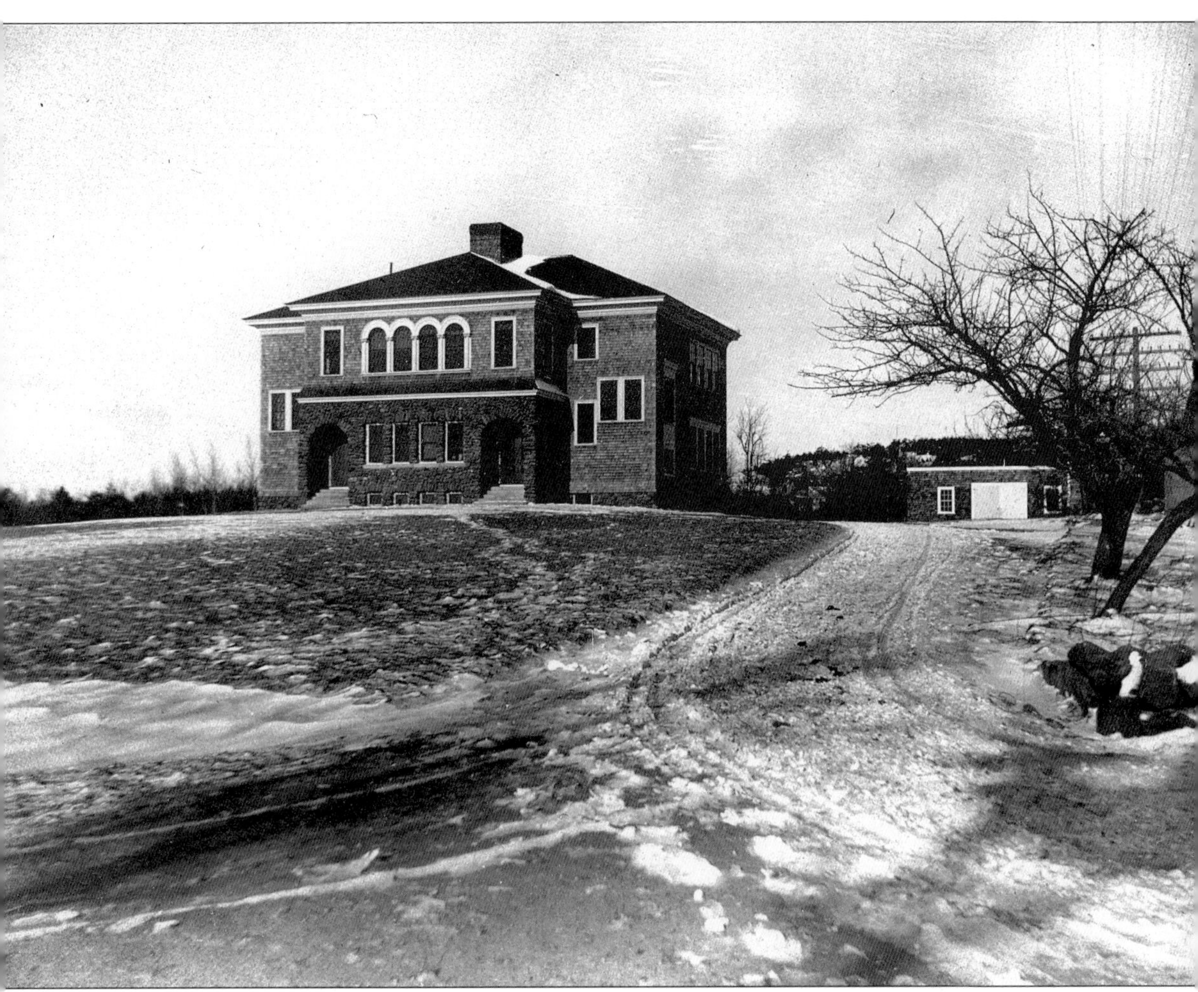

The new Princeton Center School was occupied in the fall of 1906, with two rooms upstairs for high school and another two rooms downstairs for the primary and intermediate grades. When completed, the wooden-shingle building cost $14,000. A horse barn was built behind the school, and by 1907, it was enlarged to encourage pupils who lived farther away to stay in school throughout the school year. Seventy-four pupils attended the first year at the Center School. In 1937, a gym and auditorium, three classrooms, and lockers were added. In 1937, the town purchased several acres of land behind the school for a playground. However, the hurricane of 1938 caused this Works Progress Administration project to stop midway. Additional land was donated and the playground and field were completed. Another addition (a science room) was completed in 1941. Princeton joined Wachusett Regional High School in the early 1950s, when a plan was adopted to combine five towns for a regionalized high school. (Courtesy of the Princeton Historical Society.)

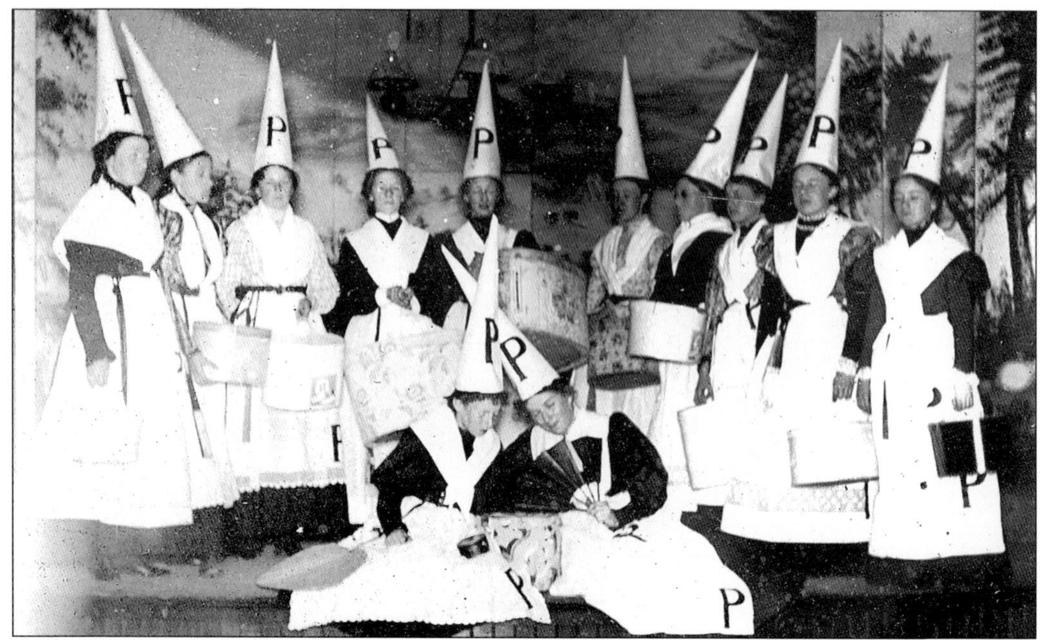

Written on the back of the original picture is "Peak Sisters," who are shown in June 1898 in the Bagg Hall auditorium. Shown, from left to right, are the following: (front row) Maude Alice Dolittle and Ethel Ruth Mirick; (back row) Florence Baker, Geneva Reed, Carrie Matthews, Edith Mirick, Bertha Goodrow, Luella Beaman, Gertrude West, Mabel Warren, Helen Eliza Goodnow, and Jennie Keyes. (Courtesy of the Princeton Historical Society.)

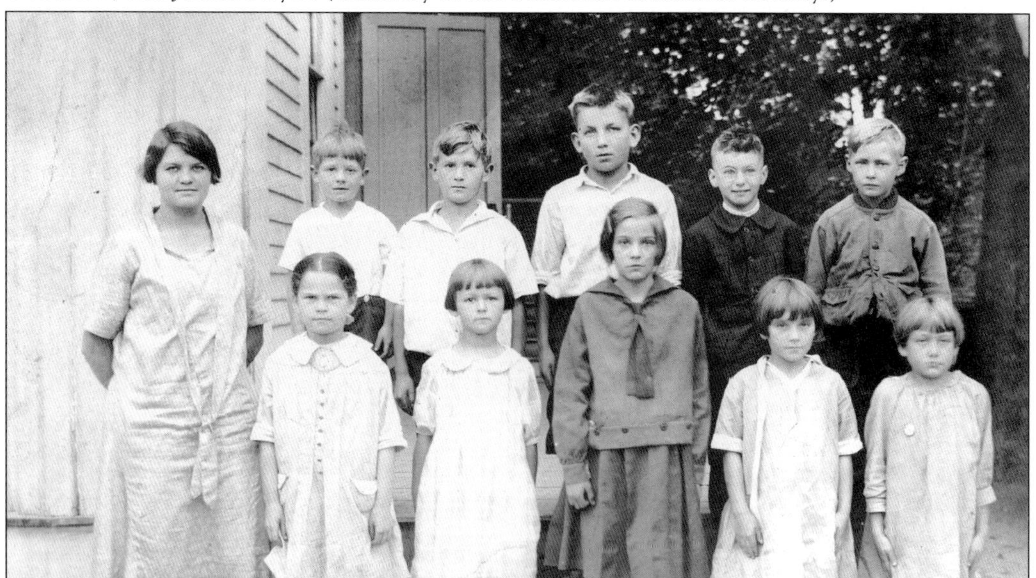

Ethel Swanson and her class are standing on the steps of Mechanics Hall in the 1930s for a school picture. East Princeton continued holding elementary school in Mechanics Hall and was the last district to close in 1945. From left to right are the following: (front row) Katherine Makosiez Kristoff, Clara Gleason Mosher, Bernice Hannah, Dorothy Slongwhite Martelli, and Dorothy Nelson; (back row) Stanley Slongwhite, Gordon Slongwhite, Towo Ahlfors, unidentified, and Louis Nelson. (Courtesy of Donald and Carolyn Slongwhite.)

Teachers Anna Mason (left) and Harriet Beaman are pictured in a classroom at the Goodnow Memorial Building in the early 1900s. (Courtesy of the Princeton Historical Society.)

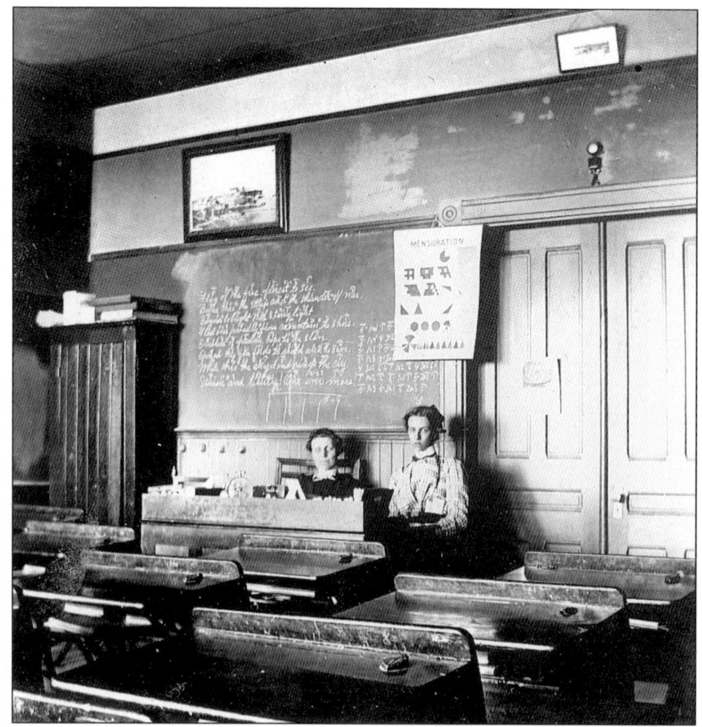

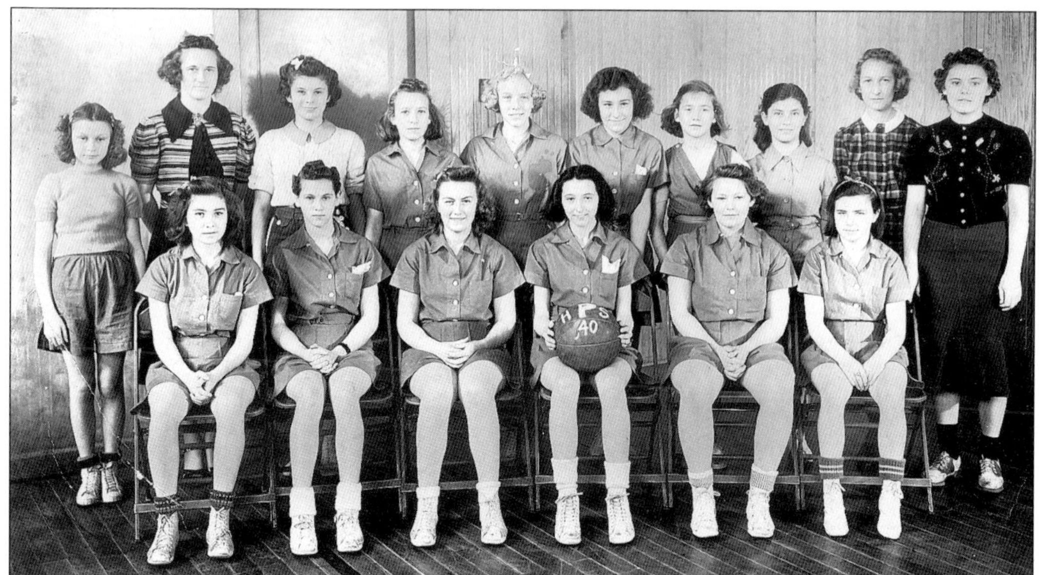

Members of the 1940 Princeton High School girls' basketball team are shown in the gym at the Princeton Center School. From left to right are the following: (front row) Frances Gauvreau Rice, Priscilla Drury, Catherine Whoriskey, Charlotte Drury, Marion Nelson, and Harriet Shepard Hubacz; (back row) Barbara Rice Cummings, Beulah Mitchell (teacher), Beverly Thompson, Phyllis Bourne Gill, Shirley Nelson Hubbard, Juliet Hamm, Irene Gauvreau, Charlotte Beardsley Gage, Jeanette Hobbs Sullivan (teacher), and Florence Thompson Ward. (Courtesy of Donald and Carolyn Slongwhite.)

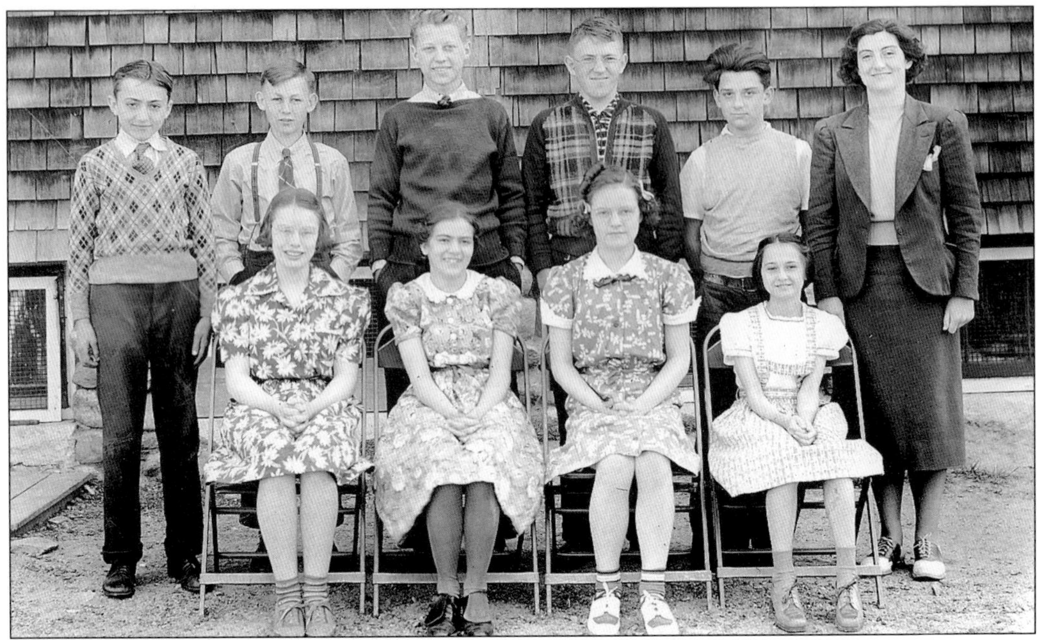

Students of the Princeton Center School pose in 1939 with their teacher, Helen Sanders Gendron. From left to right are the following: (front row) Carolyn Cooper Slongwhite, Myrtle Pouppeville, Vera Peoples, and Gladys Grosvenor; (back row) Chester Drury, Raymond Gleason, Louie Bonekevich, Scott Bryant, and Roger Gleason. (Courtesy of Donald and Carolyn Slongwhite.)

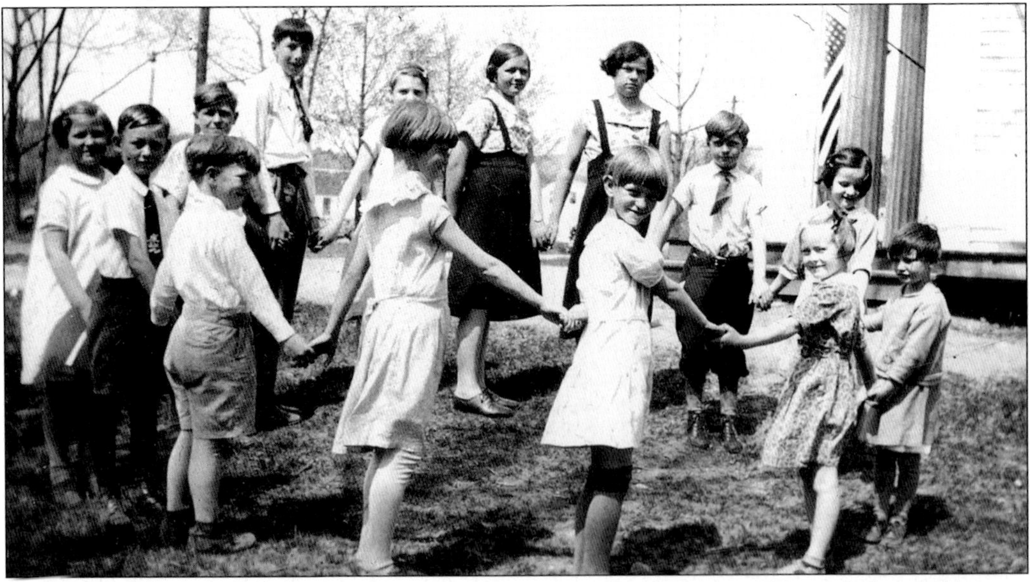

Ring-around-the-rosey has been played for generations. It is June 1933, and the children at Mechanics Hall are playing the game at recess time. Clockwise from the left are Raymond Gleason (in dark knickers), Marion Nelson, Stanley Slongwhite, Merrill Tucker, Elizabeth Peoples, Evelyn Gleason, Katherine Makosky, Donald Slongwhite, Vera Peoples, unidentified, Marilyn Towle, unidentified, unidentified, and Allen Slongwhite Jr. (Courtesy of Donald and Carolyn Slongwhite.)

Six
DAY TO DAY

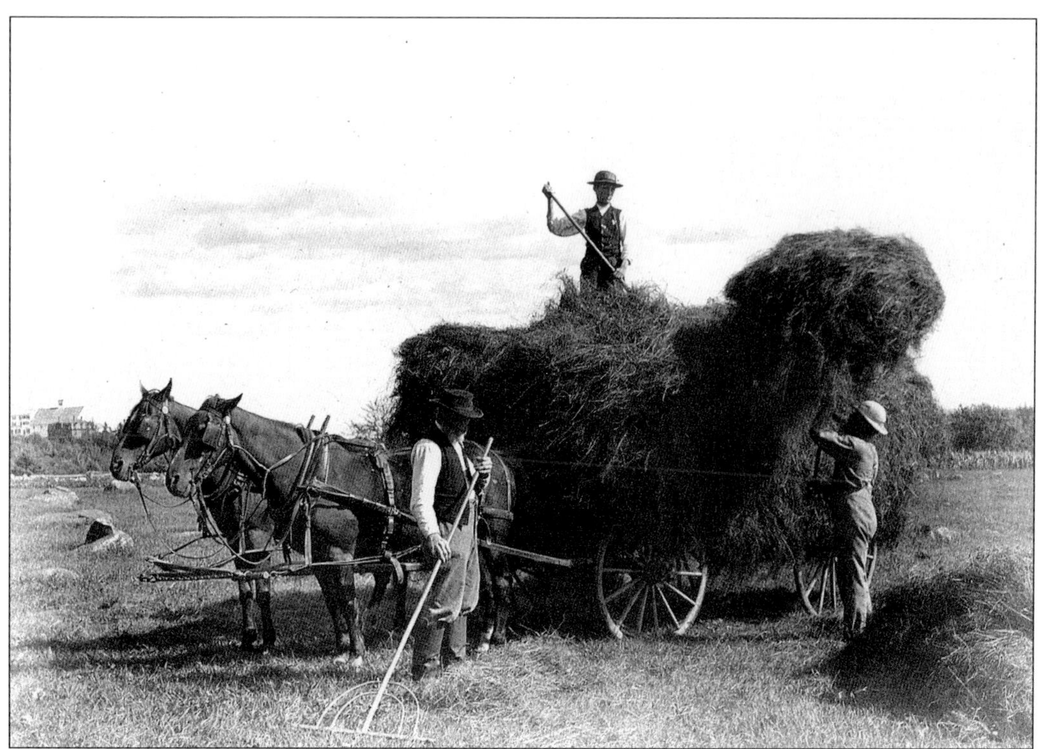

Sunny days spent haying in the fields was common in the summer for Princeton farmers. This photograph, taken before 1910, shows Wachusett House, the Wachusett House barn, and Wachusett Cottage (far left). The men in the photograph are haying in a field west of Boylston Avenue. (Courtesy of the Princeton Historical Society.)

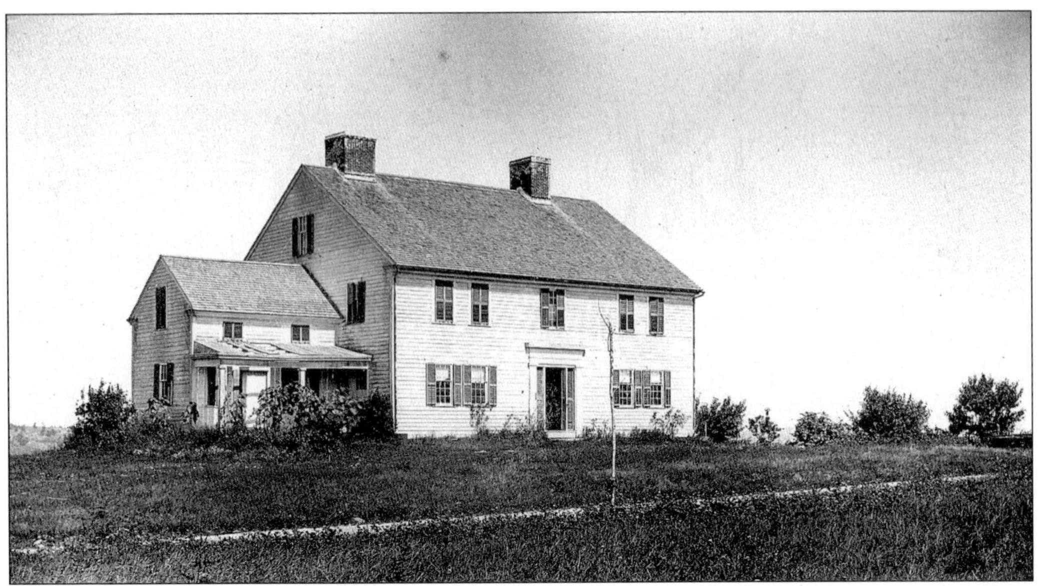

Lt. Abijah Moore came from Sudbury, built his house (now known as the yellow house at Russell Corner) in 1748, and was listed as an innkeeper by 1750. The first religious service was held here in October 1759, and the first district meeting followed on Christmas Eve 1759. Subsequent meetings were held here until 1762, when the first meetinghouse was built. This photograph, taken *c.* 1884–1891, shows the house before the ell was moved to the rear. A wraparound porch was added in the late 1800s. (Courtesy of Debbie and Charlie Cary.)

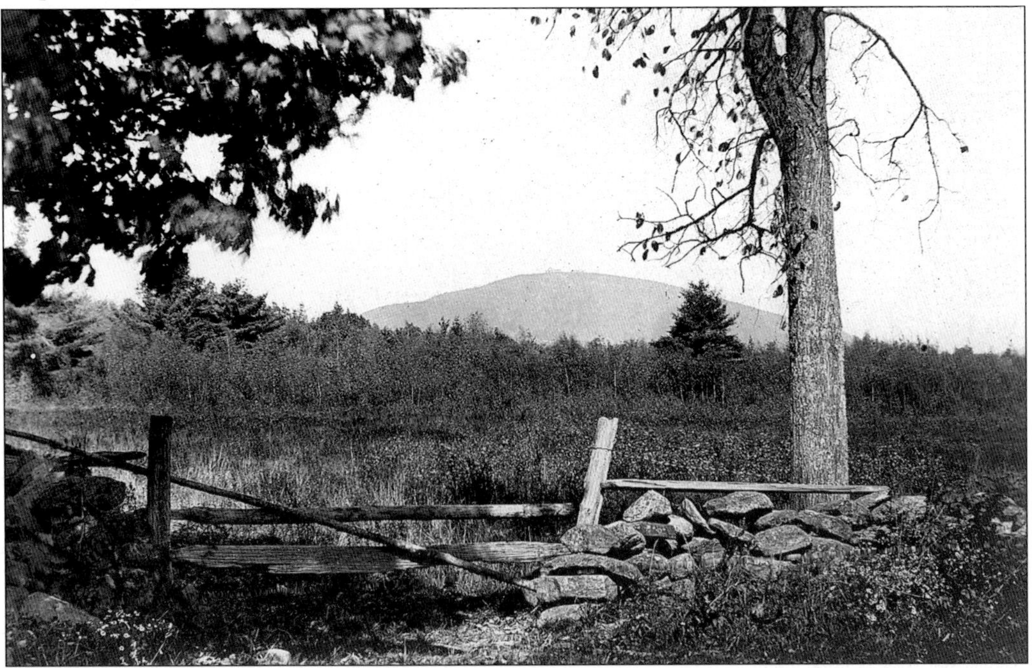

Amos Merriam's map, drawn in 1830, showed Gregory Hill Road as Goodnow Lane, which may have been named for Peter Goodnow, who built his house in 1771 in the area known later as Russell Corner. Russell Corner is one of many places in Princeton where a view of Wachusett Mountain can be enjoyed for its scenic beauty. (Courtesy of Bud Brooks.)

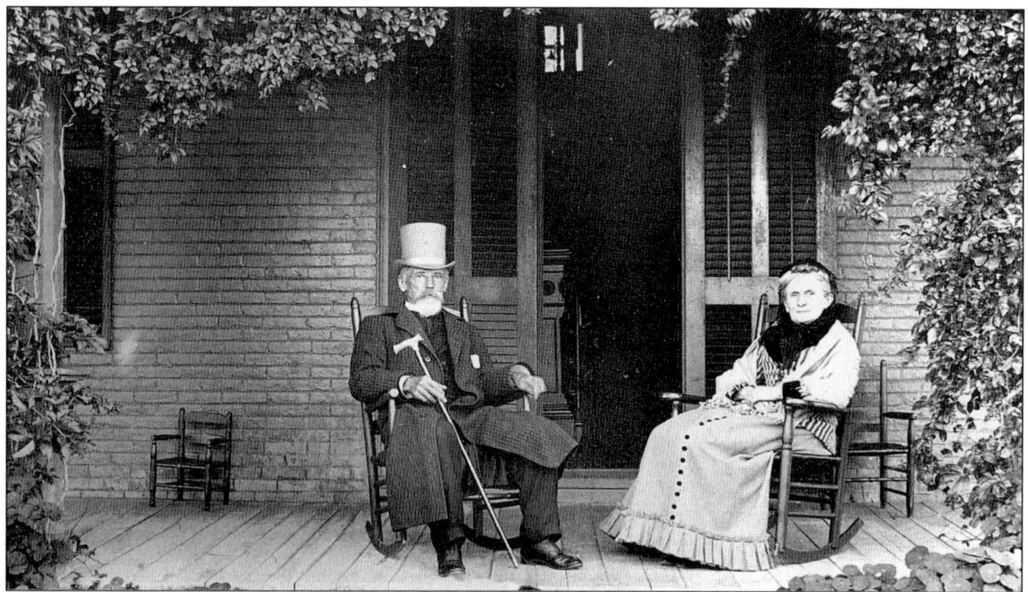

In the photograph above, taken before 1892, Thomas Hastings Russell and his wife, Maria Louisa Wiswell Russell, are sitting on the porch of the their home in their rocking chairs. The brick house, seen below, was built by Charles Russell in 1822 and housed a store and post office. Upstairs, a hall served for public gatherings. The Masonic lodge used the hall until 1826, and the Anti-Slavery Society met there from 1837 until 1843. Charles Russell was proprietor of the store and postmaster from 1817 to 1846. He instituted Princeton's first rural free delivery. Charles Russell, for whom Russell Corner was named, was a Princeton selectman, state representative, and state senator. He later served three years on the Governor's Council. The store closed in 1860, and Charles Russell retired from business and political life. In 1875, his son Thomas Russell, a Boston attorney, made renovations to the house, including a mansard roof, a wraparound porch, and a cupola. (Courtesy of Nancy Orlando.)

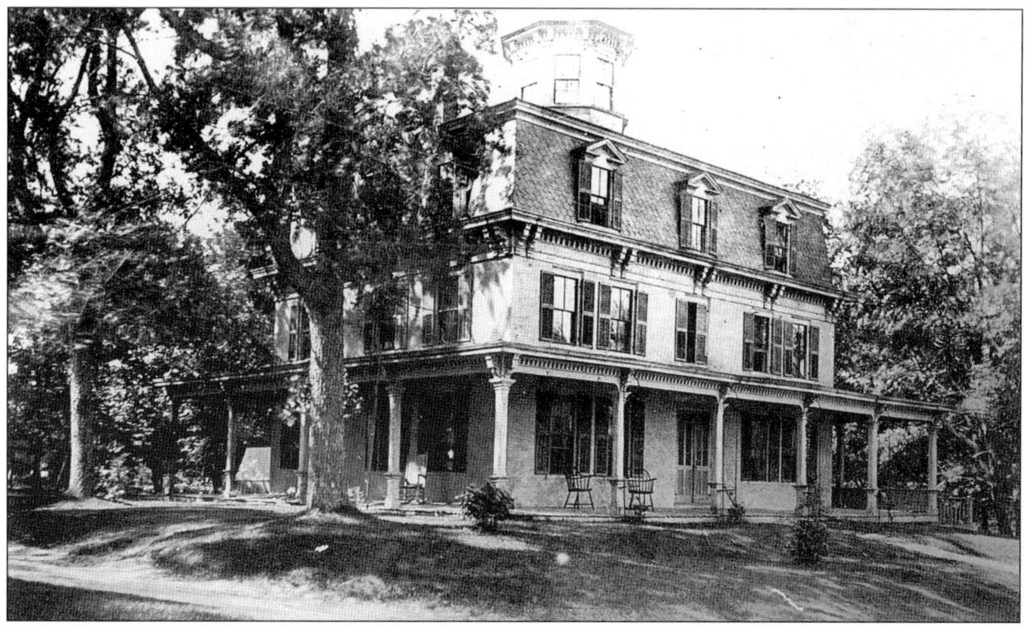

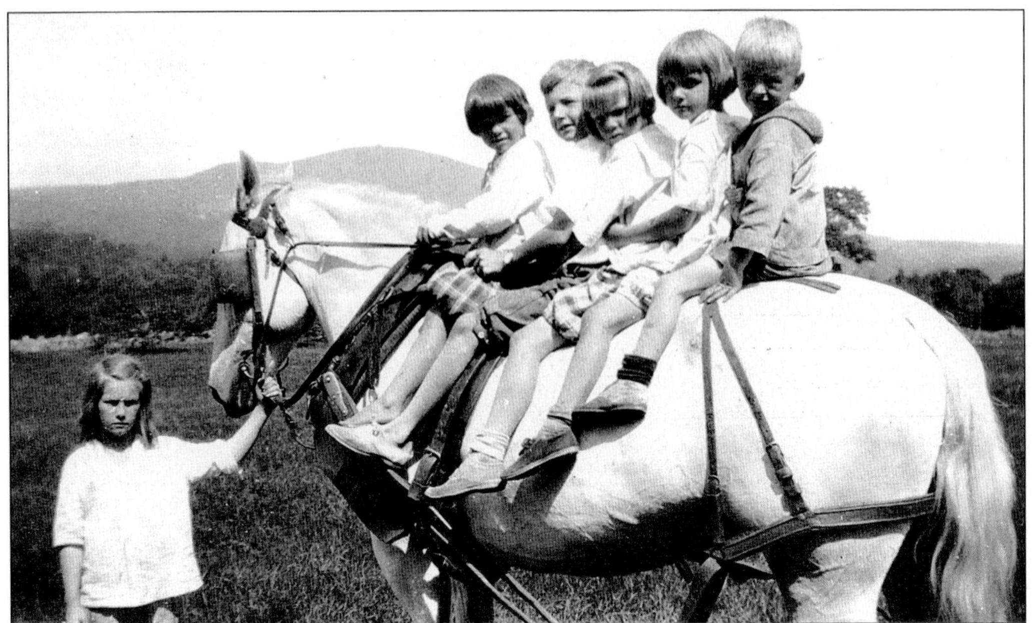

During summers, the children would gather with their parents at Russell Corner. Cousins would enjoy each other's company while swimming, playing in the fields, or fishing. Pictured *c.* 1922 on the horse Jim (owned by Frank Wiggins Sr.) are, from left to right, Elizabeth Densmore, Bancroft Littlefield, Anne Densmore Moore, Miriam Phillips Littlefield Brooks, and Rockwood Mason. Carol Densmore is holding the horse. (Courtesy of Debbie and Charlie Cary.)

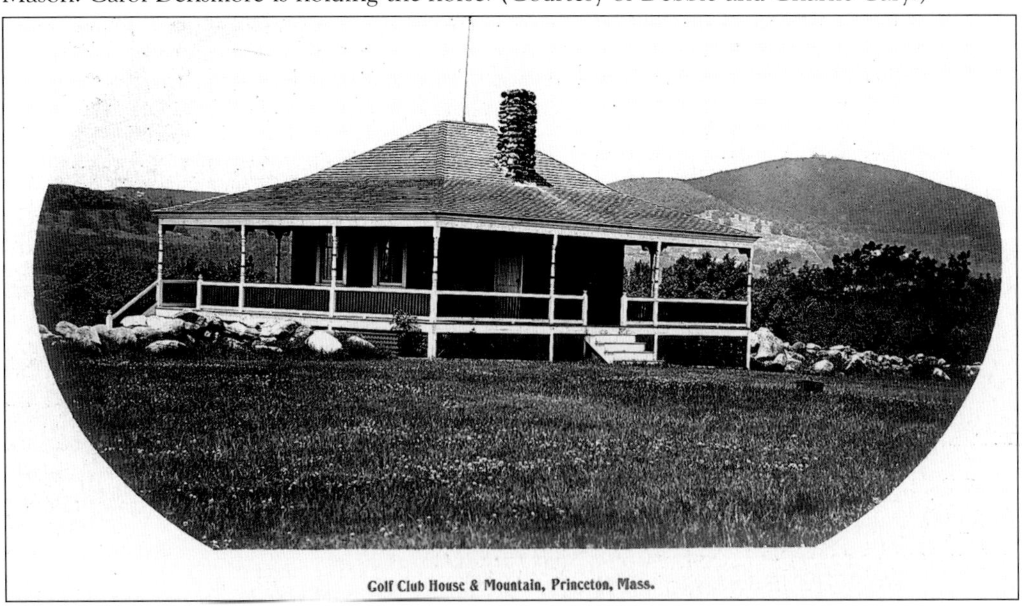

Golf Club House & Mountain, Princeton, Mass.

The Princeton Golf Club, at Russell Corner, was established in the late 1890s, when the game of golf was brought to Princeton. The Russells and Walleys offered the land, and a clubhouse was built at Russell Corner in 1902. Each Labor Day, a tournament was held on the rocky course laced by stone walls, with a silver trophy awarded to the winner. After 20 years, the Princeton Golf Club closed. With the advent of the automobile, people were able to travel to better golf courses. (Courtesy of Ed Carlson.)

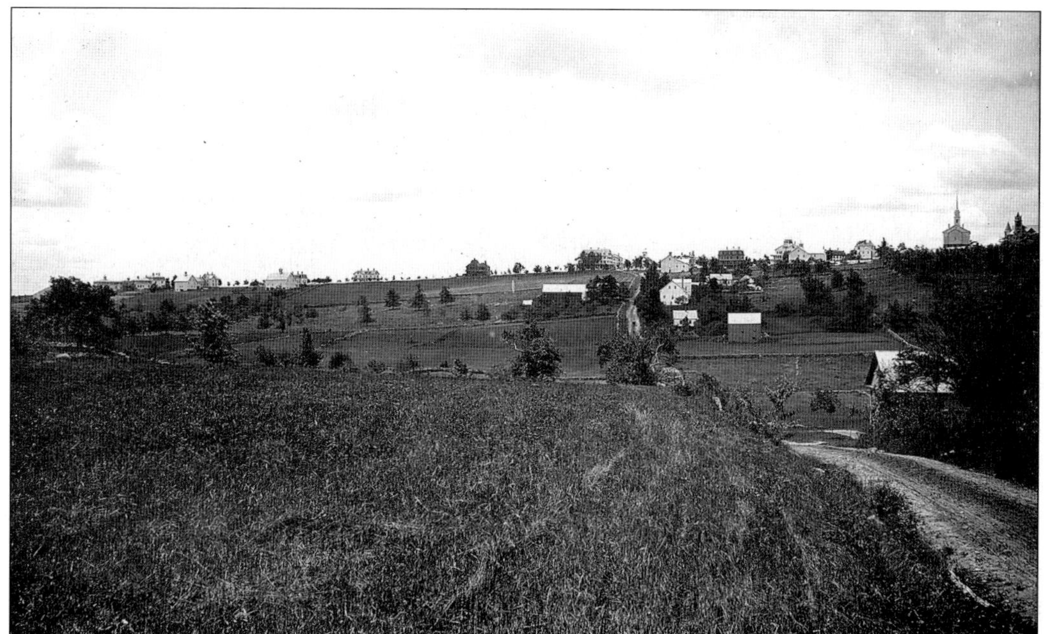

Princeton Center is seen from Russell Corner with Sterling Road at the lower right. On this hillside, in the foreground, is where the golf course was located. Schoolhouse No. 1, built in 1810, is beside the road (right) that leads up Gregory Hill Road to the center. On the horizon, to the right, is the Congregational church; to the left, Worcester Road is dotted with large farms and homes. (Courtesy of the Princeton Historical Society.)

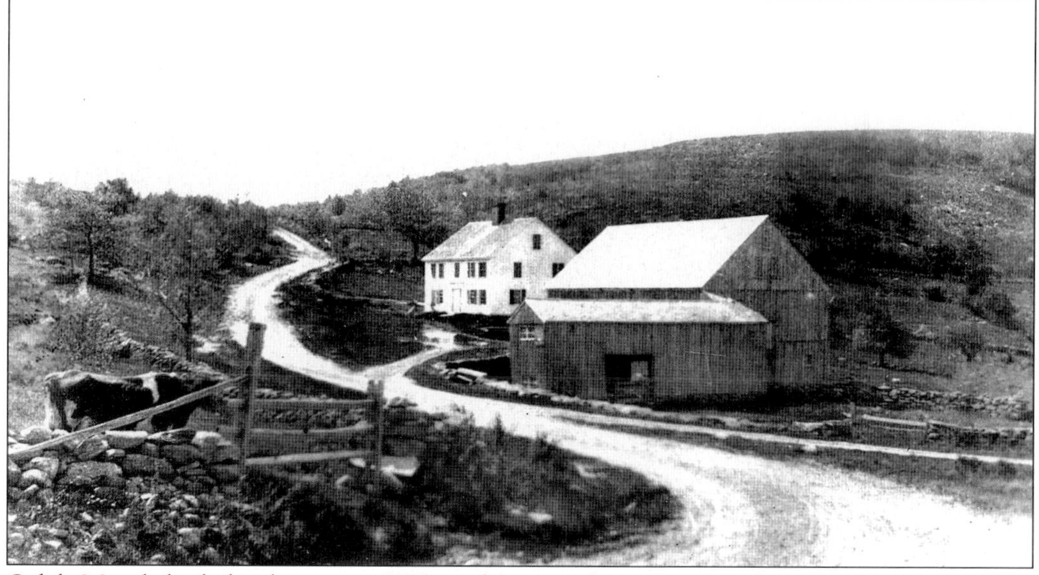

Caleb Mirick built his house in 1775, and it served as an inn and tavern for more than a century. Around the beginning of the 19th century, the Fay family purchased it. Anna Fay and her children published a newspaper called the *Laborer's Friend* and a monthly publication, *Our Commonwealth*. The Fays moved the house to higher ground in 1896 and placed the barn on the original house foundation. The house is now located at the corner of Merriam and Mountain Roads. (Courtesy of the Princeton Historical Society.)

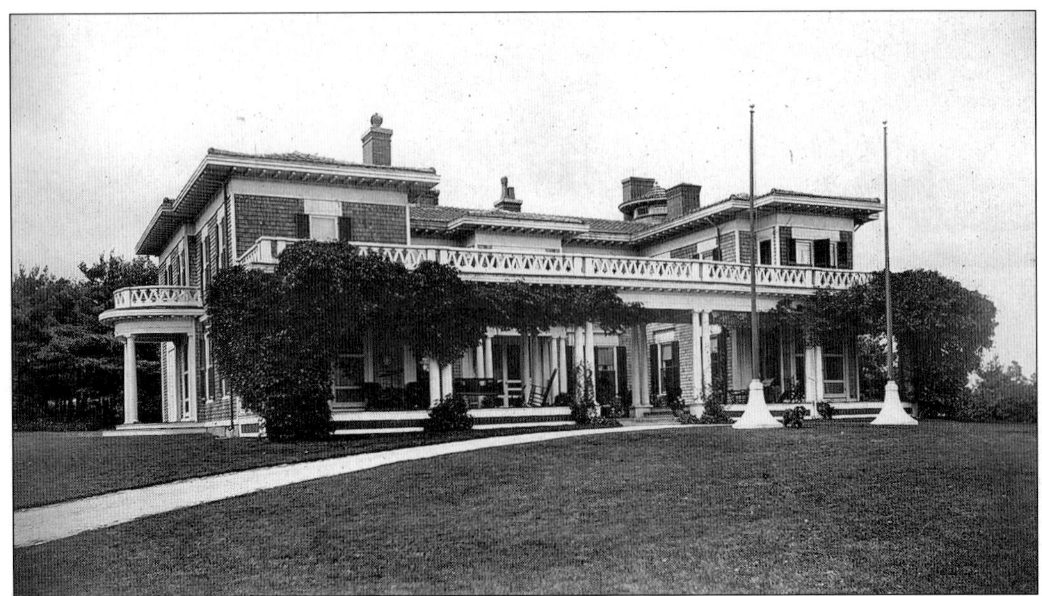

Thomas Allen Sr. built this house at the intersection of Mountain and Allen Hill Roads in 1894 after purchasing the Fay Farm and dividing the land. He operated the estate as a farm, keeping several cows, horses, other livestock, several hundred chickens, and bees. Allen also planted an orchard with apple, peach, and pear trees. (Courtesy of the Princeton Historical Society.)

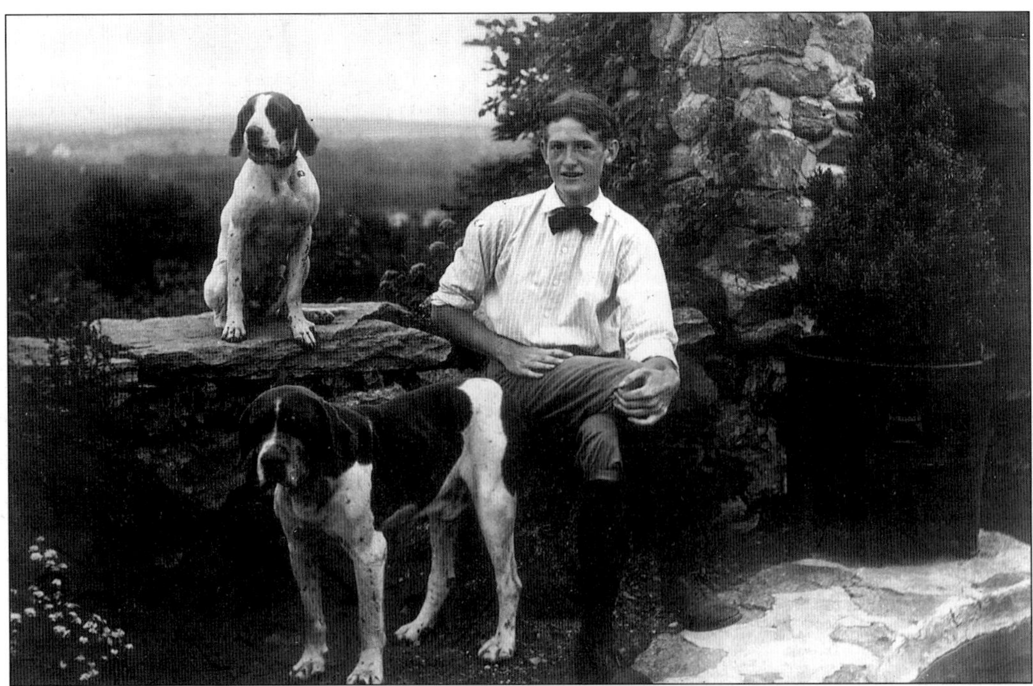

Thomas Allen Sr. is sitting on a stone wall at the Allen estate in 1905 with his two dogs. The estate, known as the Pines, was beautifully landscaped with stone walls, a pond, and private tennis court. During World War I, the Pines hosted the Princeton Dramatic Club, which raised money for the American Red Cross. (Courtesy of Fernside Inn.)

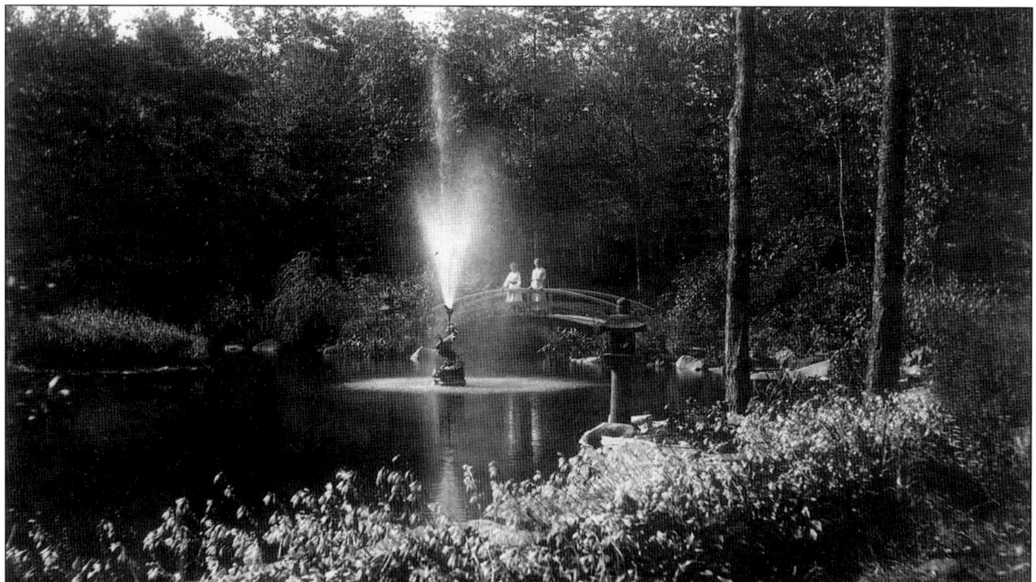

Fourth of July celebrations attended by 100 to 400 people were held at the Allen estate. The celebrations would include ice cream, which came in 25-pound slabs, and fireworks. When there were no fireworks, Japanese lanterns were hung on bamboo poles along the paths in the woods. Adding to the festivities, the Chaffins Band played as people enjoyed the celebration. (Courtesy of Fernside Inn.)

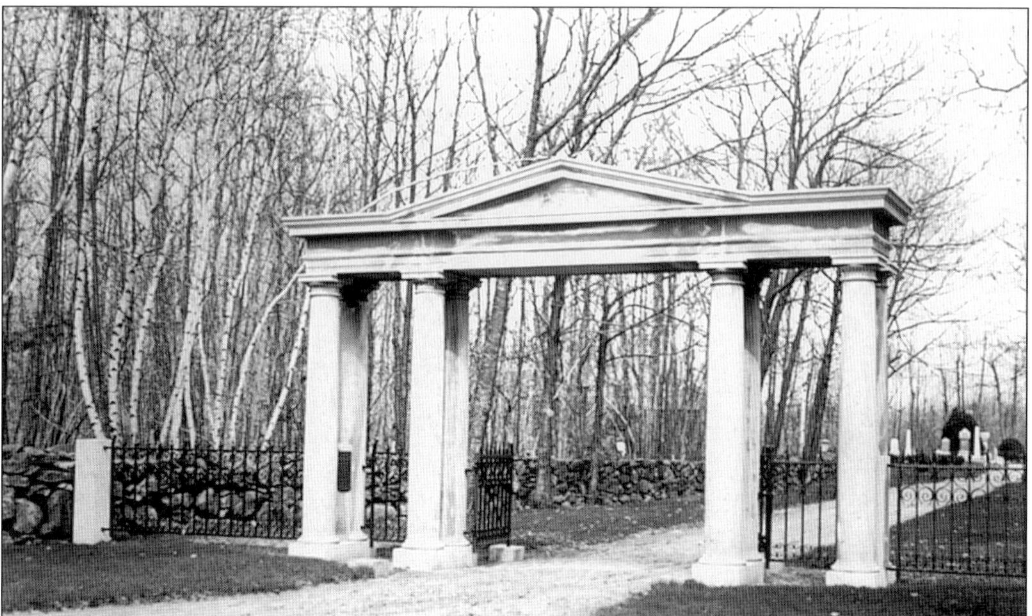

In 1852, the town purchased two acres of land for a cemetery and voted to name it Woodlawn Cemetery in 1904. The cemetery had an elaborate stone archway, designed in 1906 by Thomas Allen Sr. On October 4, 1935, Charles Gates left the cemetery after delivering a load of gravel and unknowingly left the dump bed raised. It caught on the arch and killed Gates. The Allen family replaced the arch with small pillars and an iron fence. (Courtesy of the Princeton Historical Society.)

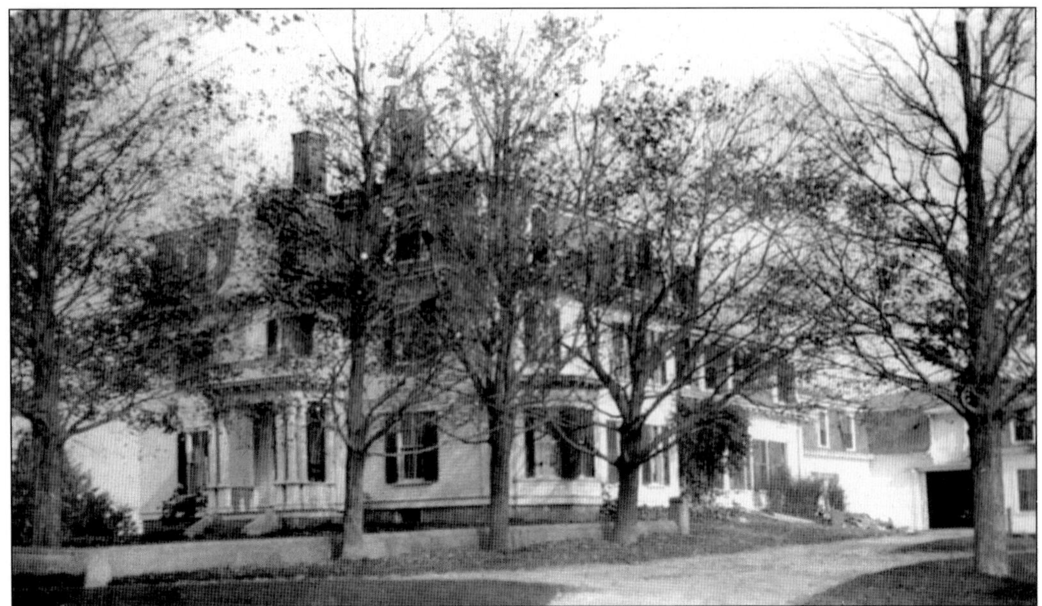

The property of John Brooks on Worcester Road was owned by three generations of the Brooks family. This large Second Empire house with attached buildings was built in 1873 on the site of a house that was destroyed by fire. Sarah Brooks Goddard, after her father's death in 1890, lived in the house until 1933. After her husband's death in 1936, the buildings were demolished and the land was sold. The carriage shed (now used as a private home), the doghouse, and a granite wall are all that remain on Worcester Road. (Courtesy of Marjorie Ollila.)

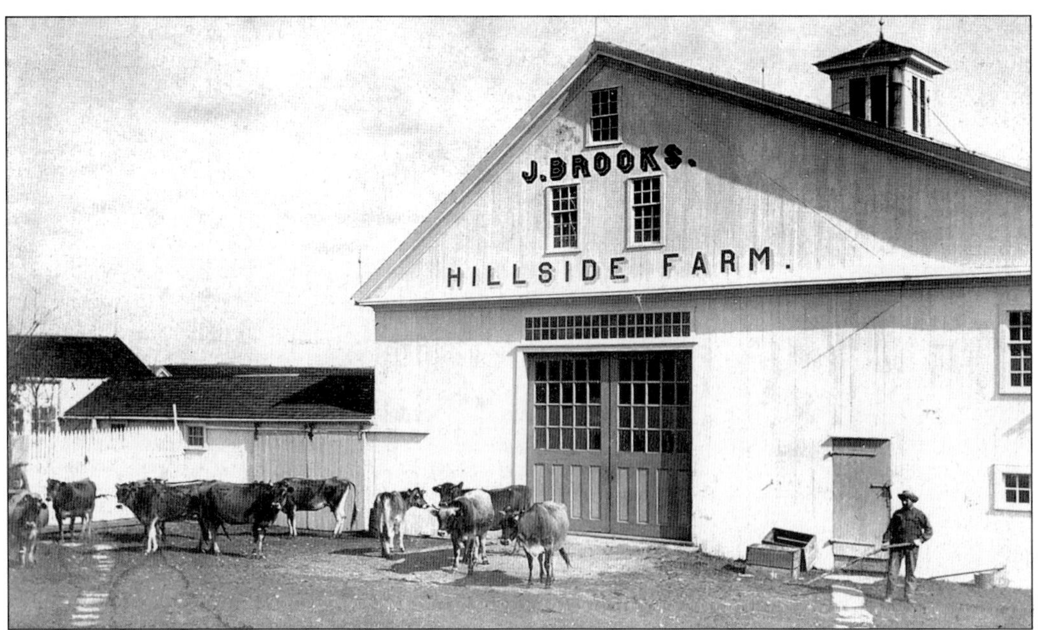

This early-1900s photograph of Hillside Farm shows the large barn associated with the farm. John Brooks belonged to the Worcester Agricultural Society, and his interest was raising and breeding Jersey cattle. The estate included 160 acres reaching from Princeton Center to the Sterling Road. (Courtesy of Nancy Beaman Flanders.)

A Second Empire doghouse on the Brooks property was home to Bob (a Boston terrier) and was built in the same Second Empire style as the house and attached buildings. When the house was razed in 1936, the doghouse was saved and taken to the Princeton Auto Museum and, later, to the Massachusetts Audubon Society. Funds were raised to restore it in 1959 as a project for the town bicentennial. The doghouse is shown after it was restored. (Courtesy of the Princeton Historical Commission.)

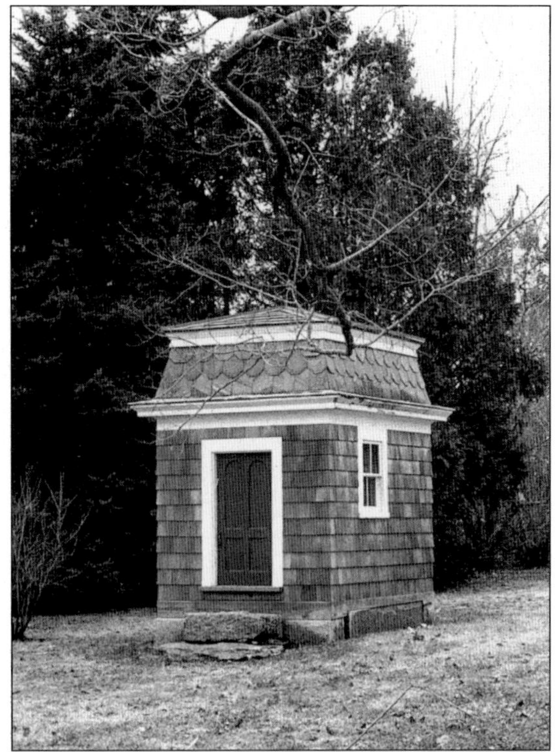

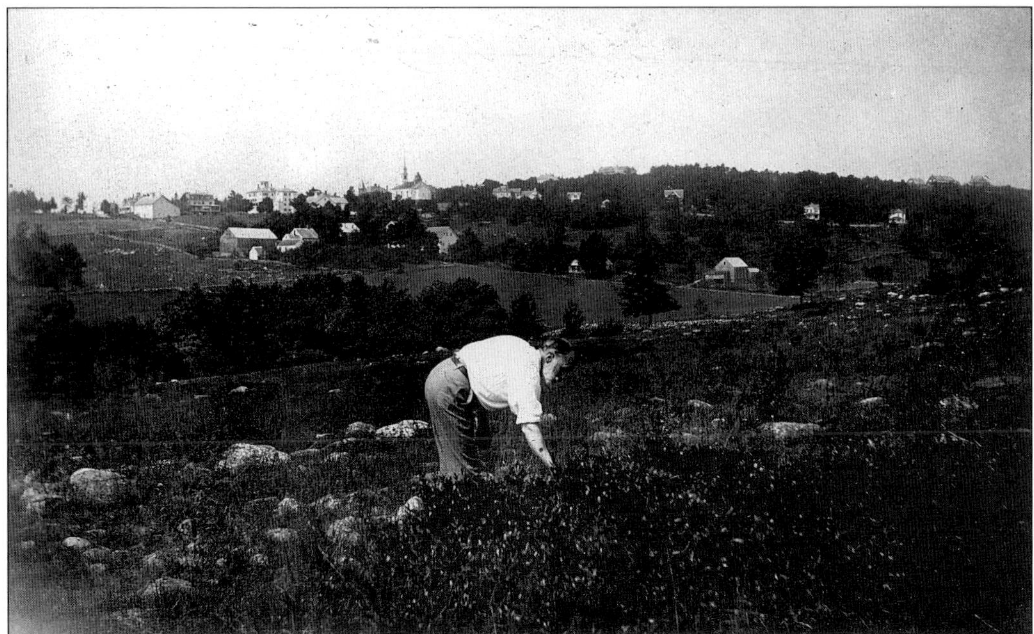

Princeton's blueberries on Wachusett Mountain and Little Wachusett were written about as early as 1793 by Peter Whitney, Worcester County historian. In this early-1900s photograph, a man picks blueberries in the Brooks pasture. As far away as the Parker House Hotel in Boston, Wachusett blueberries were advertised as a specialty on the menu. (Courtesy of the Princeton Historical Society.)

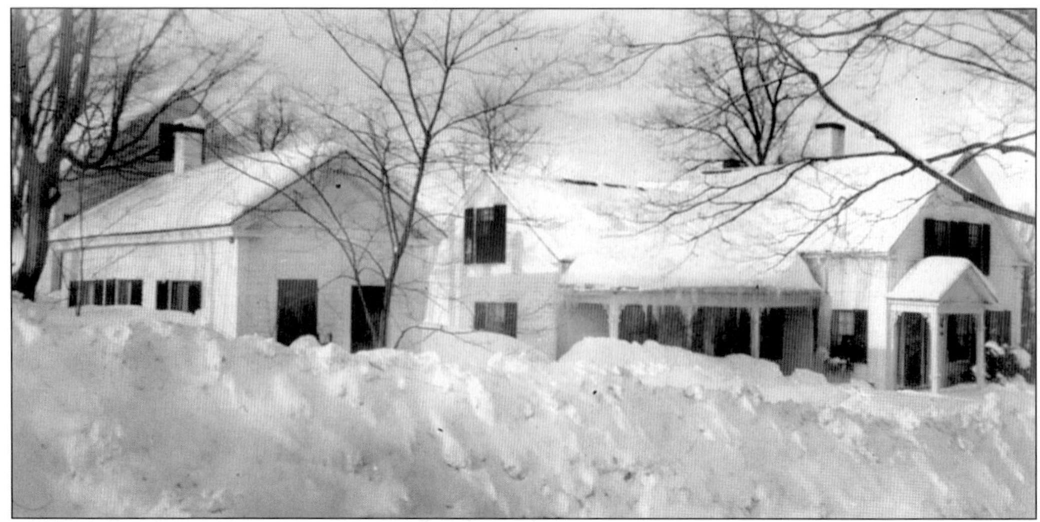

Dr. Oscar Howe, who died in 1911, was Princeton's dentist for 50 years. He lived in this house on Gregory Hill Road and used the small building on the left as an office to see patients. He was credited for being one of the first dentists living in a rural area to use anesthesia for extractions. Howe, a member of the Congregational church, received $50 a year to play the organ for church services. (Courtesy of the Princeton Historical Society.)

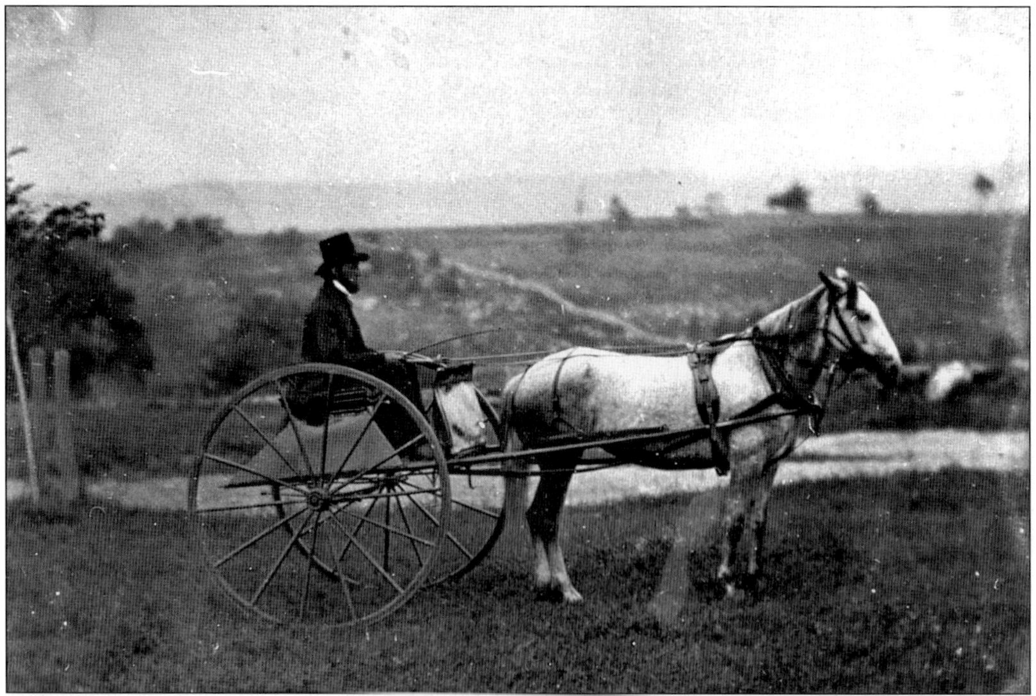

Dr. Joseph West graduated from Dartmouth in 1845 and lived in the Snuggery, on Hubbardston Road. He moved to Princeton in 1854 and became physician to the residents of the town and its many transient visitors until he died in 1887. He was once described this way: "His first thought on receiving a call was to help someone, his second, to learn something, and third to earn something." (Courtesy of the Princeton Historical Society.)

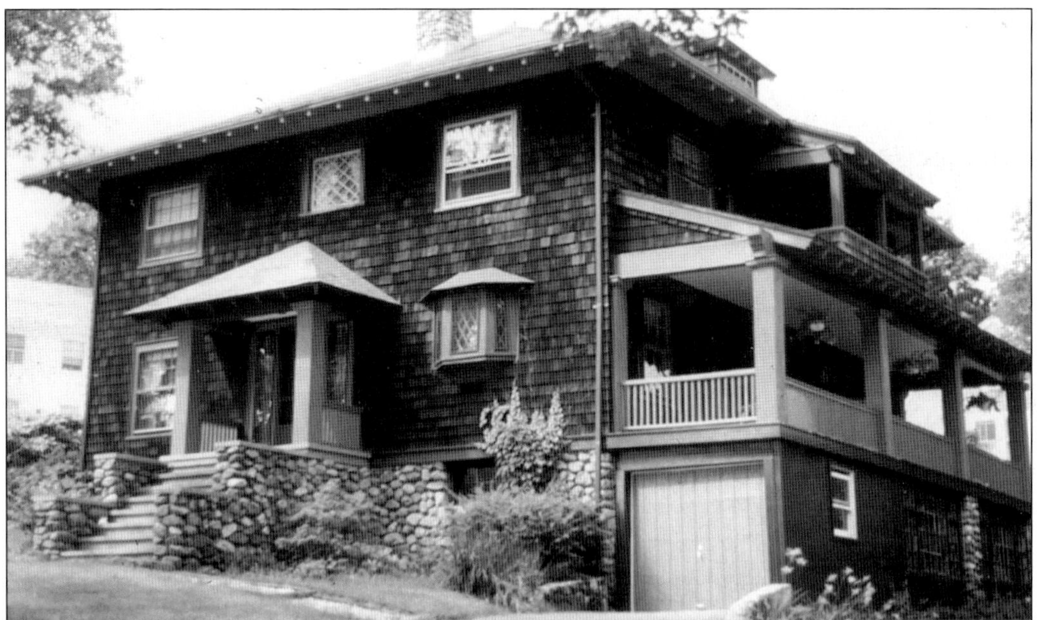

Dr. Elisha Sears Lewis built the Princeton Nauheim Institution, on Mountain Road, between 1914 and 1915. The photograph above shows his home, and below is the sanatorium (behind his home), where the patients stayed and were treated. The facility contained appliances using high-frequency electricity for the treatment of circulatory, respiratory, blood, and nervous system diseases. Lewis had enlisted in the U.S. Army by September 1918, when the Spanish flu pandemic arrived in Princeton. His wife, Catherine, who had learned from her husband how to care for the ill, helped the sick in Princeton. Young women came to the Lewis home to make gauze masks that were worn by those caring for the sick. When the pandemic was over, 69 cases were reported in Princeton and not one death. Dr. Lewis died in 1955. The flagpole on Princeton Common was dedicated to Lewis and his wife. (Courtesy of Hillary Hubbell Anderson.)

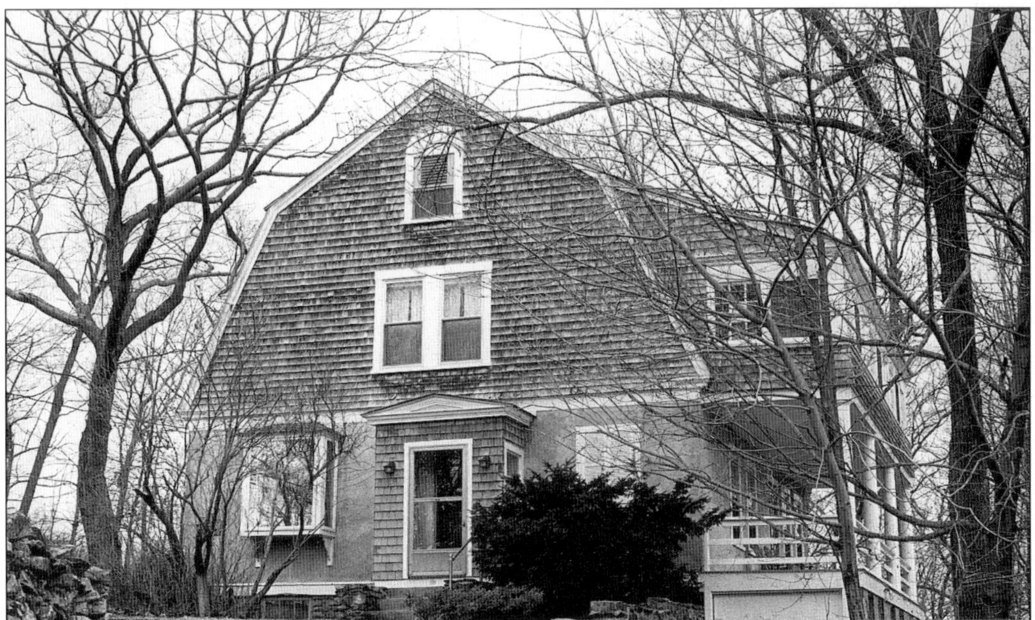

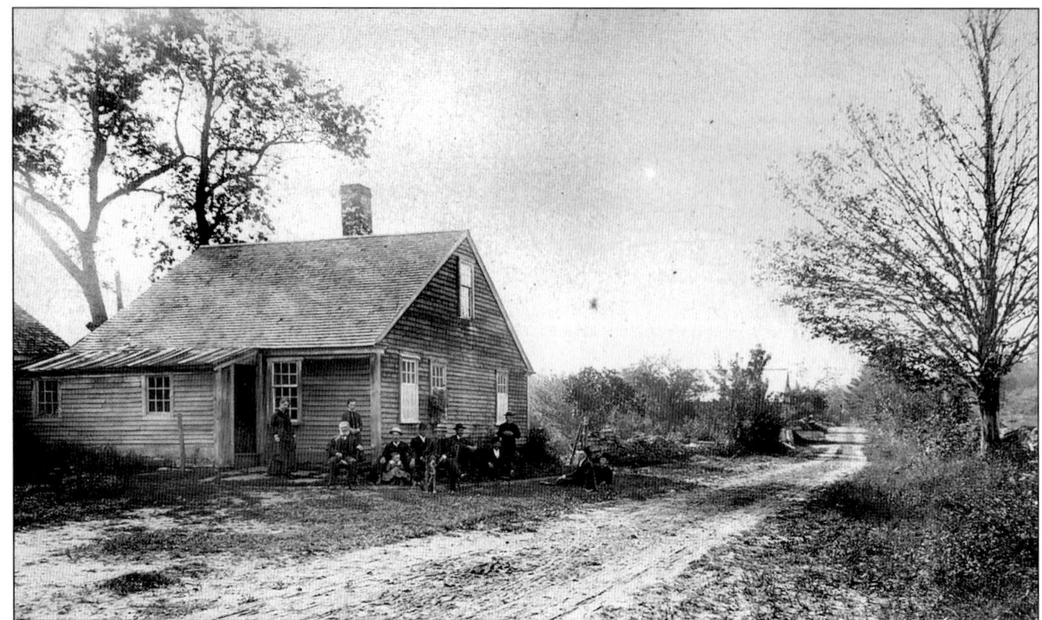

Members of the Abram Hubbard family are gathered beside their home on Ball Hill Road. Abram Hubbard was born in 1824 and had 10 children. The house is still standing and was home of Abram's grandchildren Louise and Kenneth Hubbard until their deaths in the early 1990s. (Courtesy of the Princeton Historical Society.)

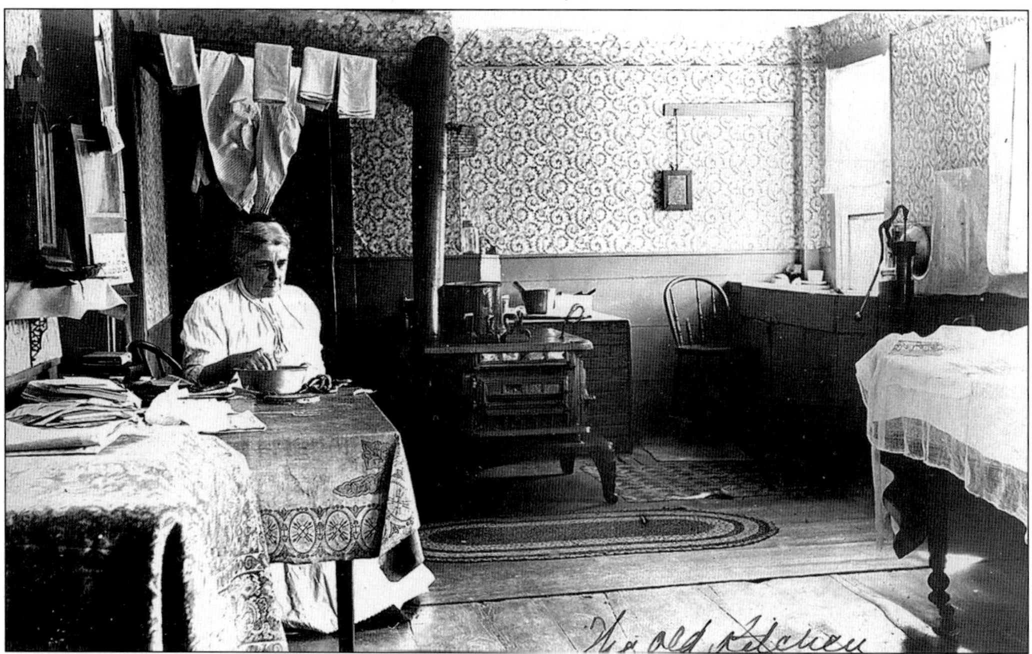

Titled "The Old Kitchen," this late-1800s photograph shows a copper water boiler, irons on the stove, and laundry hanging from the clothesline, suggesting that it might have been washday. After clearing the table, it was customary to leave the sugar bowl, salt and pepper, and other condiments covered with cheesecloth in anticipation of the next meal. (Courtesy of the Princeton Historical Society.)

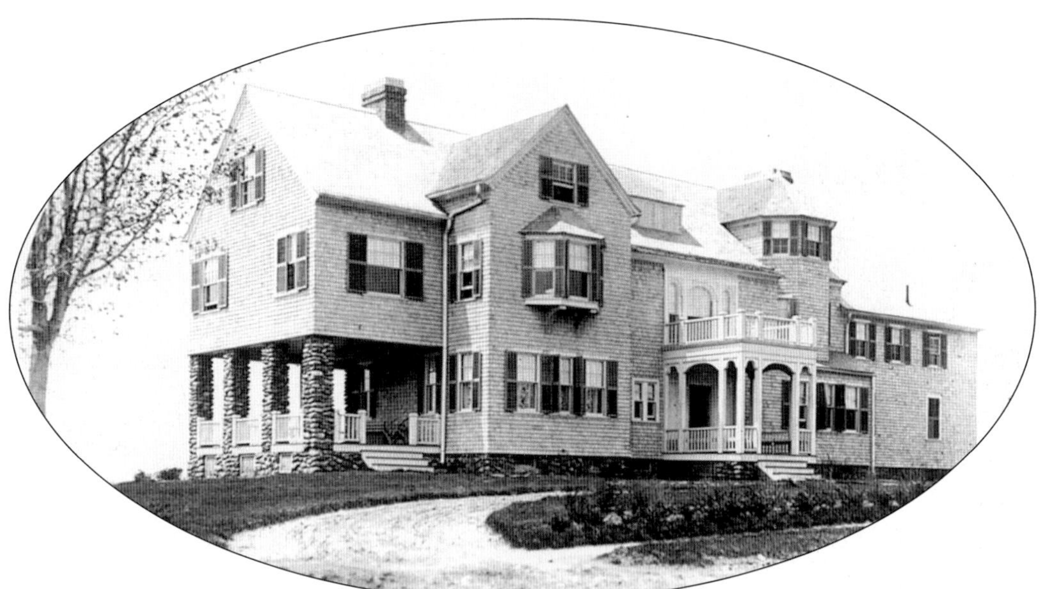

During World War I, the extensive third-floor game room of the summer home of Seth and Mary Nichols, on Worcester Road, was used as permanent headquarters of the American Red Cross. It was devoted to the preparation of supplies for French wounded soldiers. Dressings and bandages were cut, folded, and wrapped. Knitting and sewing were also done for the war effort in this room. In the view below, Mary Nichols is standing in the back. The others in the room include Sadie Goddard, Florence Bullock, Etta Bryant, Dorothy Allen, Libby Sanborn, Mrs. Kimball, Eileen Beaman, and Bessie Houghton. Seth Nichols, a wealthy resident of Boston and New York City, experimented in scientific farming at his summer home, where he owned a herd of registered Guernseys and later a chicken business. (Courtesy of the Princeton Historical Society.)

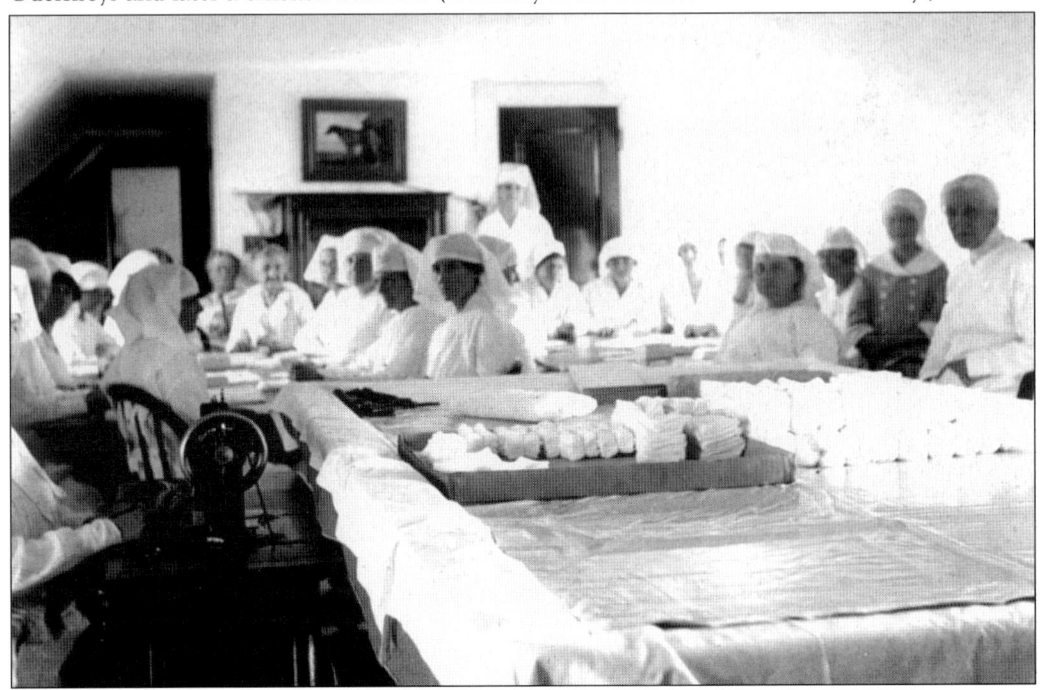

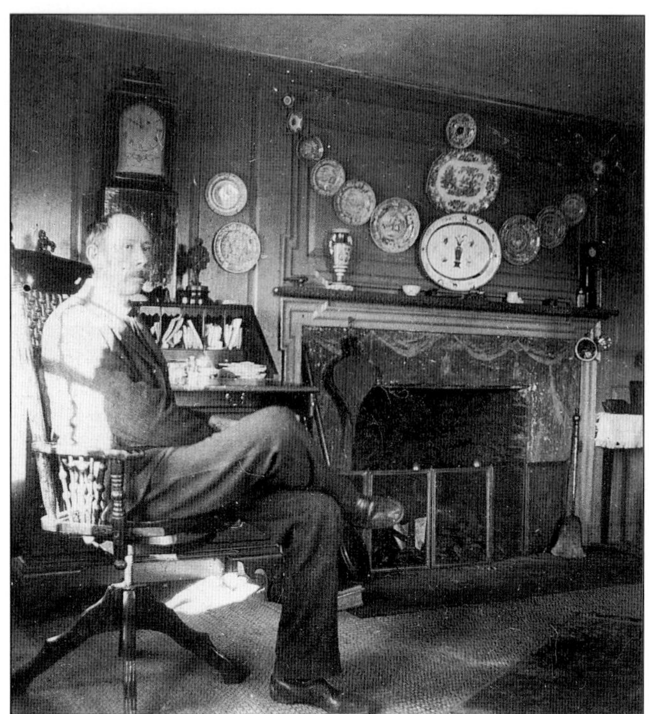

Pictured in 1897, Gamaliel Beaman, a Princeton artist born in 1852, came from a poor family. His second wife, Eileen Sherman of North Adams, saw his talent and promoted his work. In later years, his eyesight began to fail, but he continued to support himself and his family with art sales until his death in 1937. He supplemented his art sales by selling antiques in Princeton and earned the nickname "Antique Beaman." One of his paintings hangs in the Goodnow Memorial Library. (Courtesy of the Westminster Historical Society.)

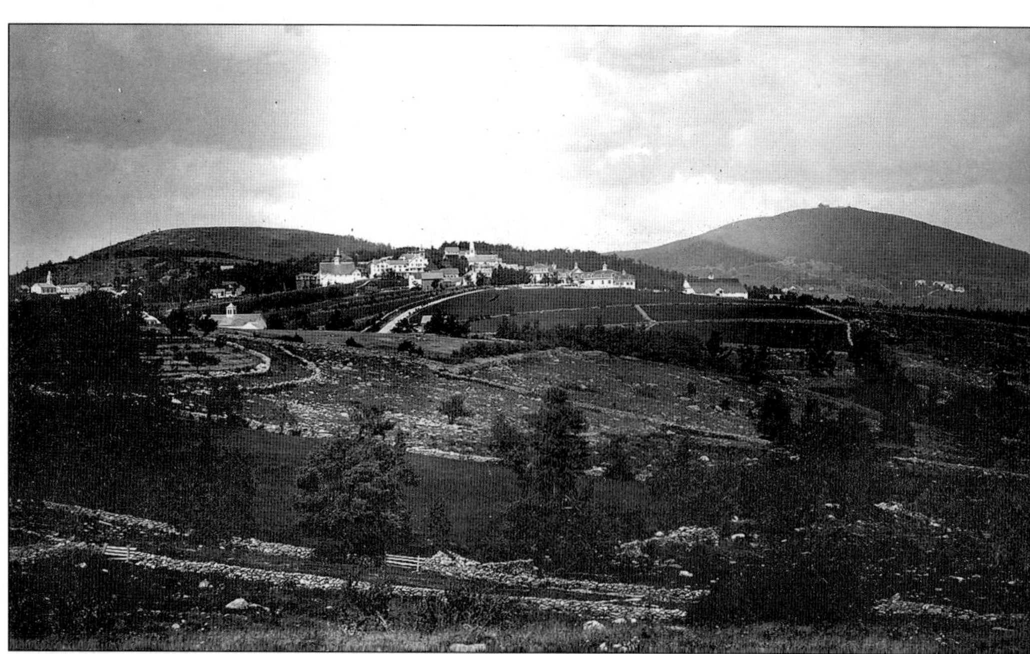

In an 1876 article for *Scribner's*, Helen Hunt Jackson named Princeton "Hide-and-Seek Town." She wrote, "It dodged in and out of view even though it was miles away. One minute it stood out on its hill, and later it was gone." This photograph from the early 1900s shows the countryside that perhaps Helen Hunt Jackson saw as she traveled around Princeton. (Courtesy of the Princeton Historical Society.)

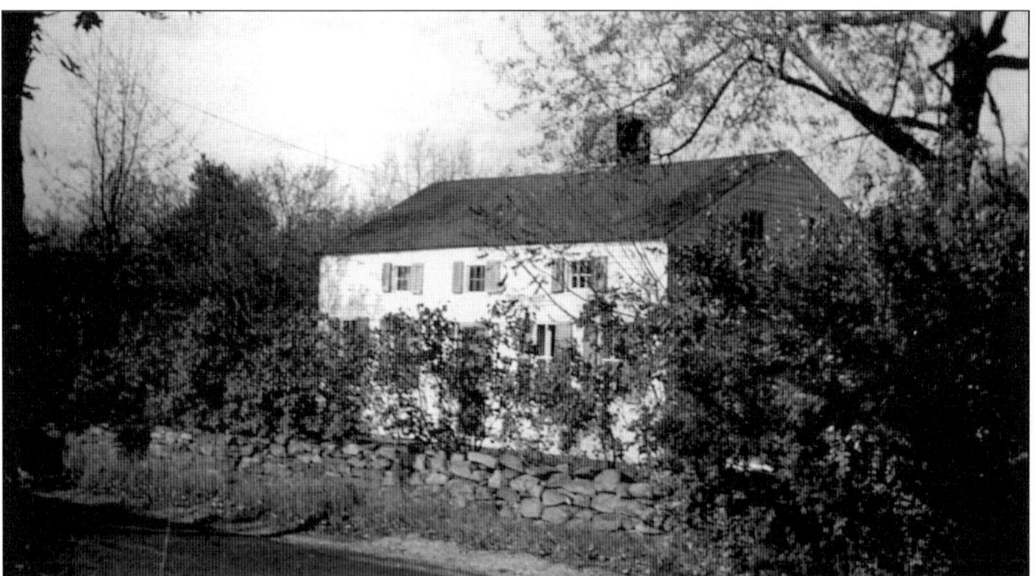

Amos and Betsey Ball and their 10 children lived in this house on Ball Hill Road from 1835 to 1867. One of the additions he made to the house created a hidden room upstairs. Amos and his family, who were abolitionists, found it the perfect place to hide slaves bound for Canada. He and his sons brought slaves to the house and hid them in the secret room, where the fugitives stayed until the next stop on the Underground Railroad. Esther Forbes, Pulitzer Prize winner in 1943, purchased the home in 1921 and lived in it until the 1960s. (Courtesy of the Princeton Historical Society.)

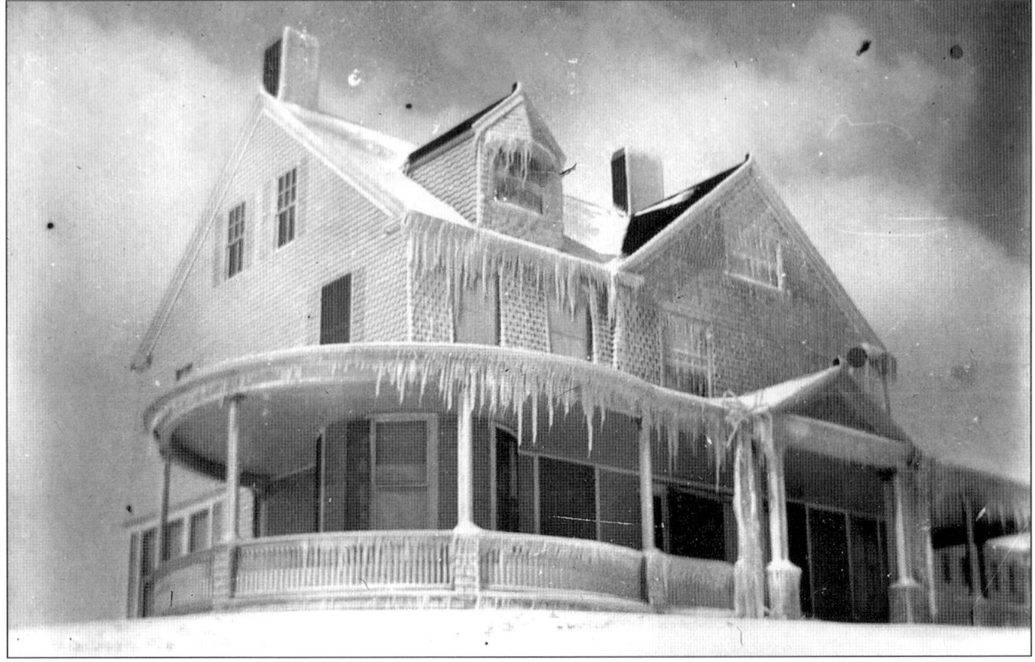

The home of Harry C. Beaman, owner of Wachusett House, was located on Worcester Road behind Wachusett House. It was built in 1890 for Beaman and his wife, Jennie Bartlett Beaman, and was demolished in 1959. (Courtesy of the Princeton Historical Society.)

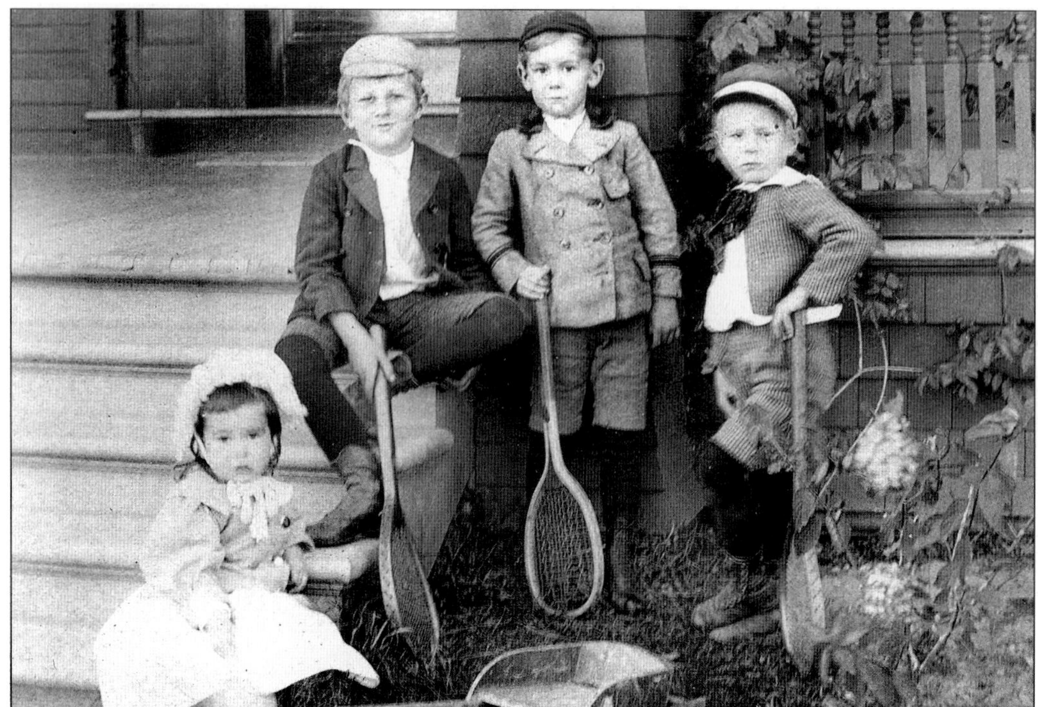

William Langley, a wealthy manufacturer from New York City, is said to have brought the first tennis set to Princeton. It was of English design, with rackets curved on one side and with multicolored strings with tassels. Employees of Wachusett House were always delighted to see him, because he would reward them with gold pieces. The Beaman boys are shown with their tennis rackets in 1894. They are, from left to right, Bartlett, Alden, Clayton, and Ralph. (Courtesy of Nancy Beaman Flanders.)

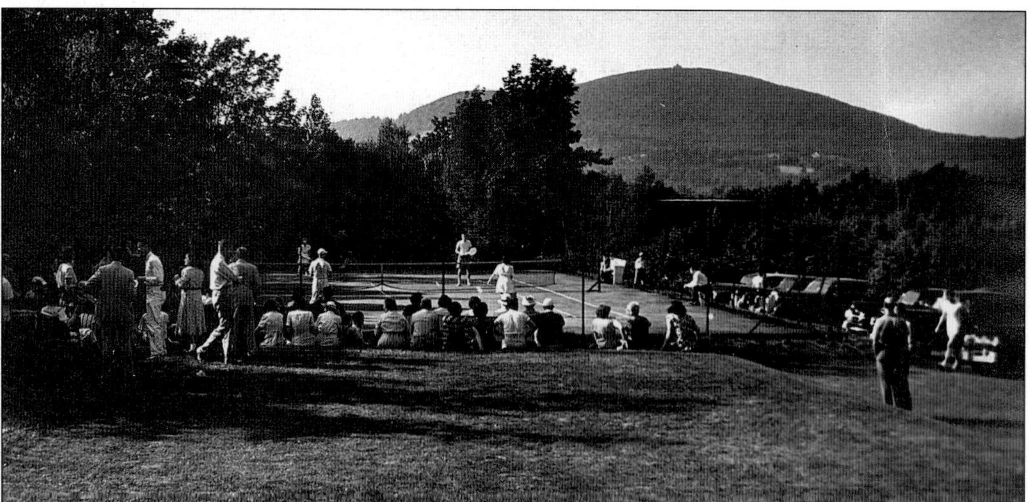

Chandler Bullock purchased a summer home at the end of Bullock Lane and built a tennis court where the Labor Day tournaments were held. This 1948 photograph shows Babbie Bullock Chute and Joe Byram, the winners of the tournament, on the tennis court with their opponents. Wachusett Mountain, with its third Summit House, and Little Wachusett are seen in the distance. (Courtesy of Judith Chandler Chute.)

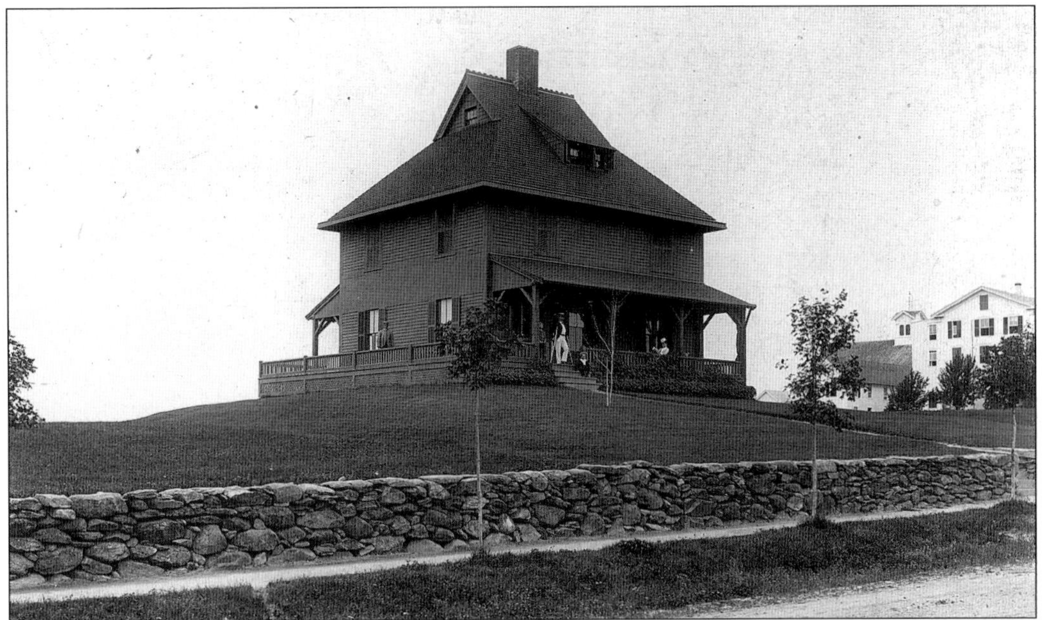

The Augustus Bullock house, built in the 1880s on Worcester Road, was one of the first large summer homes built in Princeton. When each of Augustus and Mary Bullock's three sons was born, an addition was built on the house. Located south of Wachusett House, the house was razed in the 1930s. (Courtesy of Judith Chandler Chute.)

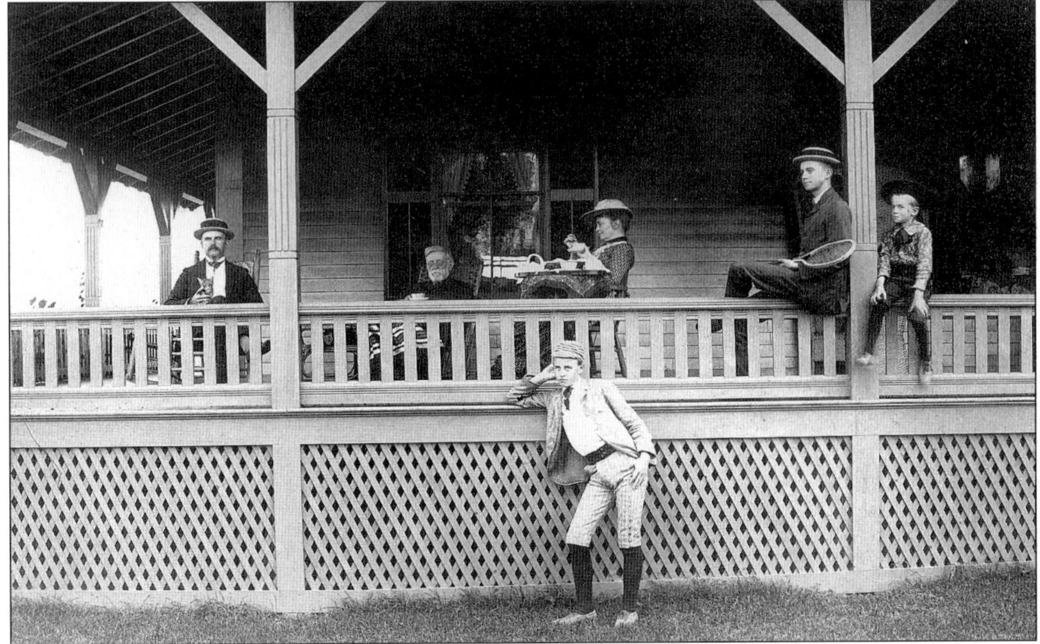

The Bullock family is gathered for tea on the porch of their home sometime in the late 19th century. Seated on the porch are, from left to right, Augustus G. Bullock (holding a cat), an unidentified man, and Mary Chandler Bullock, wife of Augustus. The young boy holding the tennis racket is Chandler Bullock, and the other two boys are his brothers, Alexander and Rockwood. (Courtesy of Judith Chandler Chute.)

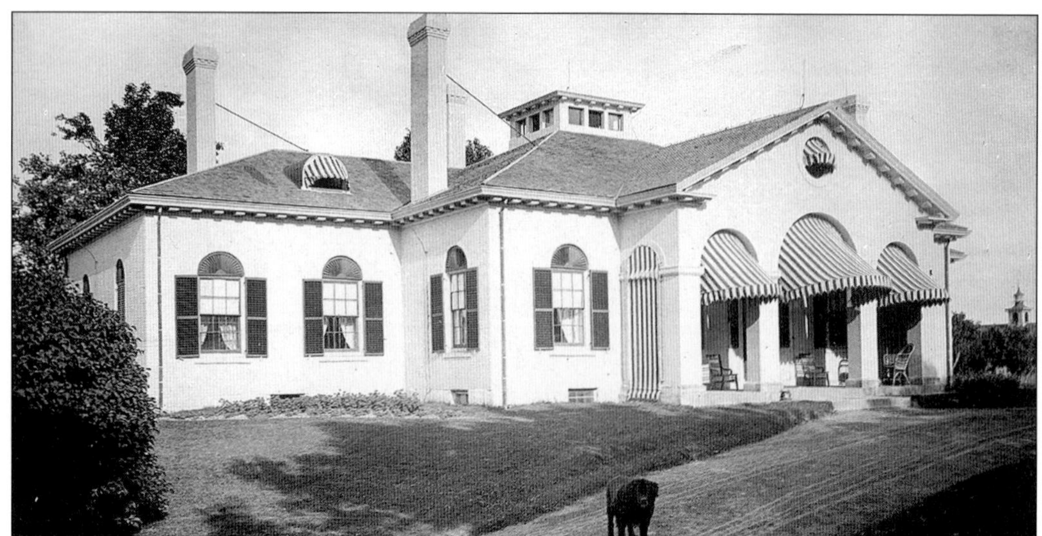

Ward Nicholas Boylston built the Boylston Villa as a summer home in 1819 on the former Governor Gill estate. Asher Benjamin, the author of *The Practical House Carpenter* (1789) and an architect in Charles Bulfinch's firm, oversaw construction of the house. When Boylston's daughters married in 1853, changes to the house were made, including the addition of the west portico with Palladian arches, a round gable window, barrel dormers, and a monitor on the roof. (Courtesy of the Princeton Historical Society.)

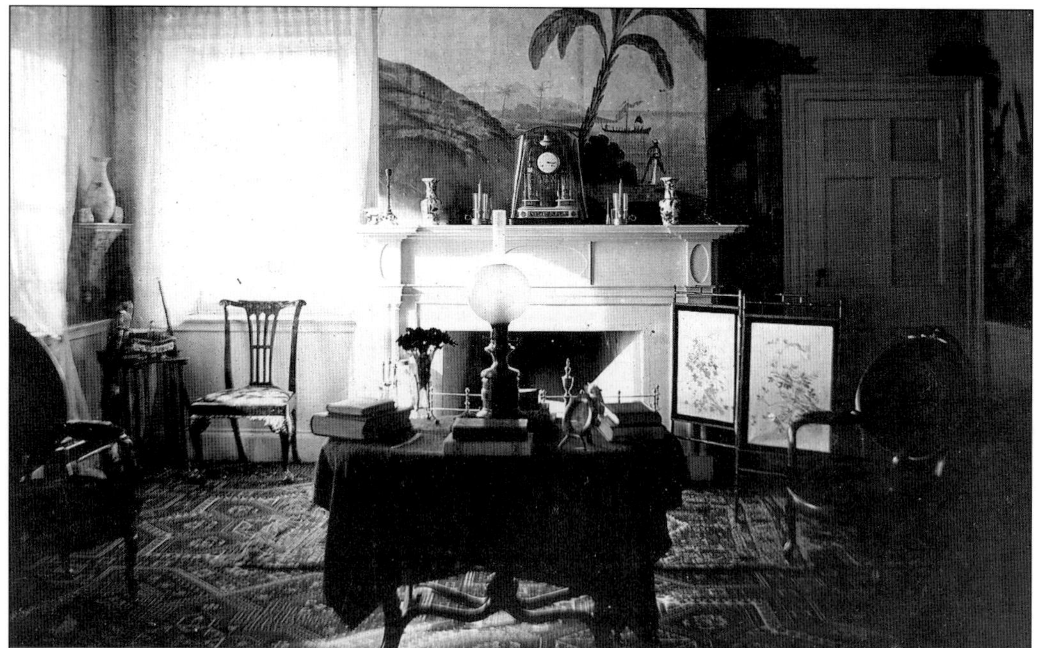

The wallpaper in the common rooms of the house was made by hand from hand-engraved wood blocks. This 1892 photograph of the front parlor shows wallpaper that was produced in France, by Dufour. With its colors of blue and green, it was named Paysage Indien, reminiscent of Hindustan scenery. It is rumored that John Quincy Adams, sixth president of the United States, brought the wallpaper from France for the Boylston family. (Courtesy of the Princeton Historical Society.)

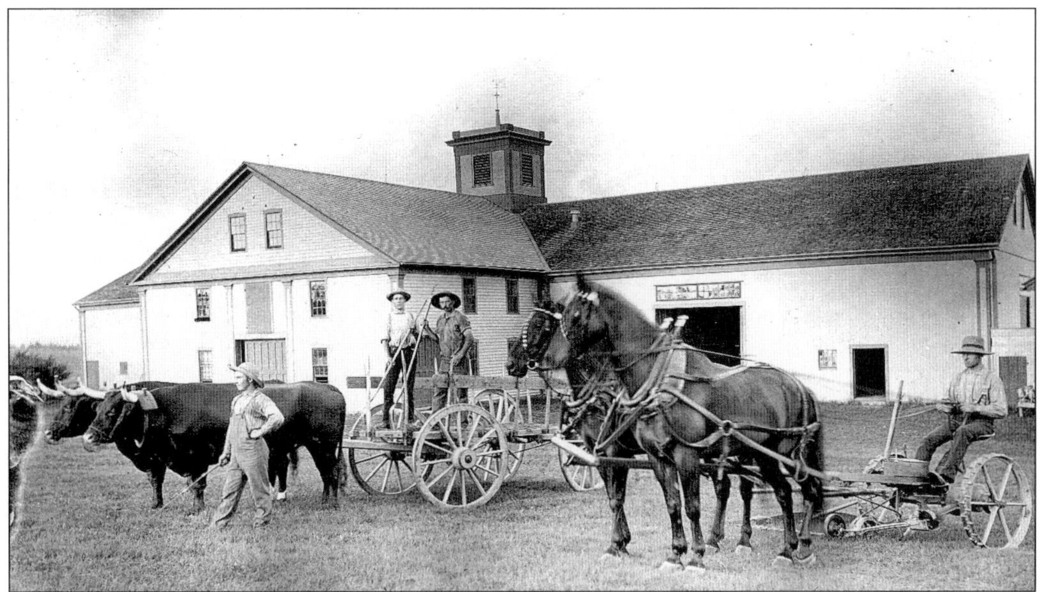

Now known as Boylston Villa, the Boylston home was given various names over the years. It was known as Homeward Bound in the 1920s and was later named Boylston Villa. Four generations of Boylstons lived in their country estate until it was sold in 1918. This early-1900s photograph of farm hands shows one of the large barns associated with the Boylston farm. (Courtesy of the Princeton Historical Society.)

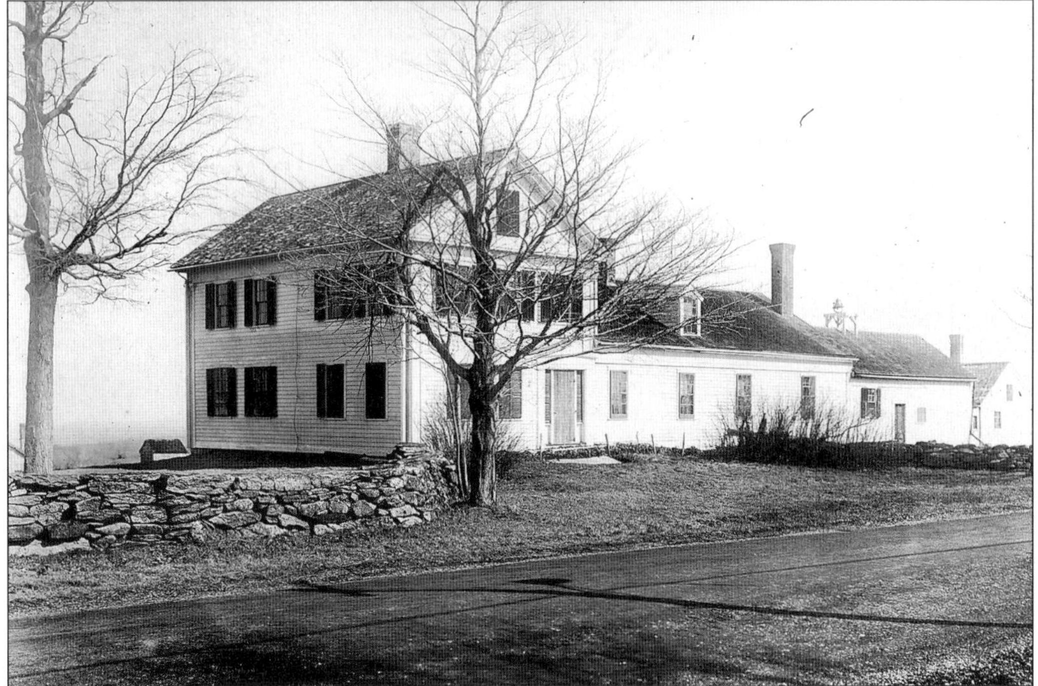

The caretaker's cottage for the Boylston Villa was located south of the home, on Worcester Road. In 1898, the employees of Ward Nicholas Boylston cared for 100 prize Jersey cows and maintained 550 acres of land associated with the farm. (Courtesy of the Princeton Historical Society.)

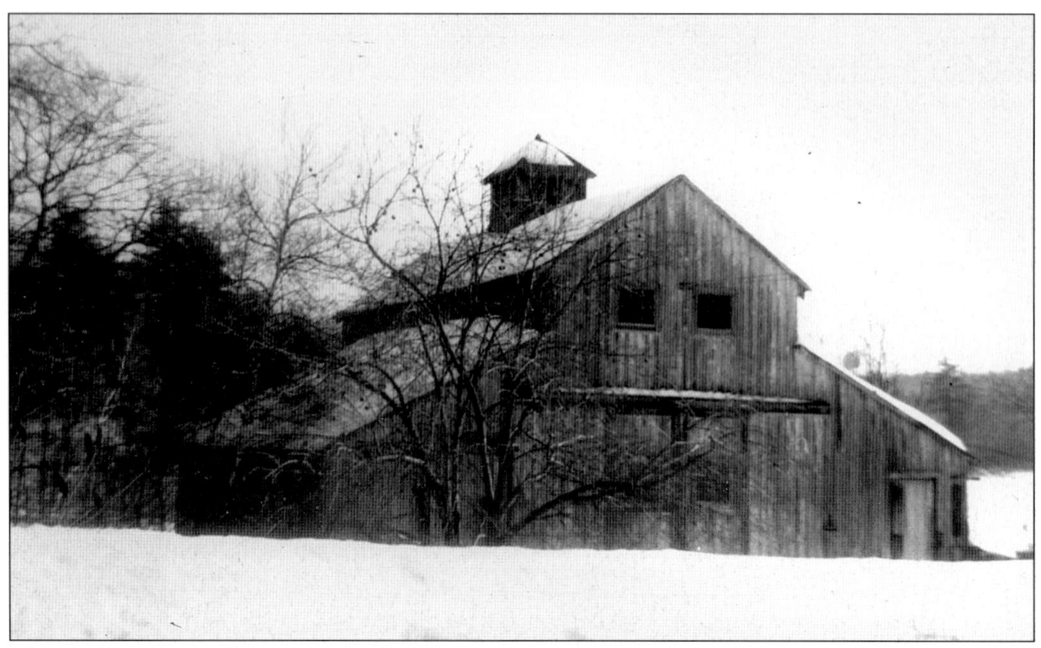

This icehouse may have stood on Brooks Station Road in the late 1800s somewhere near Brooks Station. Blocks of ice weighing 200 pounds were stored in the building. Teams of men cut the ice and brought it from the pond to the icehouse by means of a conveyor belt. The ice was kept packed in straw until it was delivered. Upon delivery, it had to be picked into blocks small enough to fit into household iceboxes. (Courtesy of the Princeton Historical Society.)

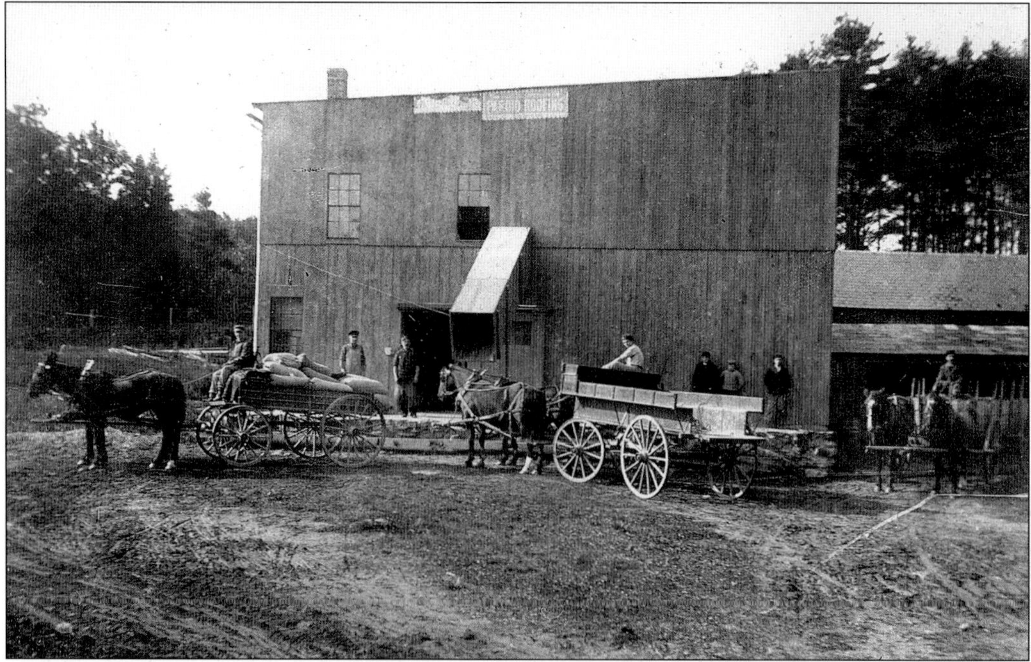

The Potter Grain Company maintained a store in the early to mid-20th century on Hubbardston Road near Princeton Depot. Grain was stored here and distributed to the members of Eastern States Farmer's Exchange for their livestock. (Courtesy of Edith Hubbard.)

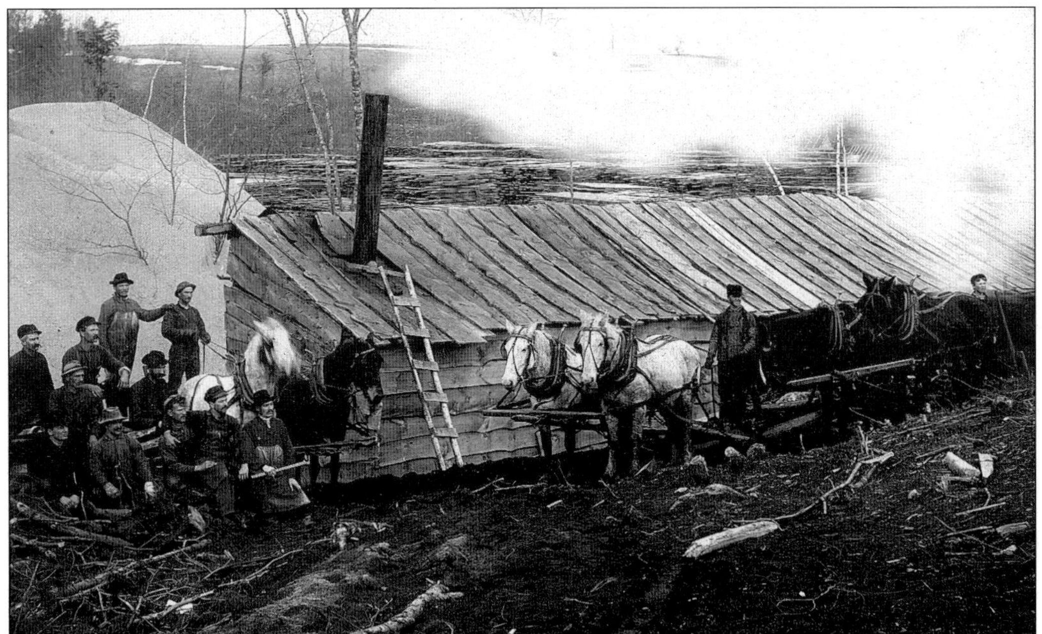

It is unknown exactly where the Whittaker Woodlot was located in 1901 and 1902. It is possible that this sawmill might have been somewhere near Princeton Depot and may have carried out the same business as the other sawmills in "Slab City" near the Hubbardston line. The lumber may have come directly from the mill and was used for the building. (Courtesy of the Princeton Historical Society.)

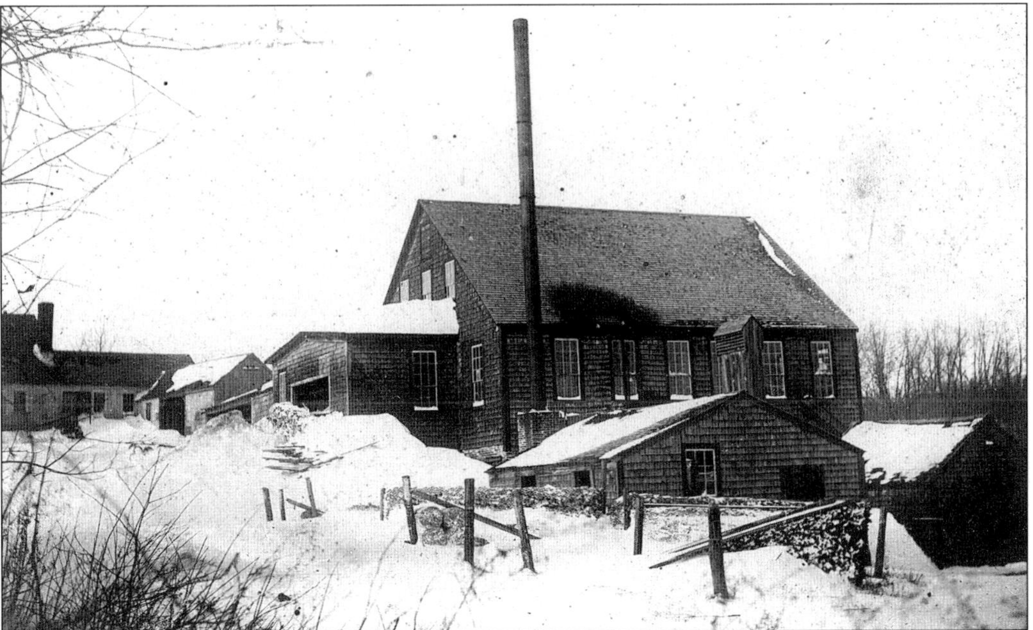

The last operating chair factory in Princeton was located off Sterling Road. It was established by Thurston and Eugene Buck in 1880 and continued to operate until the late 1940s. The Buck brothers' first mill burned in 1883, and a larger mill was immediately built. In 1914, another addition was built with two 65-horsepower boilers. (Courtesy of the Princeton Historical Society.)

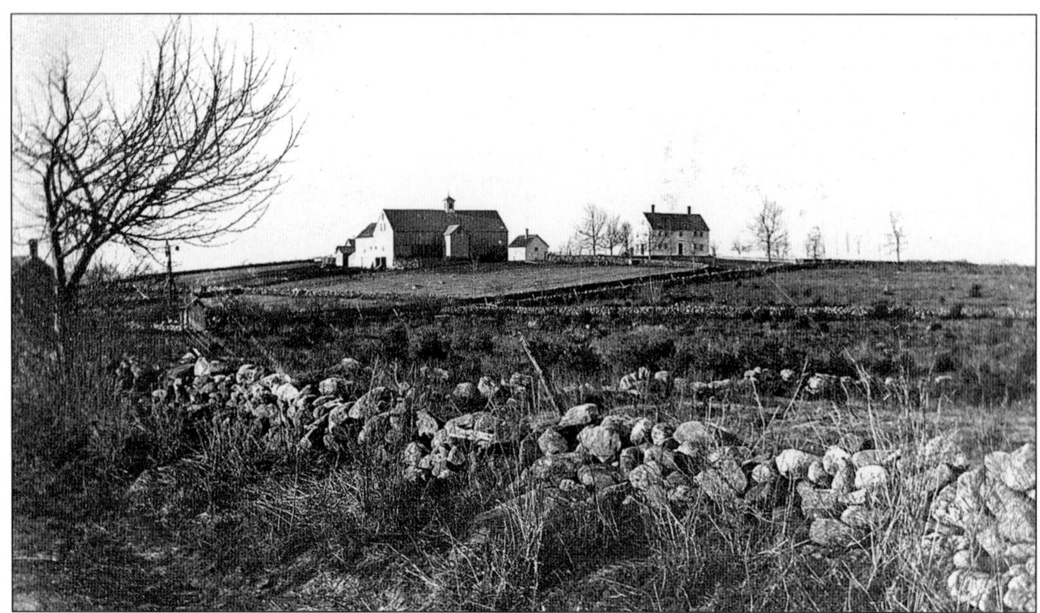

The Stimson Farm, on Thompson Road, has been in the same family since 1743, when Jedidiah Brigham purchased 237 acres for 70 British pounds. Nestled in a valley with a view of Wachusett Mountain, the historic house and barn are surrounded by stone walls. The Stimson farm celebrated its 250th anniversary in 1993 and has been passed down in the family for 10 generations. (Courtesy of the Stimson family.)

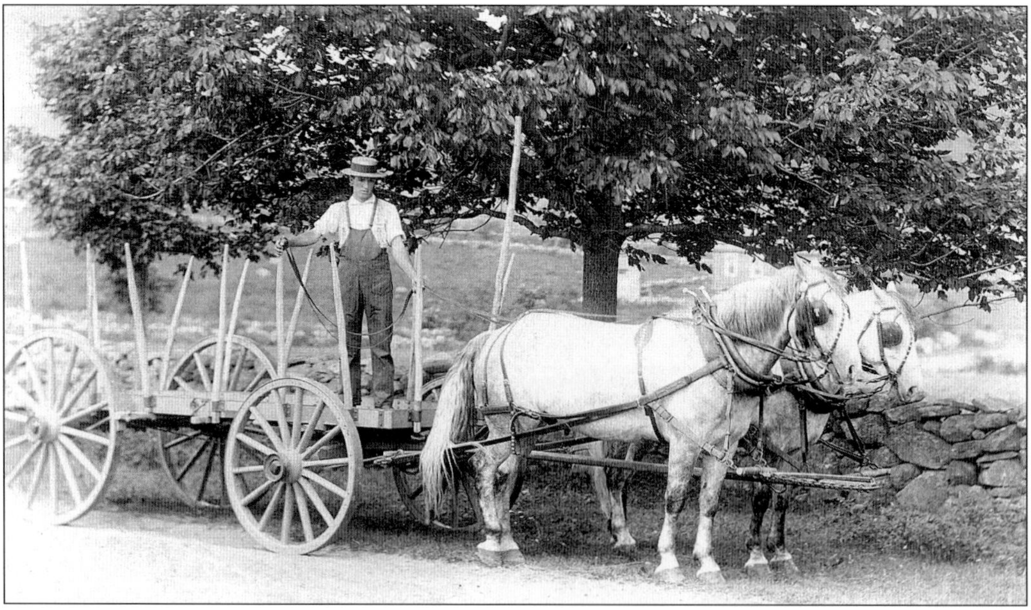

Pictured here in the late 1800s is Charles Frederic Thompson, the maternal grandfather of Charles Stimson. Thompson died in 1957 at the age of 82 from injuries sustained while baling hay. Working side-by-side, grandfather and grandson carried out the daily chores of dairy farming. The family continues to work together raising calves and heifers to milking age to sell to dairy farmers. They also produce 7,000 bales of hay for horse owners. (Courtesy of the Stimson family.)

The Princeton Farmer's Club had its first meeting on February 6, 1860, and in 1882, the name of the club was changed to the Princeton Farmer's and Mechanic's Association. The club's annual suppers were considered an important social event. Lectures and agricultural talks were given, and cattle shows were held yearly. The organization held its meetings until 1896, when it voted to dissolve. (Courtesy of the Princeton Historical Society.)

OFFICIAL PROGRAMME

OF THE

PRINCETON

Farmers and Mechanics Association

FAIR,

TO BE HELD AT

PRINCETON, OCT. 6TH, 1887.

8	o'clock	—Trial of Working Oxen and Steers.
9.30	"	—Trial Draught Horses.
10	"	—Mares and Colts.
10.30	"	—Plowing Match.
11.15	"	—Saddle Race.
12	"	—Society Dinner.
1 to 2	"	—Concert by Winchendon Military Band.
2.15	"	—Horse Trot
3	"	—Sports.

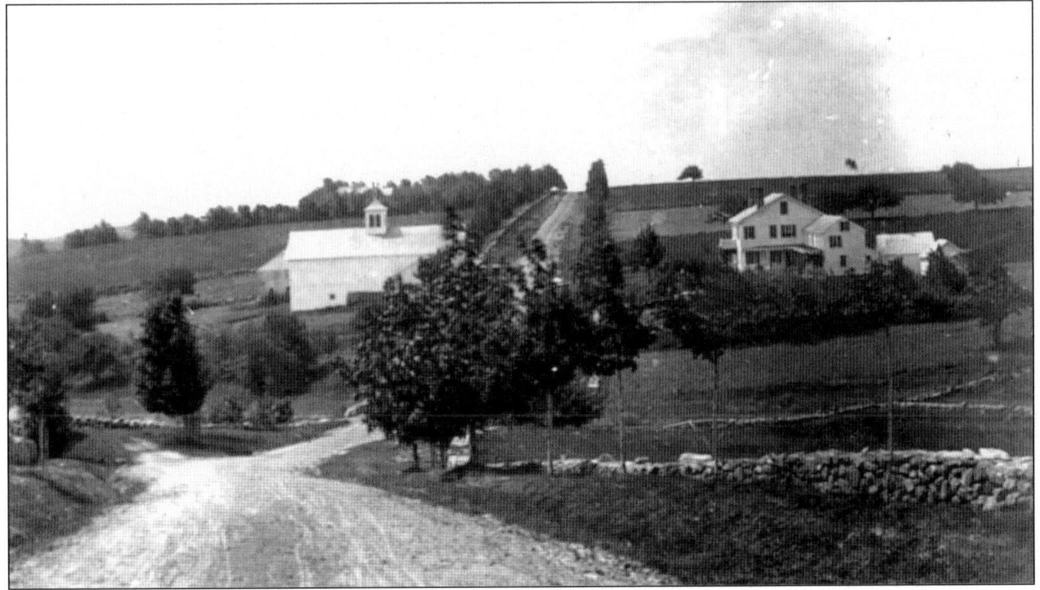

This photograph of the Brooks farm was taken *c.* 1910. Artemus Brooks purchased this farm on Worcester Road in 1859. Until his death in 1927, he and his son William worked together farming. William Brooks Sr. died an early death in 1934. There were about 600 acres of pastures to tend in various parts of town each spring after the snow melted. Sometimes, it would take all day to walk the perimeter of the pasture to make repairs to the barbed wire. Lunchtime was spent in the shade of the Model T pickup. (Courtesy of Bud Brooks.)

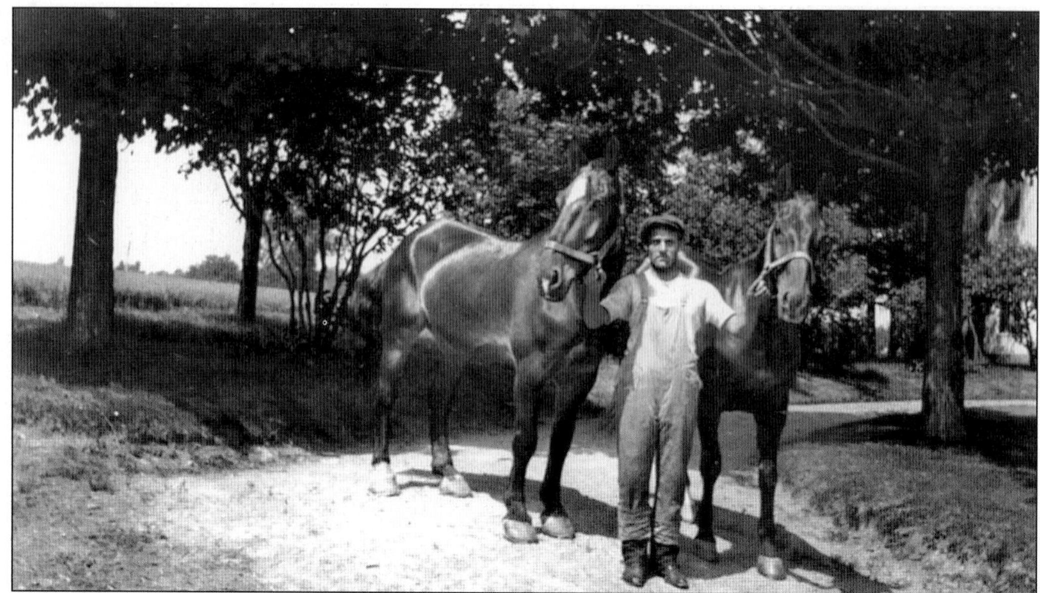

With the workload on the Brooks farm, it was necessary to hire one and often two extra men during growing season. There were approximately 200 chickens, 60 head of cattle, 4 pigs, and 2 pair of horses on the farm. One of the hired hands was Pat Shine, who was a hard worker and well-liked man. He worked for $20 to $30 a month plus a stipend. (Courtesy of Bud Brooks.)

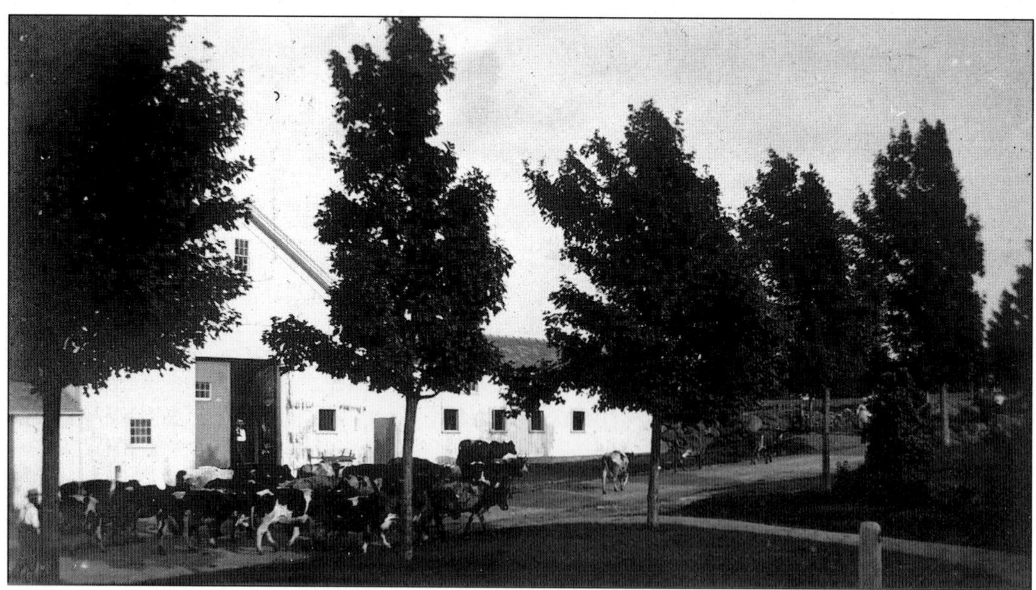

William Brooks's fields were well known for excellent pasturing. Each year, drovers brought cattle from Shrewsbury and Sudbury to graze in Princeton pastures. The drovers herded the cattle over the roads to the pastures for grazing and safely back again in the fall to the owners. As automobiles became popular, the cattle drives ceased sometime in the 1920s, and the cattle were transported by truck. (Courtesy of Bud Brooks.)

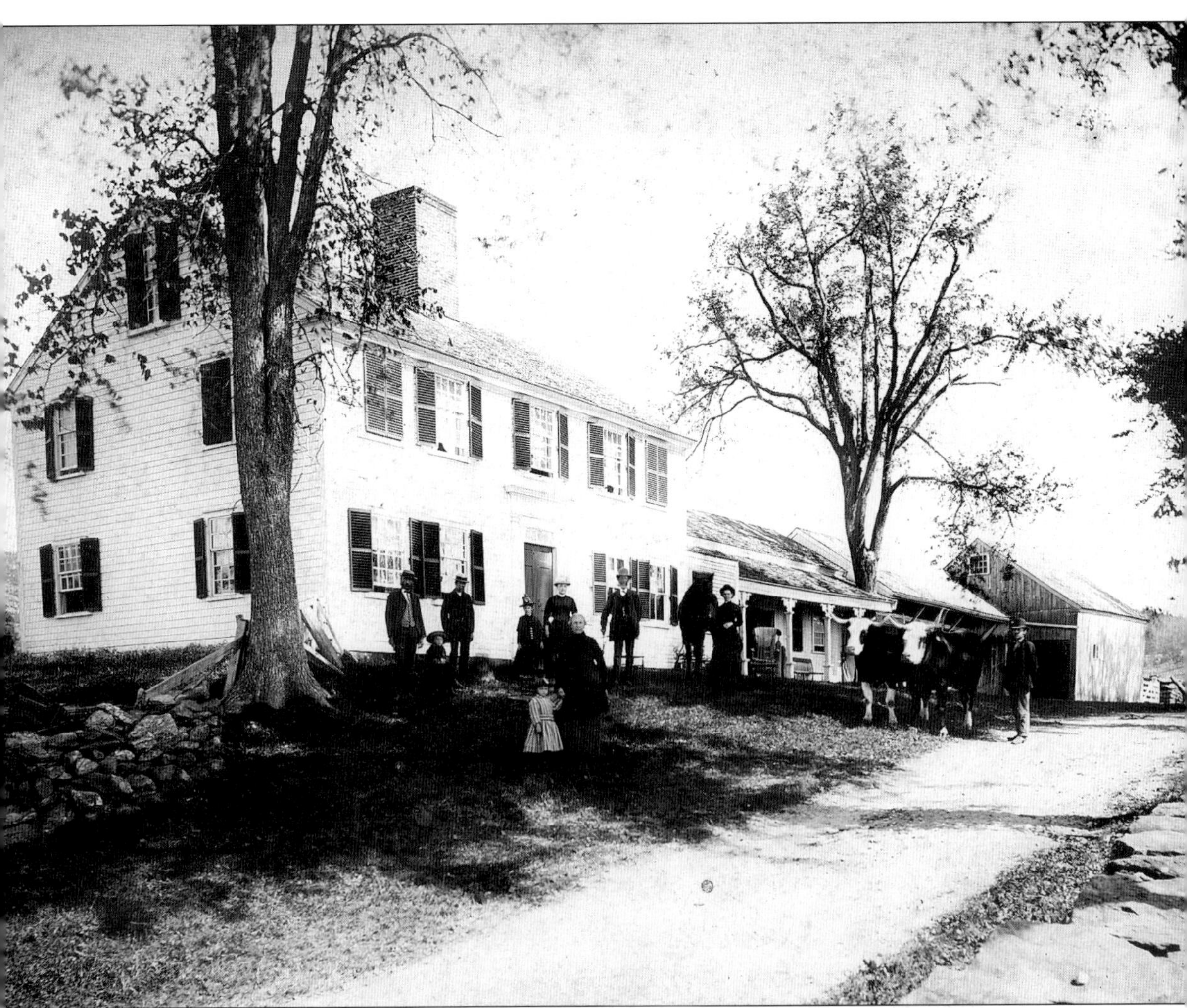

This photograph from 1887 shows members of the Goodnow family gathered in front of their home. Edward Goodnow married Lois Rice in 1770 and had 11 children. He built this house in 1786, eight years after the road was built. When Edward Goodnow Sr. died at age 56, his eldest son, Edward, began running the farm. In 1823, the Boston-Barre stage line opened, running past the house. Edward used the house as an inn for the next 21 years until the inn closed in 1844. Before the Civil War, the Goodnow house is said to have been part of the Underground Railroad. The property was sold in 1918 to Charles Crocker, who used it as a summer home. The Crockers enjoyed the farm for many years, raising sheep, dairy, and beef cattle. In 1956, the Crocker family donated the estate of 1,013 acres to the Massachusetts Audubon Society. (Courtesy of the Princeton Historical Society.)

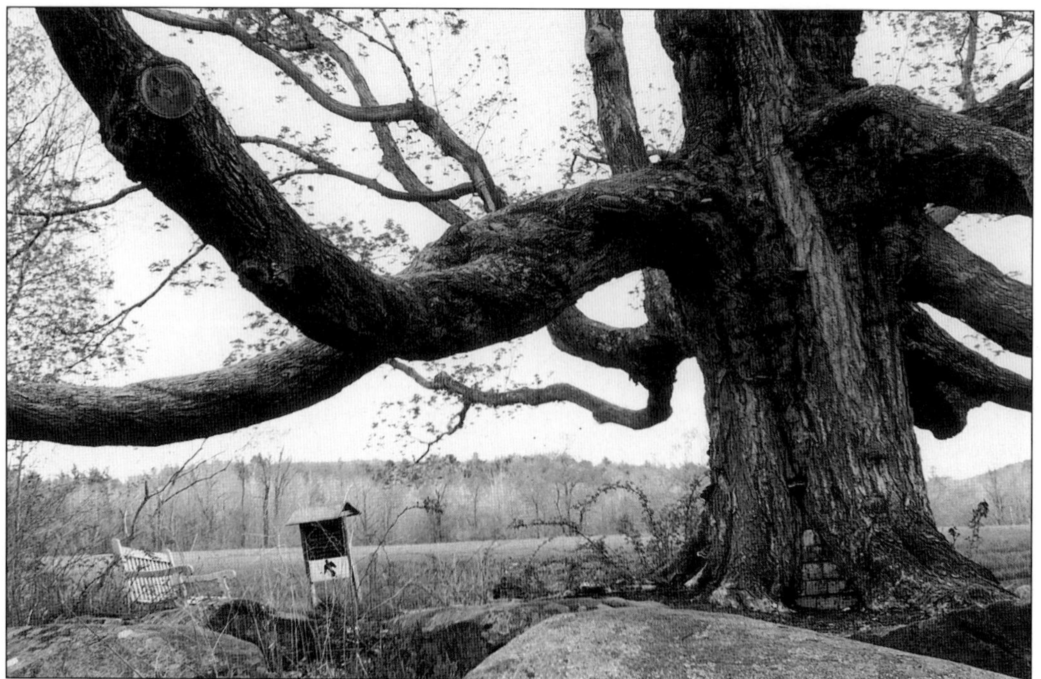

The 250-year-old Crocker Maple, at Wachusett Meadow Wildlife Sanctuary in Princeton, fell on November 18, 2002, after an ice storm. It was named in honor of Charles T. Crocker III. This mighty tree was the third largest sugar maple in New England. At the time of its demise, it had a girth of 16 feet, a branch spread of 105 feet, and a height of 85 feet. This contemporary photograph is a reminder of how magnificent the landmark was to everyone who visited Wachusett Meadow Wildlife Sanctuary. (Courtesy of Bruce Dean.)

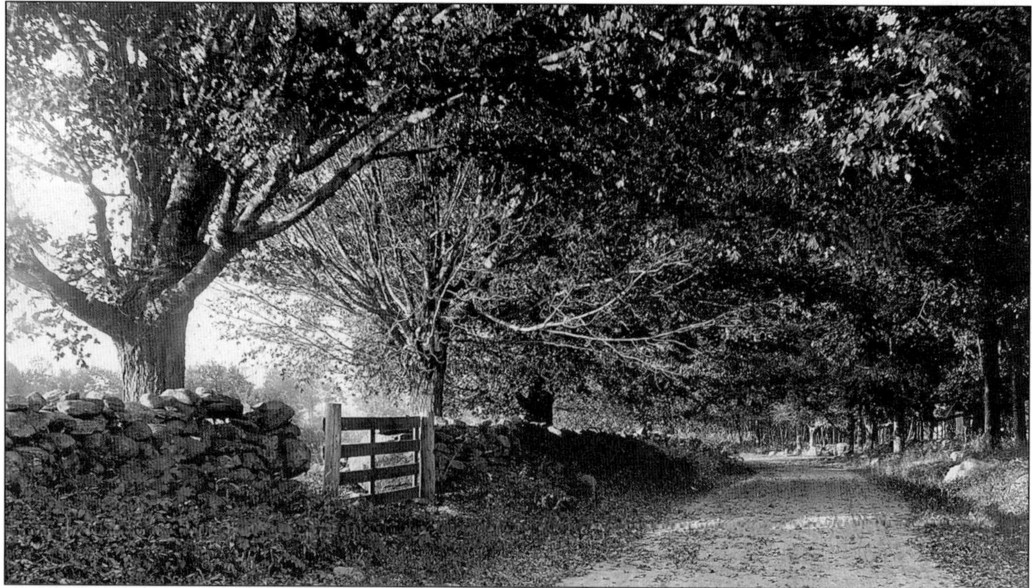

This photograph, taken in the late 1800s, shows Brooks Station Road near Woodlawn Cemetery. The larger trees form a canopy over the narrow dirt road, telling of another time and place. (Courtesy of the Princeton Historical Society.)

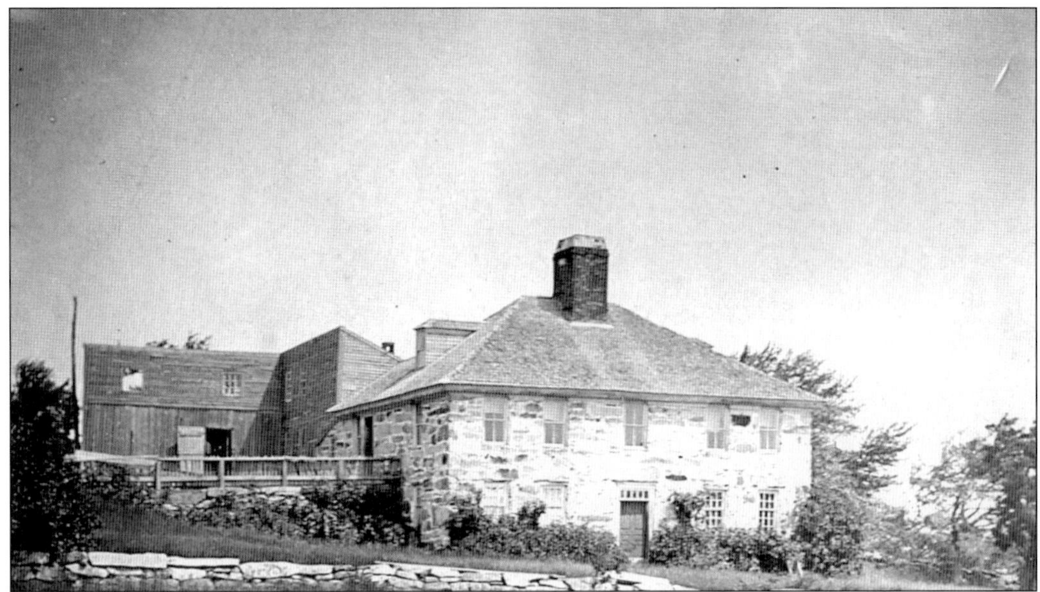

Jonas Beaman, a Revolutionary War soldier, built two stone houses on Mirick Road in 1780. Stones for the houses were quarried on Pine Hill not far from where the house was built. One house was torn down many years ago, but this one remains (although the barn is no longer standing). School was held here after Schoolhouse No. 2 burned in 1837 until a new school was constructed. (Courtesy of the Princeton Historical Society.)

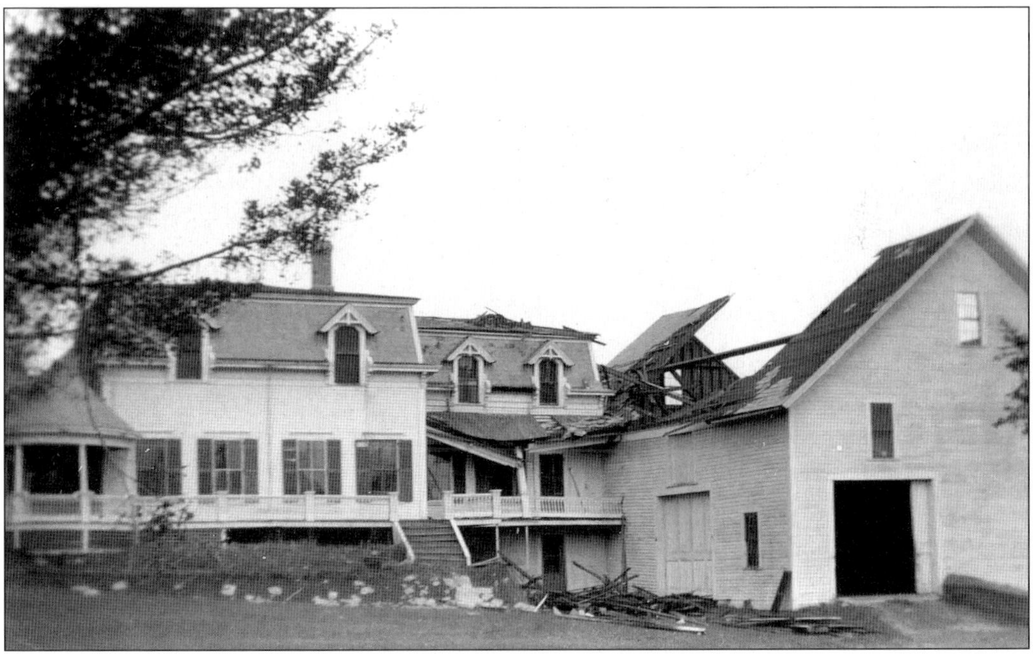

This photograph, taken in 1938, shows the home of Herbert Houghton, on Worcester Road, with its Victorian porch on the front. This house and others in Princeton and East Princeton were badly damaged by the hurricane of September 21, 1938. The barn sustained damage to the roof, and a porch roof on the side of the house was blown off. After the storm, the barn was razed. (Courtesy of Nancy Beaman Flanders.)

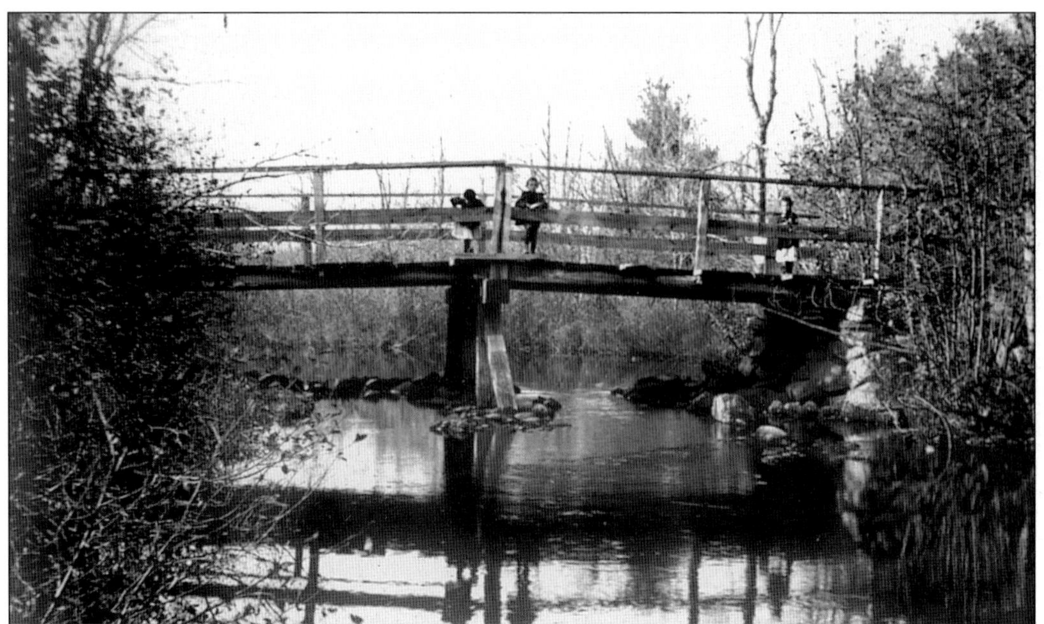

Children are standing on a bridge that spans the East Branch of the Ware River near the Hubbardston line. In 1751, Oliver Davis, an early settler, built the first sawmill on the Ware River. A cotton-carding mill was built here in 1841, and by the late 1800s, the Roper Box Company carried on manufacturing. The area was first known as Valley Village. When the sawmills and lumbermills were located there, it was called Slab City. (Courtesy of the Princeton Historical Society.)

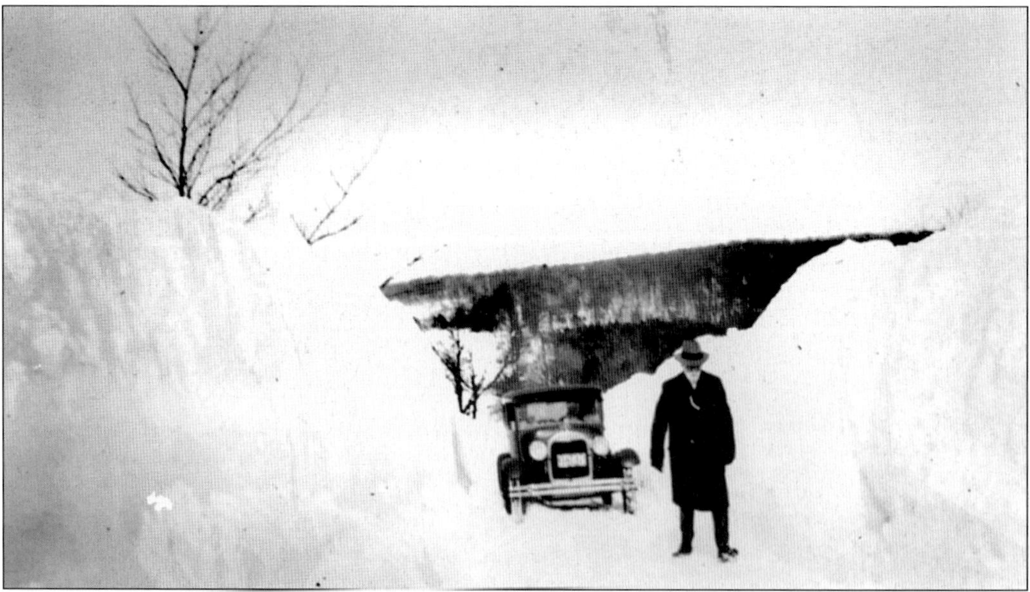

A man seeks help to get his 1928 Ford roadster out of the snow. Often, the snow was too deep for cars and even for horses. Men shoveled the roads by hand, or a snow roller would be hitched to a team of oxen. As the oxen pulled the roller, it would compress and harden the snow. When mud season arrived, people struggled again with their automobiles, and it was often necessary to use a horse and wagon. (Courtesy of the Princeton Historical Society.)

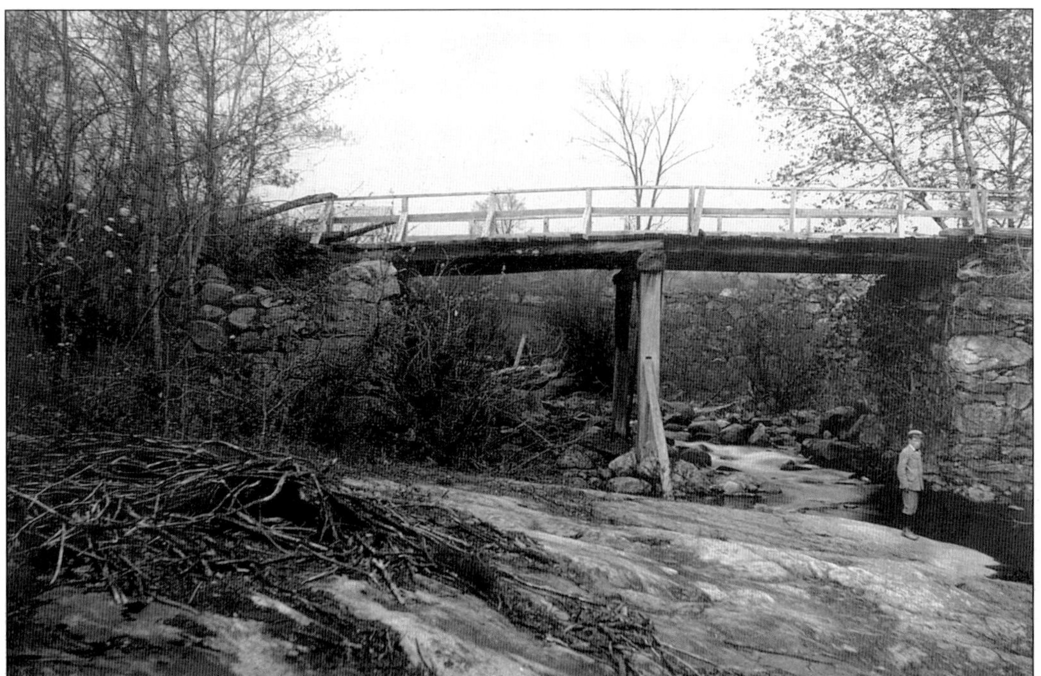

Bridges built in the early 1900s did not need to meet the standards that are required today. This May 1907 photograph shows a young boy standing at water's edge near the bridge over Skinner Brook. It is unknown where Skinner Brook was located, but it may have been near Sterling Road or Bullard Road. (Courtesy of the Princeton Historical Society.)

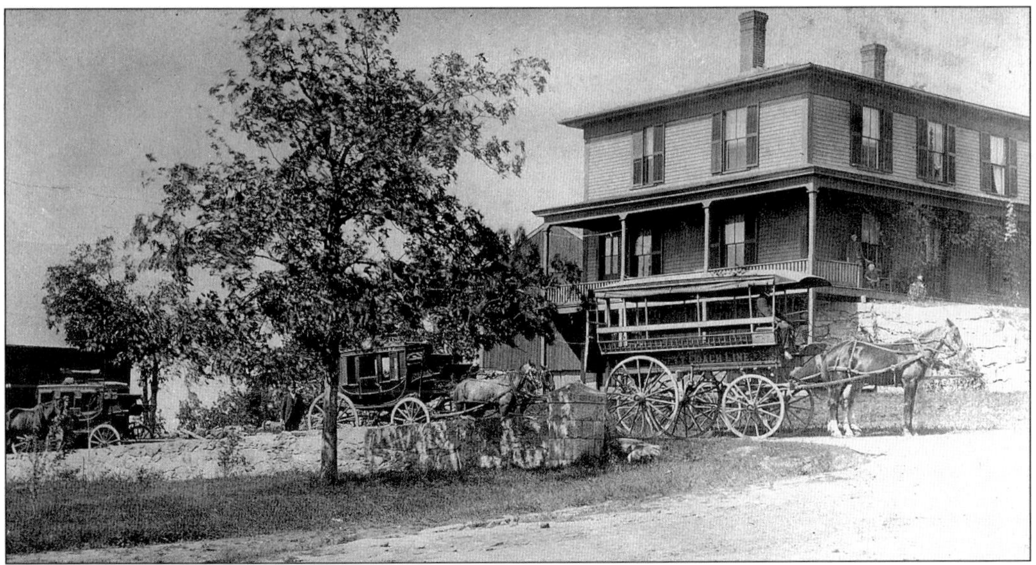

Prentice Dolittle was well known as the owner of the Wachusett Stage Coach Line from 1883 to 1909. For 26 years, he operated the business from his home on Mountain Road behind the Goodnow Memorial Building. He employed four drivers and proudly owned 17 horses, two Concord coaches, a Henderson coach, a mountain wagon, a three-seated wagon, and a baggage wagon. The fire engine was kept in his barn, ready to be pulled with his team of horses. (Courtesy of the Princeton Historical Society.)

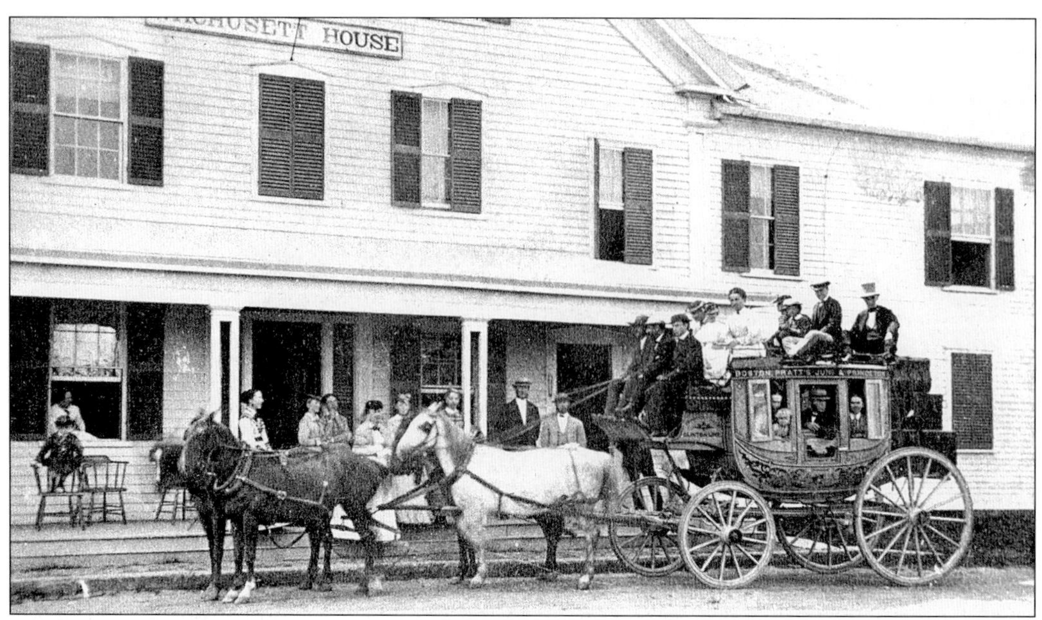

The first stagecoach line ran once a week prior to 1820 and supplied subscribers with the *Massachusetts Spy* on its way. It traveled from Royalston through Gardner, Westminster, and Princeton and to Worcester. Another line, established *c.* 1823, traveled from Barre to Boston through Princeton, stopping at post offices along the way. It ceased to operate after the completion of the railroad. A third stagecoach route began in 1849, running from Princeton to Oakdale. (Courtesy of the Princeton Historical Society.)

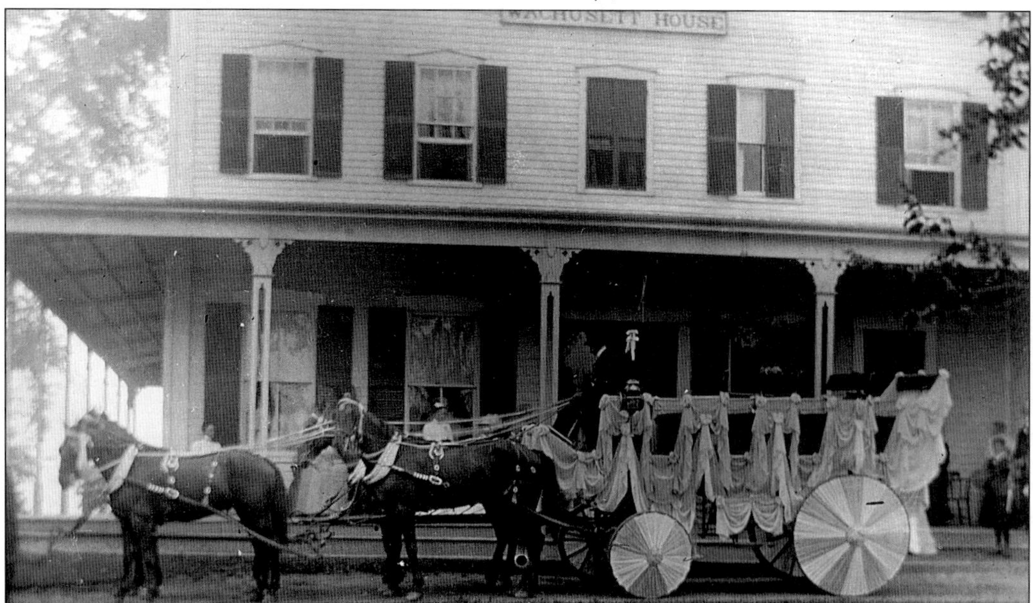

A carriage stands in front of Wachusett House, waiting for passengers to go to the coaching parade at 11:00 in Rutland. When the event was over, people would often have a picnic lunch on the Rutland common or would dine at one of the hotels. Private residences and hotels would decorate with flags and bunting to celebrate the festive day. (Courtesy of the Princeton Historical Society.)

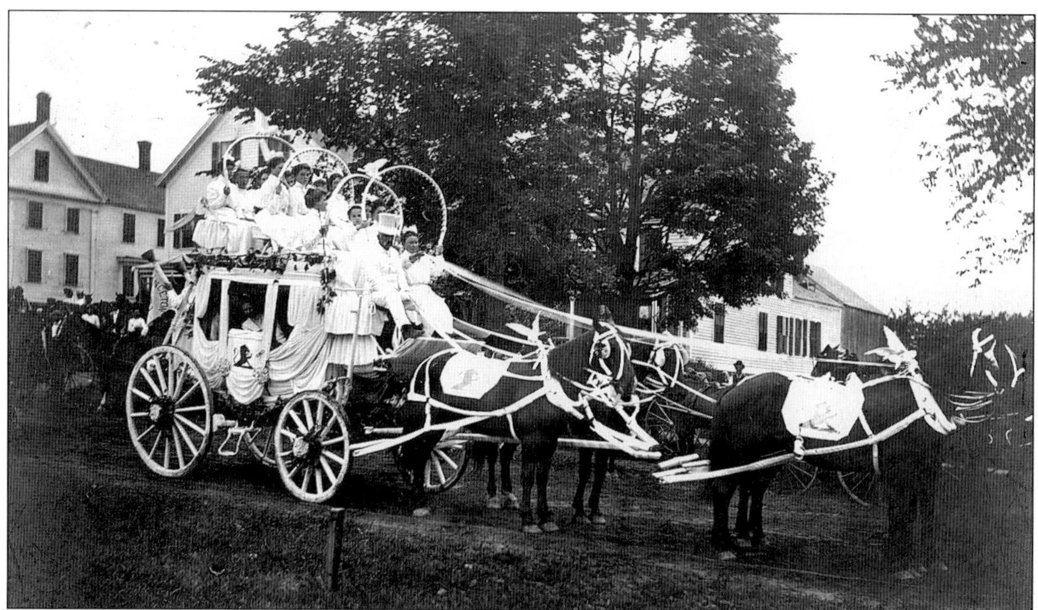

Wachusett House won the silver award in 1901 at the annual coaching parade in Rutland. Days before the event, guests would decorate the coach to be used in the parade. Prentice Dolittle, the driver of this coach, could always be depended upon to offer one of his best coaches for the event. (Courtesy of the Princeton Historical Society.)

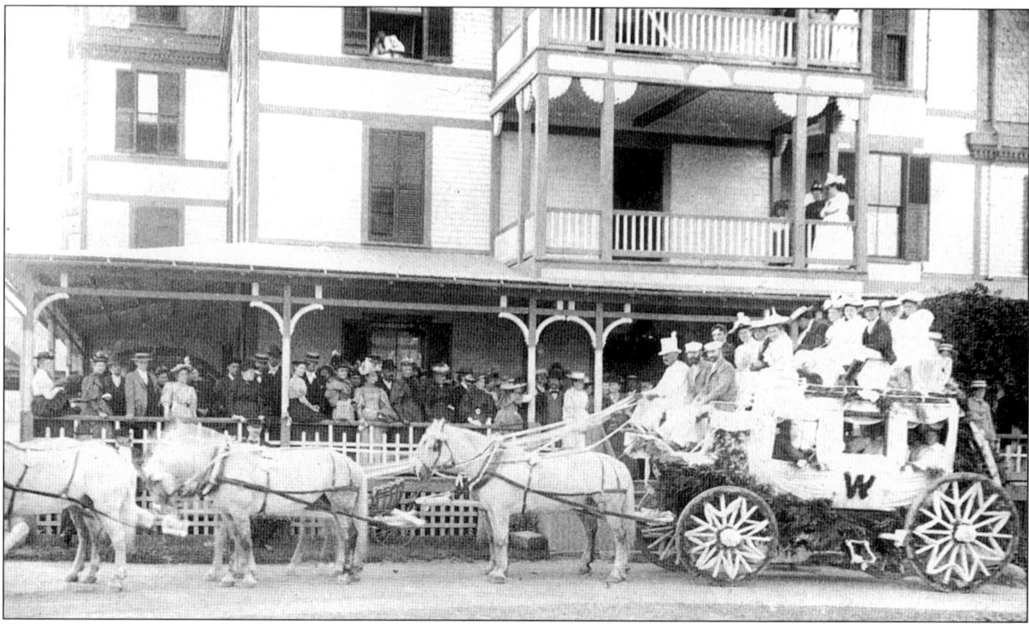

Princeton's Wachusett House coach is stopped at the side of the Bartlett Hotel in Rutland Center. Highly decorated coaches from many towns competed in Rutland for first prize. Coaches would line up and proceed down flag-decorated Main Street in Rutland while the Worcester Brass Band played on the common. Prentice Dolittle was the popular driver, and his adept handling of the horses was a factor in winning the prize. (Courtesy of the Princeton Historical Society.)

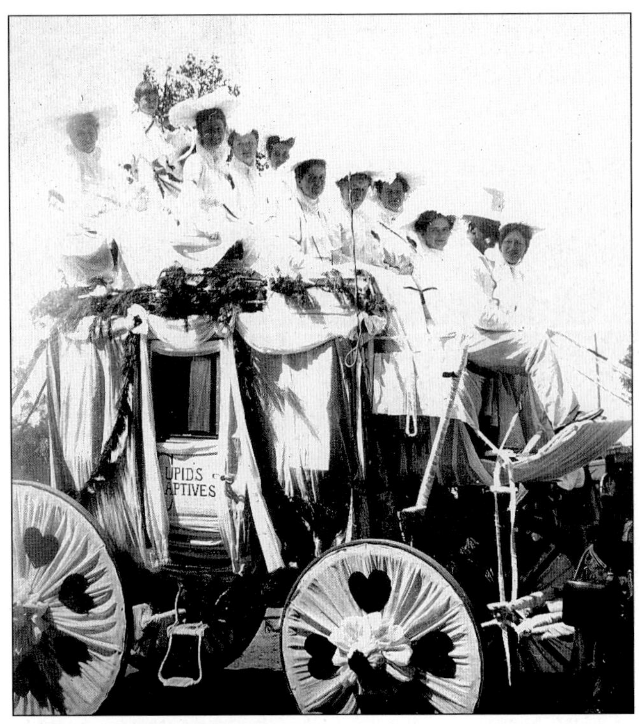

On August 24, 1904, the *Telegram and Gazette* reported, "The most unique coach in the parade to win the silver cup was Wachusett House of Princeton. Its colors were red and white with large red hearts in profusion on the coach. The women on top of the coach were cupid's captives who were gowned in white, carried white parasols, and wore picture hats." (Courtesy of the Princeton Historical Society.)

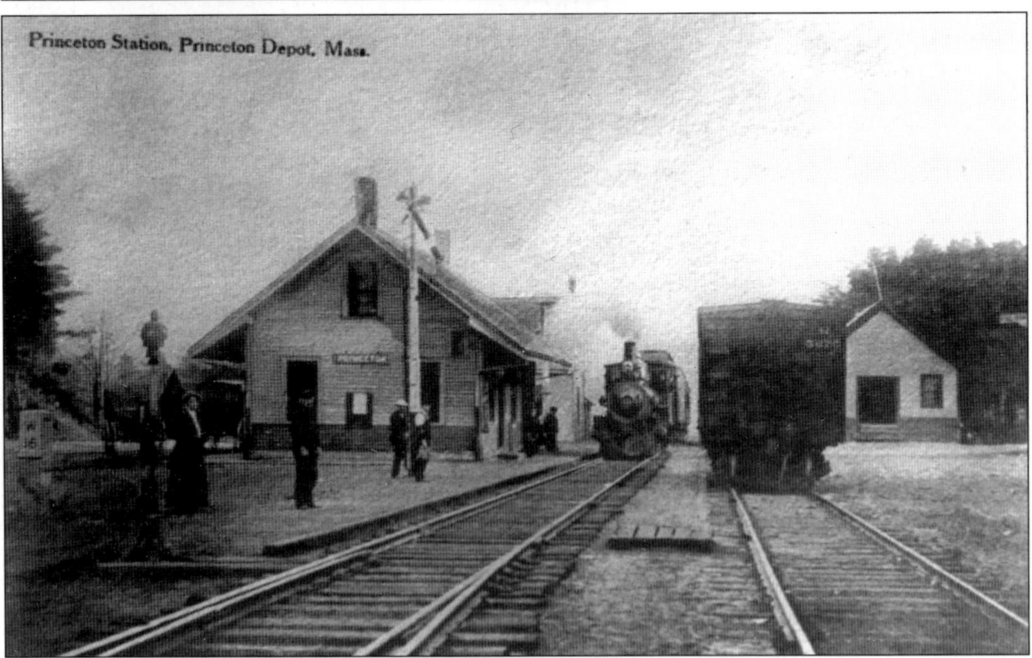

The Boston, Barre, and Gardner Railroad, which began service through Princeton in 1870, was misnamed. The train departed Worcester and stopped in Princeton. This train, known as the Blueberry Special, stopped along the way to allow people to get off the train to pick blueberries. As passenger service declined, it was necessary to flag the train to board it. The last passenger train through Princeton made its final trip on March 7, 1953. (Courtesy of the Princeton Historical Society.)

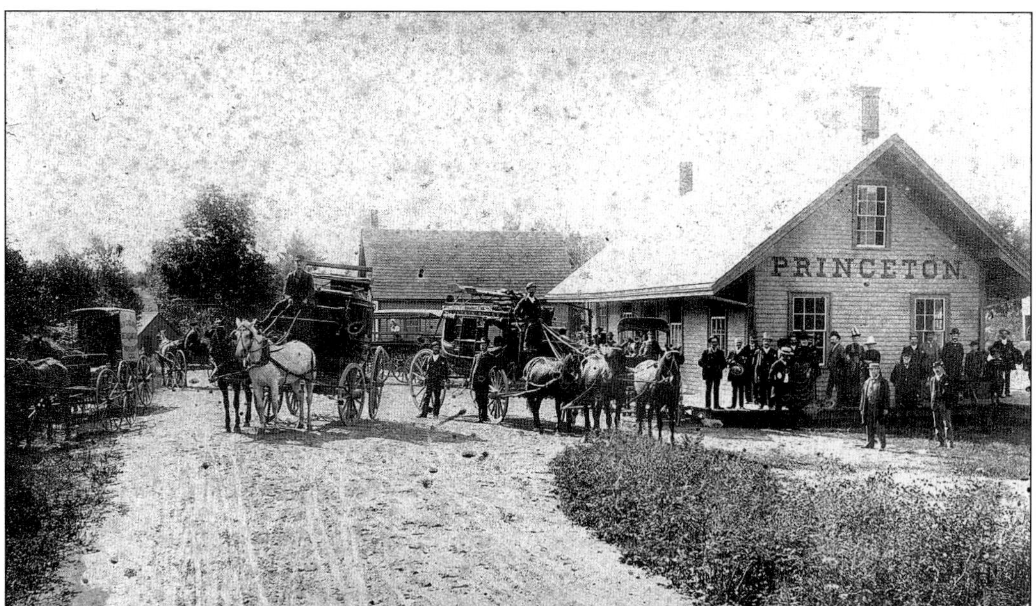

Princeton Depot, located on Hubbardston Road, was used more frequently for passenger service than Brooks Station was. In 1900, at the height of train travel, as many as eight trains a day arrived at Princeton Depot. Prentice Dolittle waited to pick up arrivals and bring them on the two-mile uphill trip to the center or to the hotels and guesthouses on the outskirts of town. (Courtesy of the Princeton Historical Society.)

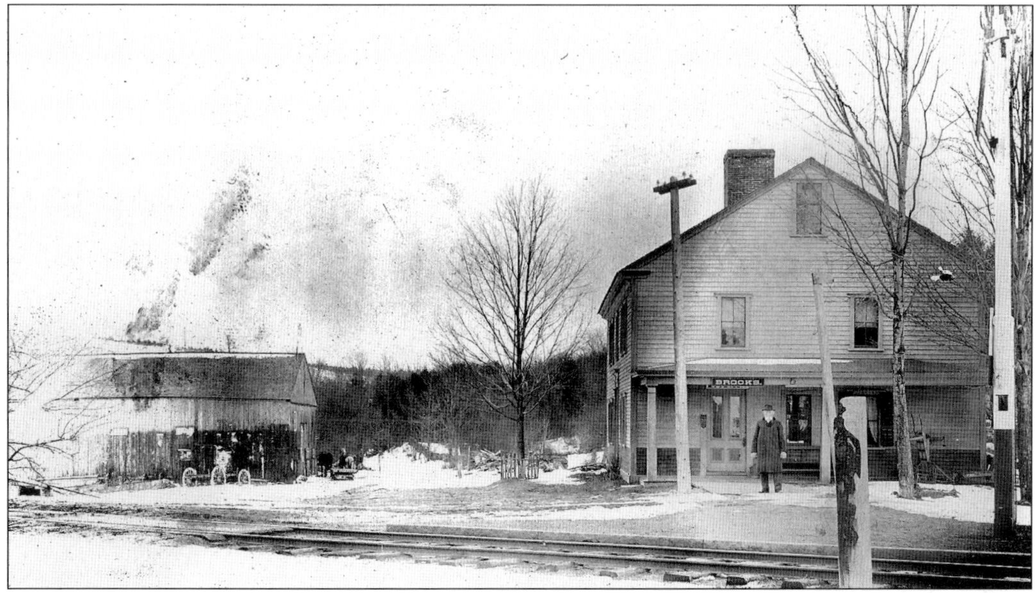

The town fathers contemplated putting a depot in the center of town; however, fearing that the location would attract undesirables, they decided the best place would be a location on the outskirts of town. Brooks Station (named after Jonas Brooks) was located, until 1924, on Brooks Station Road past the intersection of Ball Hill Road. All trains stopped here to take on water for the trip westward to Gardner until the station burned in 1924. (Courtesy of the Princeton Historical Society.)

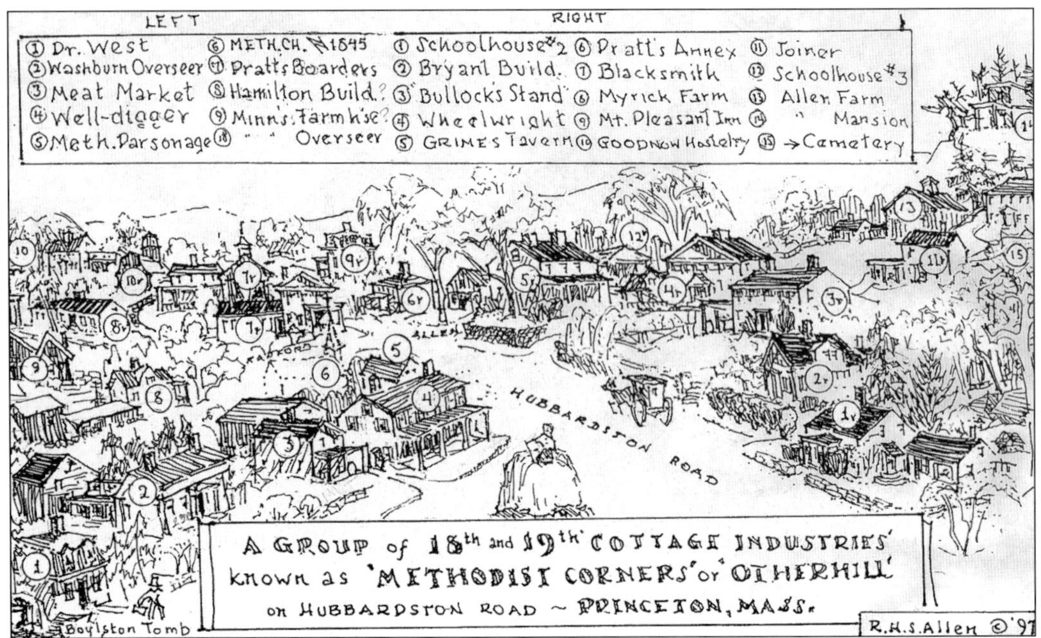

A map drawn in 1997 by Rosalind Sturges Allen, at the age of 90, depicts how West Village (also known as Methodist Corners or Otherhill) looked as a thriving community west of the center of town in the 18th and 19th centuries. Clustered together were the homes and shops of a blacksmith, a builder, a wheelwright, a well digger, and a joiner, as well as several stores, a meat market, two taverns, and Schoolhouse No. 9. (Courtesy of Princeton Historical Society.)

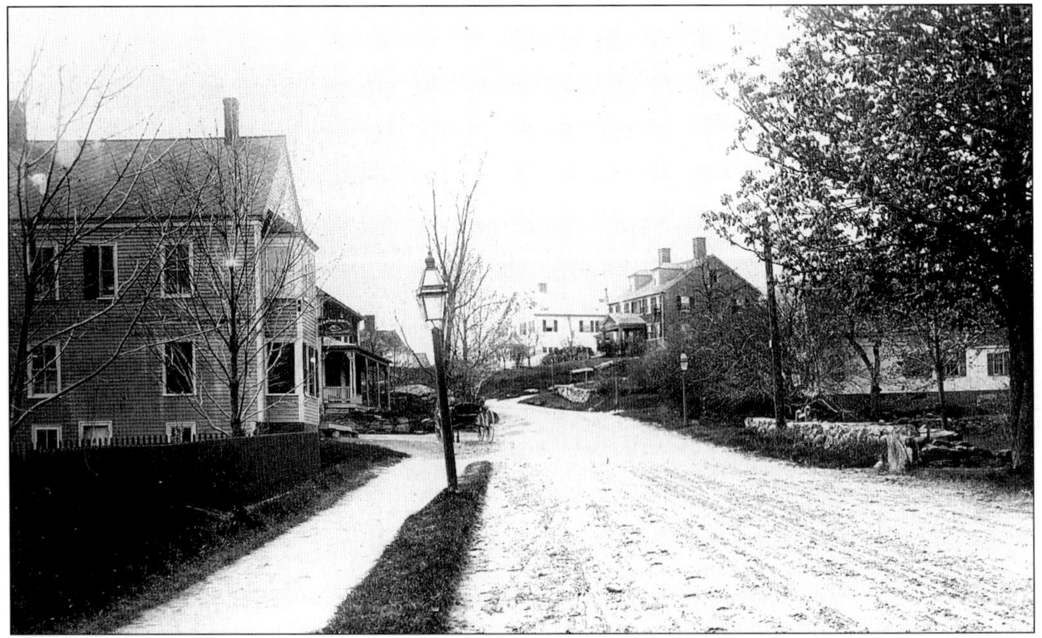

This photograph of West Village was taken after 1903, when the gas lamps were installed. At the far left are the meat market (foreground) and the well digger's house. At the right of the large tree, out of sight, is Schoolhouse No. 9. Bryant Builders (behind the tree), Bullock's Stand, and the wheelwright's house are seen in the distance. (Courtesy of Ed Carlson.)

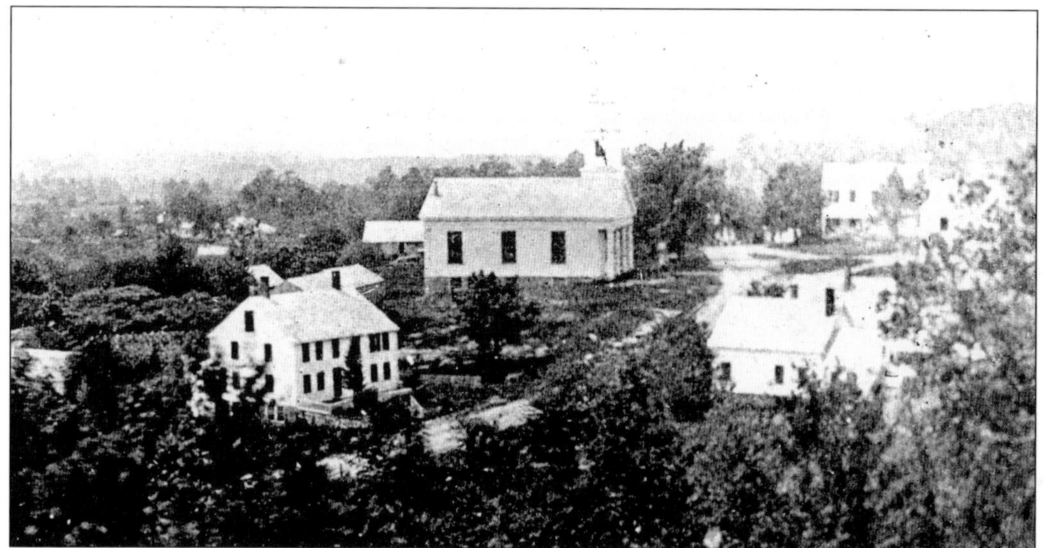

Hubbardston Road is seen in a view looking west. The Methodist church was located at the intersection of Hubbardston and Radford Roads. The church and parsonage were part of the village until the church burned in 1892. To the lower left is the well digger's house. Across the street from the well digger is Bryant Builders, and in the distance on the right is Grimes Cottage, a boardinghouse owned by Edwin Grimes. (Courtesy of the Princeton Historical Society.

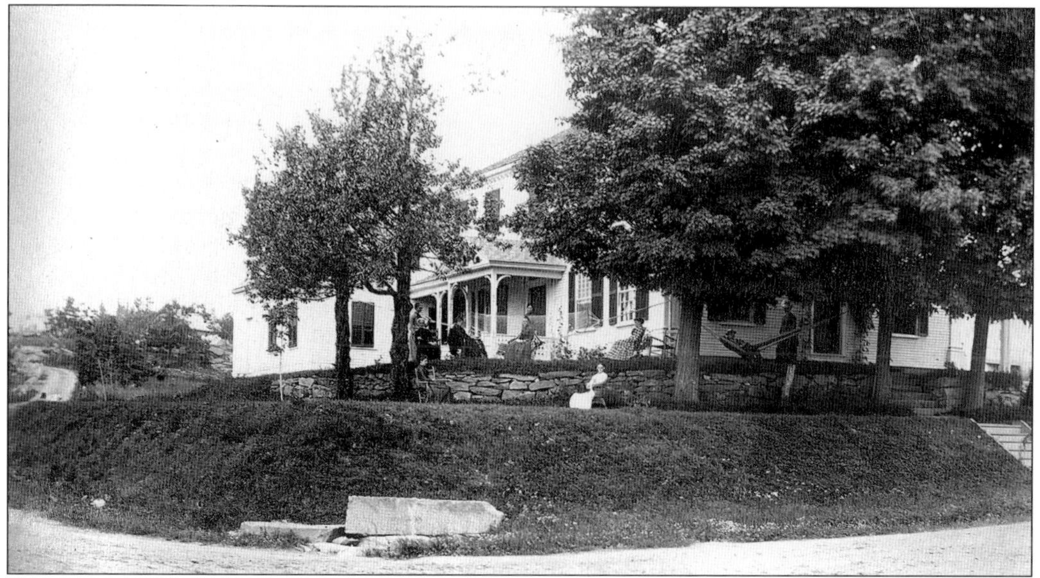

Grimes Cottage was opened in 1869 as a boardinghouse. The west side of the house, facing Allen Hill Road, is pictured in this early-1900s view. At the left, Allen Hill Road continues up the hill to Mountain Road. Guests are gathered in front of the house to enjoy the nice weather. (Courtesy of the Princeton Historical Society.)

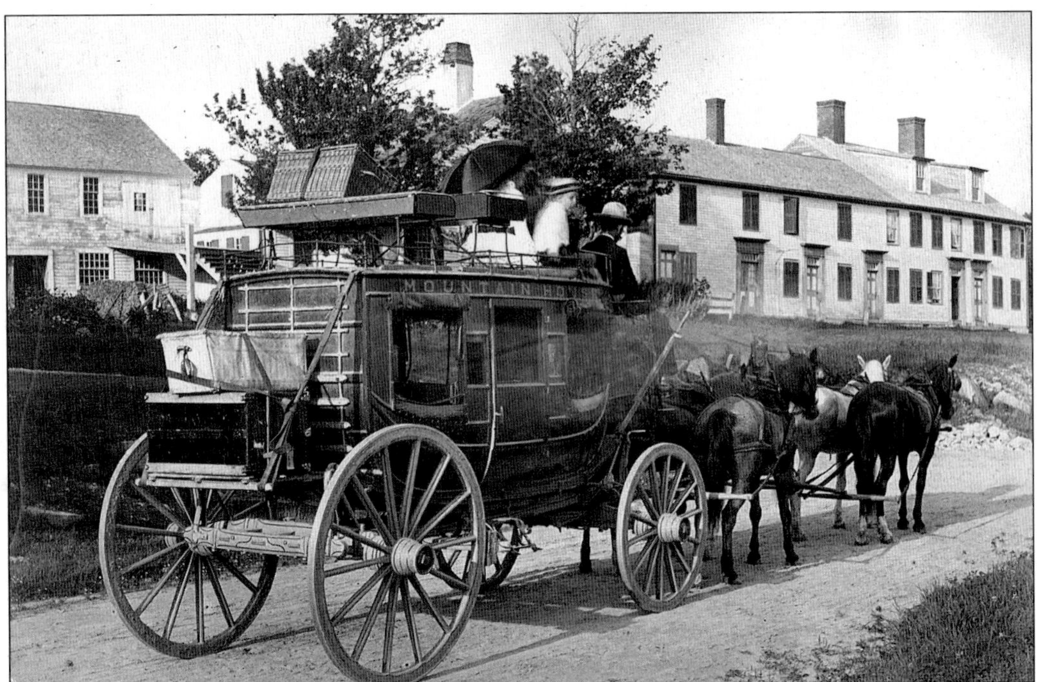

The Mountain House stagecoach is traveling east toward Princeton Center on the road leading from Hubbardston to the center of town. The building on the right is Bullock's Stand, where Calvin Bullock owned a business in 1818. The building burned in 1833, and Edward Goodnow, who owned a business there, had it rebuilt. Today it is a private residence. (Courtesy of the Princeton Historical Society.)

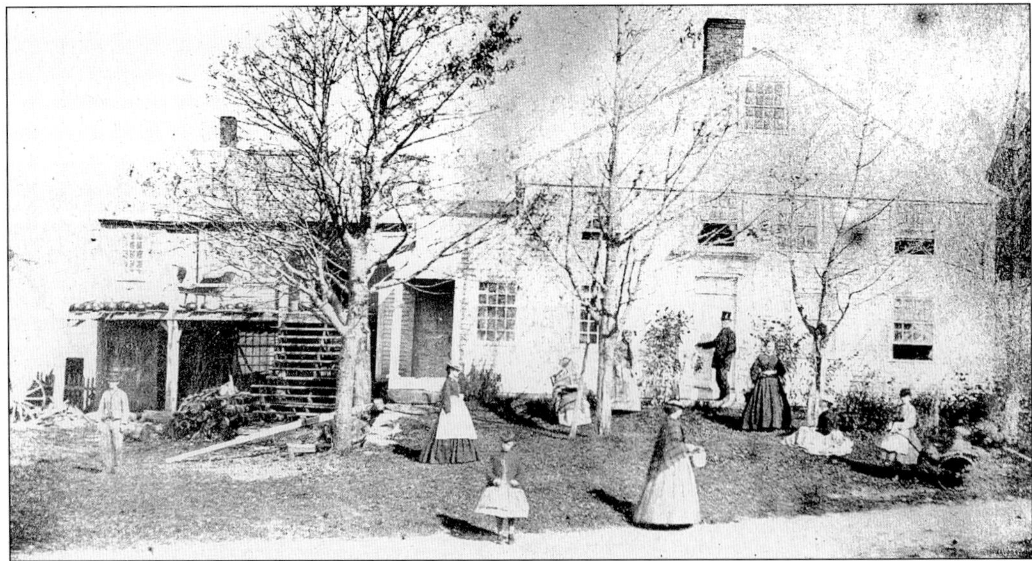

An 1856 photograph shows several people in front of a house on Hubbardston Road near the intersection of Allen Hill and Radford Roads. This house, built in 1823 by Charles Harrington, was once the wheelwright's house and shop. It was turned 180 degrees and remodeled by Isaac Jackson of Boston in 1907. It is now a private residence. (Courtesy of the Princeton Historical Society.)

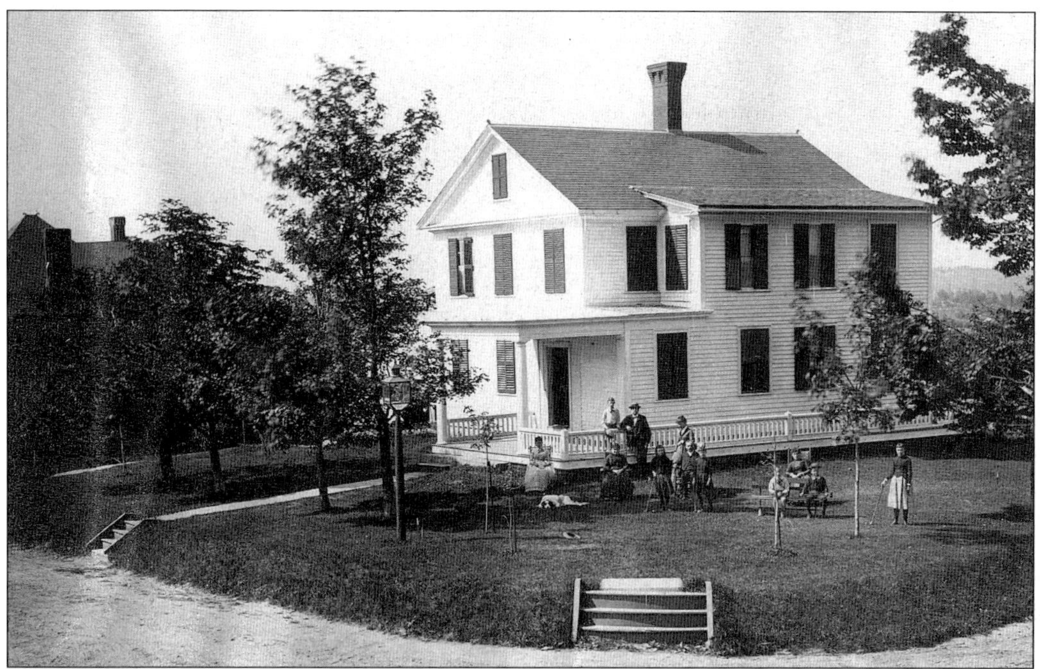

Pratt's Cottage, also called Linden House, was located in West Village at the intersection of Hubbardston and Radford Roads. As early as 1867, it was operating as a boardinghouse when James Mirick bought it from Dr. Alphonso Brooks. Harriet Pratt and her daughters, Lillian and Harriet, managed the establishment and kept it open all year long after most of the hotels closed around October 1. (Courtesy of the Princeton Historical Society.)

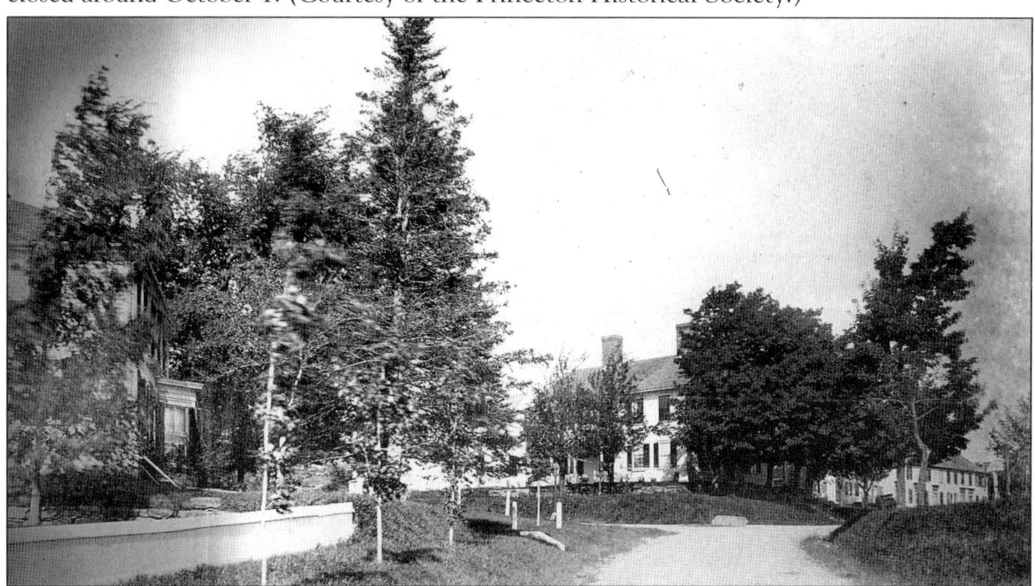

Hubbardston Road, leading to Princeton Center, is seen from the west. This photograph, taken in the early 1900s, shows Pratt's Annex at the lower left and Grimes Cottage in the center. In the distance is Bullock's Stand. When Pratt's Cottage was full, Pratt's Annex (owned by Harriet Pratt and her daughters) accommodated the extra boarders. (Courtesy of the Princeton Historical Society.)

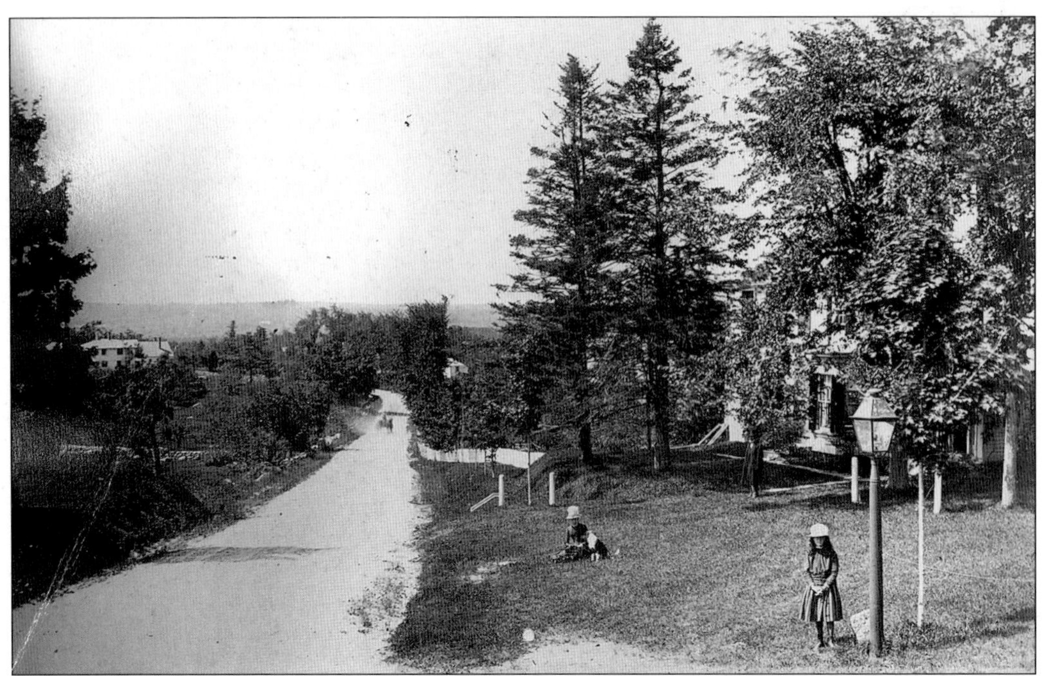

A young girl is standing on the lawn of Pratt's Annex at the corner of Allen Hill Road. Hubbardston Road is seen in a view looking west from the intersection with Allen Hill Road sometime after 1903. In the late 1800s, this road (now Route 62) was known as Westlawn Avenue. It was later named Depot Road. (Courtesy of the Princeton Historical Society.)

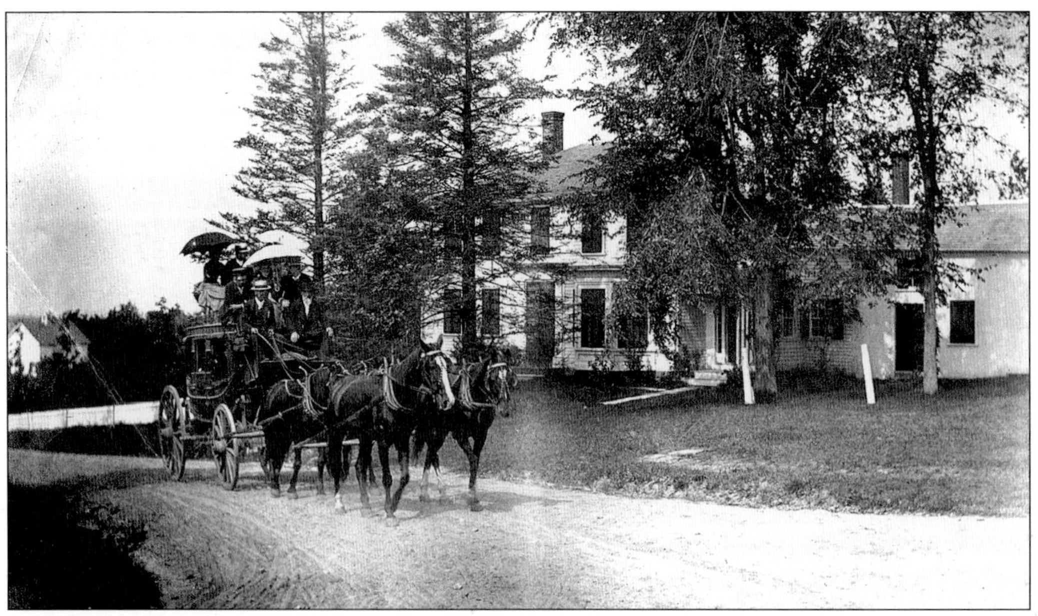

The Mountain House stagecoach, shown in the late 1800s, is about to turn Pratt's Corner and head up Allen Hill Road to its destination, Mountain House. (Courtesy of the Princeton Historical Society.)